The Complete Idiot's Ref

(Use this card to avoid reading a[...]e to.)

Idiot-Proof Command Gui[...]

To map a drive letter to a NetWare location:	**MAP** *driveletter[...]path*
To copy files and maintain the network attributes:	**NCOPY** *fromdrive:\directory todrive:\directory*
To see the listing of files with network details:	**NDIR** *[filename] [/options]*
To attempt the NetWare 4 king-of-all-commands:	**NLIST** *[class type] [=object name] [/option...]*
To redirect your printer port to the network print queue:	**CAPTURE** *[/][options][=][names or values]*
To send a brief message to another logged in user:	**SEND** *"message" [TO] userid*
To view or set attributes to a network file:	**FLAG** *[filename] [attributes] [options]*
To recover accidentally erased files:	**SALVAGE**
To change your password:	**SETPASS**
To check your security in any given directory:	**RIGHTS**

Idiot-Proof Tips for Network Troubleshooting

➤ Make sure everything is plugged in and turned on.

➤ Write down the error message, along with anything else you were doing just before the error.

➤ Check all cables and connections to make sure they are solid.

➤ Replace suspicious parts (for example, cables, keyboards, monitors, and network adapters) with known good parts.

➤ If your computer is completely locked up, reboot it by pressing Ctrl+Alt+Del. If that doesn't work, turn it off and then back on.

alpha books

Anatomy of NetWare User Tools for Windows

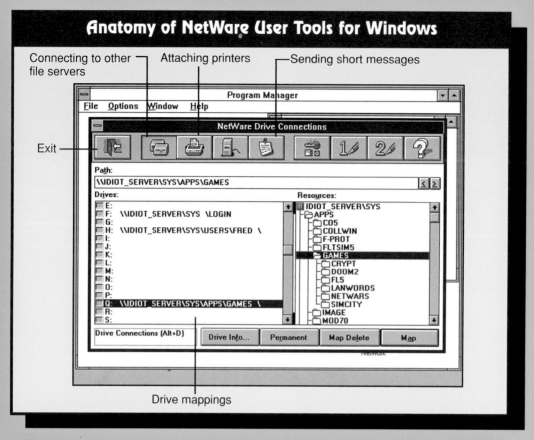

Connecting to other file servers

Attaching printers

Sending short messages

Exit

Drive mappings

Anatomy of NETUSER Utility for DOS

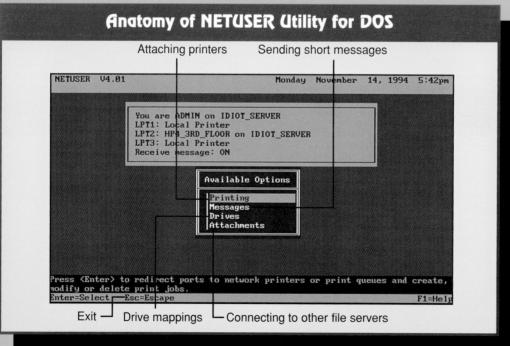

Attaching printers

Sending short messages

Exit

Drive mappings

Connecting to other file servers

The
COMPLETE
IDIOT'S
GUIDE TO
Networking

by Daniel T. Bobola

alpha
books

A Division of MacMillan Publishing USA
A Prentice Hall MacMillan Company
201 W. 103rd Street, Indianapolis, IN 46290

To Kim, my loving wife and best friend.

©1995 Alpha Books

International Standard Book Number: 1-56761-590-2
Library of Congress Catalog Card Number: 95-75172

97 96 95   8 7 6 5 4 3 2 1

Interpretation of the printing code: the rightmost number of the first series of numbers is the year of the book's printing; the rightmost number of the second series of numbers is the number of the book's printing. For example, a printing code of 95-1 shows that the first printing of the book occurred in 1995.

Printed in the United States of America

Publisher
Marie Butler-Knight

Product Development Manager
Faithe Wempen

Acquisitions Manager
Barry Pruett

Managing Editor
Elizabeth Keaffaber

Senior Development Editor
Seta Frantz

Production Editor
Michelle Shaw

Copy Editor
Barry Childs-Helton

Illustrator
Judd Winick

Cover Designer
Scott Cook

Designer
Barbara Kordesh

Indexer
Chris Cleveland

Production Team
*Gary Adair, Angela Calvert, Dan Caparo, Brad Chinn, Kim Cofer,
Dave Eason, Jennifer Eberhardt, Rob Falco, Dave Garratt, Karen Gregor,
Erika Millen, Beth Rago, Karen Walsh, Robert Wolf*

*Special thanks to Scott Parker for ensuring
the technical accuracy of this book.*

Contents at a Glance

Contents

17 How and When to Use Your Network Support Team 175

18 Problems You Didn't Cause (Don't Worry) but Which May Bug You 183

19 Problems That Lots of Us Have, and How to Fix Them 191

Part 4: Building Your Own Empire 203

20 Planning Your Own Successful Network 205

21 Installing the Network Hardware and WFW 211

26 Personal NetWare Command Reference   279

27 LANtastic Command Reference   287

Introduction

Almost all computers in the workplace are, or soon will be, connected in some type of network. Where does that leave you? Frustrated? Anxious? Aren't you just coming to grips with learning your own computer, and shouldn't that be enough?

The workforce is screaming for individuals trained in basic computer networking technology. They're also screaming *at* you for not being more effective using the network. Blaming the network for losing your files, kicking the laser printer, and spending ten hours of e-mail per day are not examples of being effective.

You don't need a book that assumes you are (or want to become) a networking wizard. You're a busy person with a real life beyond your network (which you'll be glad to get back to as soon as you can get the network to do what you need).

Why Do You Need This Book?

With so many computer networking books on the market, why do you need this one? It all depends on what you want to learn. If you want a simple "what-is" book full of fancy trivia and obscure networking facts, skip this one. But if you're really interested in a common-sense "how-to" guide that helps you to apply the basic knowledge it teaches, then this book is for you!

For example, instead of boring you with useless facts about 10BaseT hardware, this book shows you how to *use* the hardware to be more effective on the network, with helpful hints on filing, printing, and performing e-mail tasks.

After all, what does a person new to networking need to know? You need to know how to find, share, and store files on the network, as well as print, send, and receive electronic mail (e-mail), and solve problems as they arise. This book guides you through each task.

There's also a part on building your own network, written especially for beginners. You may never need to build one from scratch, but seeing how it's done can also guide you through the tasks for connecting your computer to an existing network.

Features of This Book

Part One: Getting Connected   Especially for beginners, this section describes the parts that make up a network. Just enough details will enable you to feel comfortable using and discussing file servers, network cables, server software, and fun things like modems, CD-ROMs, and printers. This background can be helpful in understanding some of the shortcuts and likely problems described in later sections.

Part Two: Being Productive   Here's the real meat of the book for people interested in finding shortcuts. What's the best way to find that lost file? How about some tips on printing? Want to save time and energy when you e-mail? This section can help by explaining (through real examples) the very best way to accomplish specific tasks.

Part Three: Staying Connected   It doesn't work the way they said it would? Getting ready to chuck the whole network into the bay? Wait! There's a chance that some of the tips in this section will help you print that big report, recover that erased file, or at least know who to call in your time of trouble (besides 911).

Part Four: Building Your Own Empire   Interested in adding another computer to your network? Want to know the step-by-step details, or even the suggested planning, cost, time, and complexity? We even take it a step further, and show you how to build your own entire network from scratch. You don't have to be a computer geek to do this! If you can find the money, we'll show you how to spend it in computer networking—and then get it up and running. Don't you wish getting a budget approved was as easy?

Part Five: Networking Command Reference Guide   I can't remember what I had for lunch, let alone what command is used in NetWare 4.1 to show whether I've enough space to store my monthly status report. I can always look it up, and this section is designed to be easier than those bulky software manuals. Those manuals have every stinking network command you can think of, whereas we've included only the stinking commands you're likely to need.

How Do I Use This Book?

For starters, don't actually *read* this book! (At least not the whole thing.) Think of it as a reference manual. When you need a quick answer, use the Table of Contents or the Index to find the right section. Each section is self-contained, with exactly what you need to know to solve your problem or to answer your question.

When you need to type something, it appears like this:

TYPE THIS STUFF IN

Just type what you see and press the **Enter** key. It's as simple as that. (By the way, if you're supposed to press a particular key, that key appears in bold, as **Enter** does here.)

There are some special boxed notes that I've used in this book to help you learn just what you need:

Notes and tips showing the easiest way to perform some task.

There's help when things go wrong!

Easy-to-understand definitions for every computer term let you "speak like a geek."

Skip this background fodder (technical twaddle) unless you're truly interested.

Acknowledgments

Thanks to the tireless crew at Alpha Books (when do they sleep?) for giving me the opportunity to write this book, and then performing their miracles, allowing this book to reach your hands.

Thanks also to all those who have enabled me to learn something about computer networking over the years. Who was teaching whom?

Trademarks

All terms mentioned in this book that are known to be trademarks or service marks are listed below. In addition, terms suspected of being trademarks or service marks have been appropriately capitalized. Alpha Books cannot attest to the accuracy of this information. Use of a term in this book should not be regarded as affecting the validity of any trademark or service mark.

3Com, 3+Open, 3+Share, and Etherlink III are registered trademarks of 3Com Corporation.

AppleTalk and TrueType are registered trademarks of Apple Computer, Inc.

ArcNet is a registered trademark of Datapoint Corporation.

Artisoft and LANtastic are registered trademarks of Artisoft, Inc.

AT&T is a registered trademark of American Telephone and Telegraph Company.

Banyan and VINES are registered trademarks of Banyan Systems, Inc.

cc:Mail is a trademark of cc:Mail, Inc., a wholly owned subsidiary of Lotus Development Corporation.

CompuServe is a registered trademark of CompuServe, Inc.

Da Vinci Systems is a trademark of Da Vinci Systems Corporation.

DEC is a registered trademark and PATHWORKS is a trademark of Digital Equipment Corporation.

Lotus Notes is a registered trademark of Lotus Development Corporation.

Microsoft, Windows NT, NT-AS, and Windows 95 are registered trademarks of Microsoft Corporation. Windows is a trademark of Microsoft Corporation.

NEC is a registered trademark of NEC Corporation.

Net/One and Ungermann-Bass are registered trademarks of Ungermann-Bass, Inc.

Novell, NetWare, WordPerfect, and GroupWise are registered trademarks of Novell, Inc.

Saber is a registered trademark of American Airlines, Inc.

UNIX is a registered trademark of UNIX Systems Laboratories.

Part 1
Getting Connected

Well, it happened. You were just minding your own business when all of the sudden a network was installed around you. Now you're a part of it, like it or not. But you say you don't know a NIC from a HUB? And you think 10BaseT is a new rap group? Yes, networking is here and life will never be the same again.

Where does someone start to figure out what a network is all about? Getting this book is a good start! Settle back and let the fog clear. The chapters in this part of the book will help you understand what a network is; what hardware, cabling, and software is needed; and the advantages of being connected to a network. There are plenty. Trust me!

Chapter 1

The Least You Need to Know About Networking

In This Chapter

➤ Stuff you need to know to get started

➤ What to do if you want to avoid trouble

➤ Common beginner mistakes, and how to avoid them

➤ Things you should not do on a network

➤ When to call in the experts

Congratulations! You've just entered the world of networking, whether you asked for it or not. Your level of happiness at work is now directly related to your knowledge of technology. Your network is pure technology. But feel some comfort in the realization that you don't need to understand the details of technology, only how to *use* that technology to get your job done. Other books try to teach you the bits and bytes of packets and three-letter acronyms. Not this one. You will learn only the minimum needed to perform the most common tasks on a network. Ready to get started?

The Minimum to Get You Started

If you think you are networked, you probably are. If you haven't a clue, don't worry. The first part of this book is dedicated to helping you understand what a network is and how it's put together. You'll be able to peek into the back of your desktop computer and locate the network cable, check to see that both ends are plugged in correctly, and prove to yourself that you are on a network. Chapters 2–8 provide a quick review of most networking components and define enough terms to make you sound like a geek. It sounds like a lot, but these chapters will teach you enough about your network to help you be more productive and solve problems later.

How to Log In to the Network to Get Started

Before you can explore the riches of your network, you must first *log in*. It's like trying to get into one of those exclusive secret nightclubs. You have to know where the door is, and then you need the password to get inside.

To log in to your network, find the DOS prompt. At the prompt type **LOGIN** and press **Enter**. If you see the **Bad command or filename** error, change to the network drive (usually by typing **F:** and pressing **Enter**) and try again. Next you should see the following:

```
F:\>LOGIN
Enter your login name: _
```

Now it's time to type your network name. By typing **login**, you've asked your computer to ask for permission to get on the network, and the network is asking you to identify yourself. Your *login name* is usually some form of your last name and an initial, like JSMITH. If you don't know your network name, turn to Chapter 17 to learn about the people at your workplace who can help you, such as the network administrator. After you've typed your network name, you should be asked to provide a password before you are allowed onto the network. Type your ***password*** and press **Enter**.

```
F:\>LOGIN
Enter your login name: DBOBOLA
Enter your password: ****** (you won't see it being typed)
Good morning, Dan
H:\_
```

4

Congratulations! You have logged in to the network! If Novell NetWare is not the product your company uses, try some commands from this listing of the most common networking products:

➤ If you are using LANtastic, try **STARTNET**.

➤ For IBM LAN Server or Microsoft LAN Manager, try **NET LOGON**.

➤ If you happen to be using Banyan VINES, try **BAN**.

➤ Windows for Workgroups would have already asked you to provide a LOGON name when your machine first started up.

➤ If you are using a Macintosh, double-click on **Chooser**. Then select what you desire on the network with your mouse.

Complete details about logging in are covered in Chapter 9. Incidentally, when you logged in, you utilized two levels of security (your name and a password). If you'd like to venture further into the topic of security, there's plenty to be found in Chapter 16. From changing your password to hiding your files from others, you'll learn enough to be secure in your knowledge of network security.

How to Find Out What's Available on Your Network

Now that you've logged in to your network, go exploring! Find expensive-looking gadgets around your workplace that may have network cables attached. Chances are that thing is on the network and available to you. You may find color printers or plotters, CD-players, or even fax machines. See Chapter 2 for an introduction to many resources, and Chapter 8 for specific examples of peripherals.

If you're not into exploring, let your fingers do the walking. Call your help desk or LAN administrator. Ask them what kind of network resources are available to you.

Easy Navigating on the Network

What's the easiest way to discover and use your network resources? It's called User Tools for you Windows fans, and NETUSER if you still live in the DOS world. With either utility you can map network drives, capture printers, and send messages to your heart's content! Learn all about these life-saving tools in Chapter 12.

How to Find That Lost File

Where did you leave it? If you answer "Somewhere on the network," that's a start, but you really should know the *name* of your file. Can you remember a drive letter associated with your file? Many people grow accustomed to storing files on a particular drive, like the A: or C: drive (even one of those new network letters like F: or H:).

If you're running an application, sometimes it's helpful to close that application and open it again. This can help restore the *default storage locations* where your lost file may be hiding. Still can't find it? Is there a chance that the file is stored on your local drive C:? Perhaps a diskette? If it was a shared file on the network, is there a chance that someone else has renamed or removed it?

Are you sitting at the same machine where you last saw your file? Are you logged in with the same name? Can you retrace your steps of the last events leading up to the disappearance? When was the last time you saw this so-called file? Tell me more about yourself. Did you raise this file in a loving environment? Do you *deserve* this file?

For further detective work, investigate Chapter 13, which deals with storing and retrieving files on the network. Feel confident about your ability to locate files. There is likely a backup stored somewhere that will contain a copy of your file, although it may be a day or two old. You can ask your help desk or LAN administrator for further assistance.

How to Print That File on the Network

Chapter 14 deals with the most commonly complained about subject: network printing. And the complaints are well deserved, because more things have to go right to print than for any other activity on the network. It's like landing a man on the moon, and when was the last time *that* happened?

You can solve printing problems by asking yourself questions. Is the printer online? Is it out of paper? Is it currently being serviced? Do you have an alternate printer to print to in times like these?

Examine your print job. Did you select the correct printer? Is your job printing somewhere else? Does it require special paper to be loaded at the printer? Have you embedded some new graphic images that you've never tried to print before? Is there an error message in your application?

Think in terms of your machine. Have you ever been able to print something like this before? Can your neighbor print today, using that same printer?

Think of a backup plan. Can you copy your file to a diskette and ask a friend to print it for you? Can you move temporarily to another machine that has a printer attached directly to it? Am I asking too many questions?

Still can't print? Take two aspirin and turn to Chapter 14.

No Time for Work—I'm Doing My Electronic Mail

Welcome to one of the biggest time-wasters of the 1990s! People now spend hours each day performing an activity that once took minutes. How many notes do you send and receive each day? How many are really needed? How few could you get by with if your life depended on it? Discover tips for reducing the amount of time spent in e-mail (and answers to many of your e-mail questions) in Chapter 15.

Problems? You've Got Problems?

And we thought our problems before networking were bad! You don't have to be ashamed or embarrassed about network problems; they're as prevalent as bad weather. You simply have to be prepared and know how to handle them.

You're staring at a screen that's telling you a file server can't be found. Not a good way to start the day. A cold sweat develops and you feel last night's supper churning in your gut. Where do you start? This book takes the common-sense approach. An alternate method might be simply to list *all* error messages and give you the best answer, but this would probably not be accurate; each network has a life of its own (besides, if I did that, the book would be a million pages long).

A good place to start is to ask yourself, "Did anything change since the last time I tried this?" Something—anything—changing is the number one reason for network problems. Someone may have updated your workstation without adding the latest software drivers. Time may have run out on your existing password. The overnight network upgrade might still be taking place, preventing you from logging in until the nuts-and-bolts work is finished. The cleaning people may have bumped up against your network cable wallplate, temporarily breaking your connection to the world.

If you have a problem right now, you may want to check out Chapter 19, which provides detailed answers to the most common problems out there today. If you're interested in general problem-solving techniques proven to work on the network, check out Chapter 16.

Maybe that problem is way over your head. You'd like to call 911, but it's not that kind of emergency. Who and where should you go for help? Chapter 17 guides you to your own support staff, ready and willing to provide you with the kind of service you may or may not deserve.

Sometimes you've done nothing at all, and there's nothing you can do but wait. Hey, at least it's not your fault. Interested in what might be going on? Or how soon you can expect to get back on the network? From file server maintenance to power outages, you'll find descriptions of common problems beyond your control in Chapter 18.

Crash Course in Building Your Own Network

As crazy as it sounds, you could easily build your own network. Chapters 20–24 take you on a step-by-step tour of connecting two machines and a printer together using Windows for Workgroups—a product you may already own. All the tips on planning, finding the right components, installing your network cards, and troubleshooting are here to help you on your way!

You could actually read this book backwards and start by building your network today. Worry about productivity later; start working on bugs now! Who's pretending? You could be a genuine *Network Administrator* before the day is out. You can even measure your installation prowess, because sample time durations are given for the various activities. Can you really install a network card during a lunch break? How long did it take you?

Sound like some exciting stuff? OK. Maybe not as exciting as getting that new game you've been wanting up and running. So, turn the page and let's learn how a network works and how to get connected.

Chapter 2

Just What Is a Network, Anyway?

In This Chapter

➤ What a network is

➤ Examples of good things you can do on a network

➤ How to tell whether are you on a network

➤ What the real benefits of networking are

Life Before Networks

How much do you need to know about the history of networks? Not much; that's why this chapter isn't hundreds of pages. But it's helpful to see how technology evolves, and how people like you and me should try to take advantage of technology to make our everyday work easier. Think about it. Is your work any better since you were put on the network? If the answer is no, maybe you are still in a transition period. This chapter explains some of the major transitions (some serious, some not) that have occurred in the evolution of networking.

Cavemen and the Invention of the Network

In the beginning, there were no computers. Humans were forced to scavenge for food and clothing, but they were hungry and found little to wear. Squirrels simply did not cut it. The meat was barely worth the effort, and you needed dozens of pelts to make comfy underwear.

Humans lusted after the woolly mammoth, but no individual was strong enough to bring down this beast. If only they could talk to each other, they could organize a massive hunt and share the wealth, defeating the beast with their combined intellect. So they invented language. Now they could argue. They realized they all wanted the same thing, so communication was good. But they were still hungry.

To capture the mammoth they needed technology. So they invented the network. It was an early version of a network, with rocks instead of computers and vines instead of cabling. But they leveraged what they had, worked together closely, and threw the whole shebang at the mammoth. Its feet became entangled in the vines and the rocks hurt. The woolly mammoth succumbed, and we've never been the same since.

The Middle Ages of Networking

Humans now lusted after technology. It came in the form of a computer. Not the big ones, really; you had to be over the edge to fall for something like a mainframe. It was the personal computer that would take away our White-Out forever, transport us from Pong to DOOM in the entertainment department, and save vast forests through electronic mail (though we quickly chopped them down anyway to *print* our e-mail). Everyone had to have a PC.

Our lust wasn't satisfied on the desktop. We wanted more. More computing power, better graphics, better printers, better access to our company records and the football point spread. But these *peripherals* were too expensive for the average worker; only a few could be purchased, which then ended up on the desks of executives who hardly knew how to turn them on.

During the Middle Ages, somewhere in the 1970s, it became fashionable to start tying together these expensive computers and other gadgets. Some say even ARPANET got started around this time as a hedge against Ma Bell getting nuked. Brilliant minds were set to the task of how to connect all of this technology together. The *network* was invented.

10

The first networks did very little because computers did not have much memory or storage capacity. Any kind of useful product created on the computer (like a file or a program) had to be stored on big floppy diskettes. Then came the invention of the hard drive, which was soon stuffed into personal computers. This was nirvana for computer lovers; they could store hundreds of more things on a single hard drive inside a computer, and not have to worry about the floppy disks. But there were two problems. First, the things were so darned expensive that few people could afford them, so they were scarce. Second, they were still accessible to only a single machine. You had to sit at that computer to get at the information.

Network   Two or more computers connected together for the purpose of communicating or sharing equipment.

Peripherals   Valuable pieces of equipment, such as expensive printers, modems, CD-ROMs, etc., that can be attached to a network and shared.

Marvels of Today

This was the first opportunity for the network to creep into our lives. A network was capable of letting another computer, or person, share the hard drive! Someone strung a cable between two machines and *kapow*, I could see yours and you could see, well, I didn't have one! So the first networks were a bunch of computers without hard drives connected to a single, central computer with this wonderful storage device.

Time for a geography lesson: Networks are classified by the amount of real estate they take up. A network within the confines of a single building is called a **local area network**, or a **LAN**. If you have satellite links or lots of cable across the city, country or planets, it's considered a **wide area network**, or **WAN**.

About this same time computer printers came into use. They were expensive, and were often paired with computers as a replacement for typewriters. Printers, like hard drives, were also considered a valuable *resource*, and a prime target to be networked. Once again, the lucky machine with the hard drive also got the printer. People wanted to be connected to the LAN so they could get to these resources.

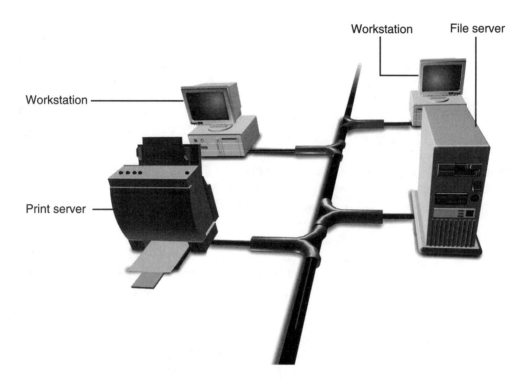

A typical network.

Expensive Gadgets

Your workplace is probably filled with expensive equipment just waiting for you to make the network connection. Just as the remote control has added inches to the waistline, so will the network attempt to replace all forms of human exercise.

Gutenburg, Xerox, and Mrs. Facsimile

The first books (sentences?) were simply carved into stone, a big effort for anyone. Very few copies were made of these rocks; people got enough of a workout just lugging them around. With the invention of the printing press, more people had access to information, and society became smarter. Then the copy machine was invented and we were all inundated with pizza ads. There was no place to store all that stuff. The fax machine made us smarter *faster* (because we didn't have to wait for the mail), but there was still the problem of where to put all that paper.

Computers give you a great place to store all this stuff. It's the hard drive—especially those big networked drives. Your fifty-page document is merely a smudge on a metal disk somewhere on the network. And there's room for lots and lots of your stuff to fit inside computers. Your desktop now looks clean! When you need to actually create paper, you can do so with the greatest of ease with a laser printer, and it looks better than it would fresh off the printing press. Finally, someone discovered how to use the scanner to suck in all the faxes that were lying around.

Resource
A general term used by computer people to describe something of value, usually connected to the network. Typical resources include printers, scanners, CD-ROMs, storage locations, and modems.

Who exercises anymore? As much info as your local library might hold can be stored on multiple CD-ROMs on the network. You can actually connect a copy machine to the network. We're not even walking to the fax machine anymore, because—yes—it's on the network. Who said networks weren't hazardous to your health?

Learning to Share This Wealth

People and technology don't often mix well. The problem exists today. Waste is rampant. Technology is underutilized. It's hard to share, it's easier to hog. That's why this book was written. And perhaps why you're reading it.

The network helps us share all this wealth. We've outgrown a single computer. We use the network to improve the way we communicate, through writing, sharing of files, graphing and printing information, and performing a CYA by carbon-copying the boss on that e-mail. Your computer helped you by making your writing better (spelled correctly, formatted nicely, stored conveniently); it's easier to compose and print your thoughts. The network helps you by tying all that good stuff together with everyone else (sharing documents, e-mailing notes, using equipment on another floor, sending your spreadsheets to the IRS).

13

What a Network Consists Of

Network is a term that encompasses all the parts that make it up. Computers play the biggest part. Some computers have special functions and are given special names on the network, such as *server*, *database*, *gateway*, and *print server*, to name just a few different types.

Hardware Identification

Hardware is the word for the physical chunks of metal and plastic that make up a network. Computers require help in getting connected to the network. They require a special adapter card that gets installed inside the machine. Once installed, the network cable can be attached and the computer is on the network.

Lots of other special pieces of equipment can be connected to the network—for example, printers, plotters, CD-ROMs, modems, and ice machines. All of these (except the ice machine) are available to you as a network user. The network, however, also controls access to them, so you may have to ask permission from your network administrator before you are allowed to use them.

Cabling and Connectors

All of this hardware is tied together using *cabling*. In good networks, this cabling is out of your way so you don't trip over it. Each computer gets a cable. Printers get cables. Modems can get cables. The list goes on and on, just like the cabling in your walls.

Cables are connected together using connectors. They have to be designed to work with each other to run the network correctly. When a cable fails, it's usually that the wire has broken away from its connector.

Just when you thought you understood network cabling, someone invents wireless networks to confuse you. These are still rare, but are gaining in popularity. Instead of a cable attachment, your computer connects to others through the use of radio frequencies or invisible light. This will be a great option for laptop computers—once it's stable, cheap enough to afford, and secure from spying or eavesdropping.

Software: DOS/Windows Applications and Network Stuff

All computers need some type of software to help them run. With a network installed, your computer needs a bit more than simply DOS and Windows. This extra software, once it's installed on your computer, works with DOS and Windows to let you see and use all those gadgets on the network.

Your word processor, database, spreadsheet, and graphics program can also take advantage of the network by using the increased available storage space, the computing power of other machines, and the special capabilities of equipment such as printers and scanners.

The earliest forms of networks were attached to central mainframe computers. That's what you had to connect to to get your computing work done. The early mainframe computers wanted to reach you on your desktop, but the PC hadn't been invented yet. So *dumb terminals* did the job. The name fit because these machines didn't have any brains themselves, just a display that sat on your desktop, controlled by the mainframe.

> **Emulator** A type of software product that fools a mainframe into thinking your PC is a dumb terminal. It's often used on networks that have a connection to a mainframe, so users can get to it for whatever reason.

When personal computers were invented, users wanted to use them instead of the dumb terminals, but often their jobs still required them to get to the mainframe. They could either keep both machines on the desktop, or run a software product called an *emulator* on the PC.

Everything Else

We can toss everything else into a big bucket called "other." One of these might be very important to you or your organization, so get to know how to use them.

Special-purpose computers Sometimes your business invests in computer systems that specialize in doing very important things for your business. This might include automating your *workflow*, such as inventory, order entry, payroll, accounts receivable, or human resource systems. It may help you prepare complicated

15

Internet Also known as the "Information Superhighway." It's made up of zillions of smaller networks form around the world, all connected together. If you can figure out how to use it, you can access resources around the world.

legal documents (or manage them); it might store important info as pictures or images, so you can refer to them later.

The Internet Many people think if their computer is connected to a network, they must be connected to the *Internet*. It is confusing because the word "net" is thrown around a lot these days. No, your computer network *isn't* automatically connected to the Internet, unless a technical person has set up a special piece of hardware called a *gateway* that connects you to things outside your local LAN. Even if your network is connected to the Internet, not all users may be given that right. Ask your network administrator.

The Least You Need to Know

Those of us ignorant about the history of networking are condemned to repeat it. So we learned:

➤ The basic function of most networks is to help users be more productive and efficient by enabling them to share data such as document files and to share resources such as printers, hard disks, modems, e-mail, CD-ROMs, and so on.

➤ A network consists of hardware, cabling, and special software that ties two or more computers together for the purpose of sharing information.

➤ Two or more computers can be connected for the purpose of sharing and communicating with a LAN.

➤ Networks help us stretch our dollars by sharing expensive resources instead of buying one for everybody.

➤ Big projects that used to be too burdensome for a single person can now be shared on a network, and be burdensome to many people.

Chapter 3

The Big H (Hardware)

In This Chapter

➤ The truth about file servers

➤ What is a NIC, and why should I care?

➤ How is my computer different from the file server?

➤ How is my computer similar to the file server?

Of all networking components, you should be most comfortable with *hardware*. Your computer is an obvious example of hardware. So is a hammer. Forget the hammer. The hardware we will focus on is a whole other category: the things used by computers or networks. They could be inside or outside, really big or really small.

What Is a File Server?

Start by thinking about a small network of perhaps three or four computers connected with cabling. Call one of the computers the *file server*. This should be the most powerful and expensive computer, because its role is to serve the other computers on the network, by providing necessities such as files, e-mail, printing capabilities, or databases. You'll learn about those in the next few chapters.

How did that machine become a file server? Someone loaded special software on it. What software? It's called the network operating system, and is covered in Chapter 4. The file server is important because it holds the brains of the network (the software) and performs important network duties.

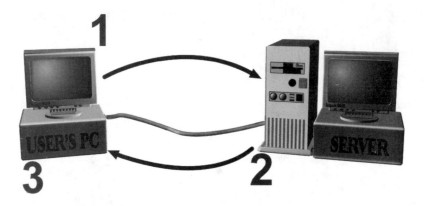

The File Server shares information to and from users.

Introducing the File Server

Your computer may hold a special place in your heart, but if you look throughout your office you may notice a pattern. Most businesses purchase computers in bulk, and they all start looking the same. These are good computers, but you may find yourself wishing for something a little faster, with more disk space, or just plain bigger. Have you ever wanted to see a machine that has it all? Then introduce yourself to a file server!

File server: A computer that contains and runs the software required to make it act as a central storage facility for connected computers.

Historically, the *file server* has been by far the largest and most powerful computer on a network. It's not as easy to see that anymore. Sure, today's file servers are more powerful than million-dollar mainframe computers were just 10 years ago. But so is your desktop computer! Typical file servers are about the size of a large suitcase standing on end. It's a given that things like computers will continue to get bigger (at least in terms of what they can *do*) and better each year; it's what keeps advertising people in business.

Actually, bigger is not always better. The general goal in making computers has been to make the inside parts smaller, which can make them faster, and more economical because they take less power to run. Your current desktop machine is likely smaller than the first one you had, and the next will be smaller still. Physically, smaller is better.

The difference in pure speed and function between the file server and your desktop computer will get smaller each time your machine is upgraded or replaced. Your computer will become so powerful over the next few years that you may no longer need a traditional file server to assist you in certain tasks. You'll still want a file server to assist in sharing files with others, however.

Just because the file server sounds intimidating doesn't mean it is so. If someone let you actually sit at your file server and do something familiar, like play Windows Solitaire, you wouldn't see that much of an improvement over your own machine (unless you have a real dog). So, you may think, if this super machine can't impress me with Windows Solitaire, what's the big deal? The big deal is comparing apples to apples. A file server doesn't need to waste its engines running the graphics to play Solitaire.

The role of the file server has changed over the years. Instead of being just a storage area, it's now more likely to *manage* your files, by making sure they are always available, even if some hardware in your file server dies. And the server's focus is equality for all, giving everyone the same right to compute. This means if it's slow for you, it's slow for everyone (doesn't that make you feel better?). With proper care and feeding, a file server can live a long life of three or four years before it's obsolete. File servers become obsolete much faster than ordinary computers because so much more is demanded of them, forcing them to be improved at a faster rate.

Other Server Parts That Help You

You probably have a standard hard drive in your machine, on which you store your files. These files are said to be kept "locally." The file server has several *huge* hard drives. If you store your files here, they are said to be "on the network." It continues to grow as your support people add more hard drives to keep up with demand. Network users demand lots of disk space on their file server as they become more productive and have more things to store.

Crash: Slang for a network that has stopped working—or (in more traditional usage) when a hard drive can no longer understand what is stored on it. Often the entire hard drive has to be replaced. Dropping a hard drive often causes it to crash in more ways than just the loud one.

Hopefully, the hard drive in your computer has never *crashed*. It would really inconvenience you to replace and reload and retype things that were lost. Could you imagine the pain and suffering if your *file server* hard drives crashed? Many, many people would really be devastated and your business could go *out* of business, so this is no joking matter. Your file server should be designed to prevent such accidents or failures. How? By sticking in duplicate drives and storing everything in *two* places instead of one!

How's Your Memory?

How much memory is in your ordinary computer? You can watch the numbers count up on screen when you first turn on your machine. If you are running DOS, you probably have 640 to 2,000 of memory units, called *kilobytes* (The following sidebar can tell you more about kilobytes). A Windows machine should have 4,000 to 8,000 kilobytes.

Speed and storage capacity are measured in bits and bytes. A *bit* is the most basic unit of measurement for information. A *byte* is eight bits lined up in a row. Each letter of the alphabet is made up of eight bits, or one byte.

Most information is stored in amounts so large that we abbreviate the size to make it easier to say. One thousand bytes is a *kilobyte*. One million bytes is a *megabyte*. To help you relate to these sizes, a typical single typed sheet of paper contains 2,000 bytes of information, or 2 kilobytes, or 2KB.

Likewise, information travelling on a network speeds along at a certain rate. These speeds are measured in bits, not bytes, so don't be confused. The standard Ethernet runs at 10 million *bits per second*, or 10-Megabits, or 10 Mbps.

A file server, on the other hand, usually has between 16,000 and 64,000 kilobytes of memory, and some have even more! What does a file server do with this memory? It can make the hard drives of the file server even faster for the users by keeping the most commonly used things (such as important files and software) right in memory, rather than asking the disk for it (which takes much longer).

Protecting the Important Data on the File Server

You know the importance of *backing up* your files. If your job depends on some really important files, you should keep a copy of them on diskette, and protect that diskette.

The file server is treated as though *every single file on it* is important, mainly because it would take too long to ask everybody on the network what's really important. To protect all these files, your file server uses a piece of equipment called the *tape backup*.

Once your company has a tape backup of the network, you can rest assured that anything stored on the network can be recovered in the event of a disaster. Sure, an earthquake or tornado qualifies as a disaster, but more common day-to-day disasters are often saved by these tape backups. For example, you may need to:

> **Memory** has nothing to do with remembering. Computer memory, also known as RAM (Random Access Memory), is the working area used by the computer. Memory is the holding place for data to be processed. The more you have, the better your computer functions. Memory is measured in bytes, and is sold in increments of megabytes.

➤ Find an earlier version of a data file you used last week

➤ Bring back something that was erased accidentally a few days ago

➤ Fix a file that has become corrupted by replacing it with the copy from yesterday

➤ Determine whether an important file has been changed

Tape backup: A set of cassette tapes holding a copy of the contents of a hard drive. Most businesses should have a good tape backup of all file servers. Also used to describe the equipment used to copy the hard drive's files to tape.

You can arrange these common requests through your network administrator. Of course, you can bring back these files only if they are really stored on tape somewhere. And tapes aren't recorded once and locked up forever, not even in the Pentagon. Several days' or weeks' worth of tapes are used, stored, then used again. This process is called *tape rotation*, and determines how far back something can be restored. Find out what the tape-rotation policy is for your company. If it's not long enough for your comfort, store your important files to diskette (which is always a good idea anyway).

UPS and Downs

With all of this important gadgetry attached to the file server, you wouldn't want something as common as a power failure to stand in the way of its effectiveness. Neither does your network administrator—that's why a *UPS* (Uninterruptible Power Supply) was installed. It sits next to the file server, and weighs as much as a car battery (because basically it *is* a car battery).

A UPS is used as a battery backup to keep electrical equipment running during a power outage. In a total blackout, typical UPSs keep the file server running for 5 to 10 minutes (which is longer than most power failures last), or enough time for the network administrator to shut it down properly.

Where's It Hiding?

Where might you find this magnificent piece of machinery called the file server? Probably locked up safely in a room somewhere, with all the related fun gadgets. There's no need to know where it is—unless your business has lots of network problems and you want to know where the action is.

How Can My Computer Play with the Server?

Here's what you need to participate on the network:

➤ A special adapter card for your computer

➤ Configuration software that comes with your adapter

➤ A network cable and a cable outlet to plug into

➤ Network software for your computer

➤ A name you can use on the network

➤ A password, as well as permission to see (and access to use) the stuff on the server

If this sounds like a lot, it is, but all these activities are performed by support people, so you don't have to worry. It just helps to know what the pieces are, in case one of them breaks.

What Is a Network Interface Card?

To connect to the network, you have to plug the network cable into something on your computer. The standard connectors that came with your computer aren't enough—those are for a printer, modem, keyboard, mouse, and display. You (or somebody) must take the cover off your computer and install a network adapter. This is commonly referred to as a *Network Interface Card*, or *NIC*. Once installed, you must run software that came on a diskette with the NIC so that your computer can recognize it. After that, you're ready to plug into the network.

> NIC: Network Interface Card. The adapter card that fits inside your computer and provides the capability to connect to the network.

Where did it come from? Someone in your company bought lots of them, probably on sale. Yours should be the same as your office partner's. They should match the cabling system, or else they won't work.

Who gets the NICs? All machines that connect directly to the network cable require a NIC. Besides ordinary computers, this includes the file server, printers, and cool things like networked CD-ROMs.

Can I install one myself? Installing a NIC is not difficult as long as you have the NIC, a few tools to get into your computer, and the software that came with the NIC. If you want to do this yourself, it's detailed in Part 4, where you learn how to create your own network. A typical NIC installation takes about 15–20 minutes, and should last years. One is all you need.

How can you tell if your NIC's working? If you're lucky, it has a little light on it that glows green or yellow (and sometimes blinks) while your computer is turned on. If it's not working, the little light isn't lit. Or else it's red, and that means something outside, other than your machine, needs attention. The only problem with this light is its location—the back of your machine. Not too convenient for the paranoid. If your NIC doesn't have a light, you have to hope that it works. The good thing about NICs is that once you get them working, they tend to stay working.

Does everyone on every network have a file server? No. Most companies that are networked do have one or more file servers, but you can be networked and not have a server. *Peer-to-peer networking* is discussed in more detail in Chapter 6.

How Is My Computer Different from the File Server?

➤ Your computer strives to be the best for you, one person.

➤ The file server is usually a much more powerful machine, intended to be used by many people.

➤ Because it's more powerful, the file server is usually much bigger, and stands on the floor instead of the desktop.

➤ Nobody sits and works at the file server, unless it is very sick or is being morphed into a more powerful machine.

➤ Your machine probably has better graphics and a better display attached to it, because you need it. The file server doesn't. Your machine probably has a mouse. The file server doesn't need one, because nobody is sitting in front of the server day-in and day-out.

➤ Your machine is plugged into the wall. The file server is plugged into a special power source called a UPS that keeps it running when the power fails and the other machines on the network (yours, for example) die.

How Is My Computer Similar to the File Server?

➤ Both machines are constructed from the same parts. Your machine has good parts in it, while the file server has super-duper parts in it.

➤ Both machines have a NIC and a network cable.

➤ Both machines are designed to help you perform your work.

The Least You Need to Know

In this chapter you learned more about the hardware components of a network and what a file server is.

➤ A file server is a big computer where you can store and protect files. It's stored in a secure location (such as a closet or special room) somewhere in your building.

➤ NIC is the common name and acronym for Network Interface Card, which lets your computer become a part of the network.

➤ A computer needs a NIC to work on the network. Once installed, NICs need to be configured to work properly.

➤ The main difference between your computer and a file server is who uses it. You use yours, while everyone can use the file server. Everyone has an opportunity to see files on the server, but not on your computer. Your computer is easier to use—you can't even run DIR on a NetWare file server.

The Big C (Cabling)

The goal of this chapter is to help you identify your network cable. You should be able to point to it and say, "That's my network cable!" This will be enough to help you solve common network problems later on. Better still, you might say something like, "That's my 10BASE-T cable!" after picking up some additional interesting facts about your cabling system, which will help you tackle the really tricky problems much faster.

How much should you understand about cabling? Sound like an incredibly boring topic? Sure, but so is flossing your teeth. You have a feeling that it's good for you, but you don't want it to take too long. It won't; it's another short chapter.

Besides Tripping Over It

Your network cable is important. Every print job, e-mail, and file you request from the network travels through your cable. Take a peek in back of your machine. What a mess, huh? Sometimes these cables get damaged and prevent you from doing work, so it's good to have a very basic idea of who's who and what's what.

How Can I Identify My Cabling?

Ignore the power cord. Ignore the mouse cable. Ignore the keyboard cable. Ignore the video monitor cable. What's left? Odds are it's your *network cable*.

The **network cable** is the wire connecting computers together to form a network. It has connectors on each end of it. Sometimes it's inside the walls where you can't see it.

Jumper cables are way too big to use on your network, so leave them in the car.

Don't ever remove a network cable while a computer is turned on! You could lose files and other important stuff. For some of you, it could even bring down the network.

After you've identified your network cable, you'll notice that it's removable. Removing your cable can be a disaster, so leave it alone. Remove someone else's. (No, I'm just kidding! If you are interested in following along, ask your network administrator for a spare cable to look at. Then you'll understand another important topic—spare cables!) Notice that it has a connector on both ends. One end connects to your Network Interface Card or NIC; the other connects into a holder or outlet on the wall somewhere. These wall outlets are called *wallplates*. Once this cable connection is made, your computer can reach file servers, printers, and e-mail heaven. But only as long as the cable stays healthy.

Take a close look at the connector. See those tiny wires? Some tiny people with tiny hands attached that connector to the cable. It's fragile. If you start playing with your cable, those connections will break—and though the cable may still look fine, it will be as dead as microwaved dirt. Worse yet, these critters don't usually die a quick death. They keep popping in and out of various states of health, confusing the heck out of your network administrator or Maytag repairman.

So how can you take care of your cable?

➤ The obvious—don't run over it with your chair.

➤ Also obvious—don't yank on it. It's not meant to bend or stretch.

➤ Don't chew on it—you or your dog. Seriously, this is a big problem with networks installed in some health and veterinary clinics. Coat the cables with Tabasco sauce if necessary.

➤ Don't hang things from it, like plants or baskets of snacks.

➤ Don't tie things up with it, like your office partner.

➤ Don't use it as a hammock for your feet.

➤ Don't play circus games (test your strength with the cable tug!).

If you ever have to replace your network cable, it's a quick process. Removing a connector from your NIC or the wall is not difficult. If it's round, you can try to turn it counterclockwise. You can also try to push it in and turn it, like one of those childproof caps. Other connector types have a little plastic tab you can squeeze against the cable, which releases the cable. Still others have thumbscrews (or regular screws) that have to be loosened before the cable is released.

Is My Cable Better Than Your Cable?

It depends on what you mean by "better." Some cables last longer than others. Some are sturdier. Some are less expensive. If your company buys cheaper cable and passes the savings on to you in the form of a raise, then your cable is better.

Why on earth should you care what kind of cable you have? To make it easier to fix if it ever breaks. All you have to do is scream for another *"Patch cable—10BASE-T!"* and replace it, and it will work.

Get to know your cable. Hold it. Is it thick like a garden hose, but tougher to bend? If so, you are holding the original Ethernet cabling called "ThickNet." It's known by other names also, like RG-11 or 10BASE-5, "thick coax," Standard Ethernet cable, or even "yellow" cable if it's colored yellow.

29

Patch cable is another name for the short cable connecting your computer to the connector on the wall.

Coax (short for "coaxial cable") is used for cable TV and some networks. A central conductor is wrapped in an insulator, which in turn is wrapped in a braided-wire outer conductor, which is then wrapped in still more insulation.

Is your cable not that thick? Is it about the thickness of a pencil? Easier to bend? Does it feel like your cable TV cable? If so, it's likely to be the more common Ethernet cabling called "ThinNet." It has many names also, like RG-58, 10BASE-2, or "thin coax." It's usually black, but most cables *are* black, aren't they?

Maybe your cable is thin and flimsy. Does it look like your telephone cable? Then you've got the most common cabling around, and its common name is *twisted-pair*. You may hear geeks call it 10BASE-T and sometimes "Type 3" or "Category 5" (which makes you wonder about the other categories).

This twisted-pair cable is easiest to recognize when it is *unshielded* (a.k.a. UTP— Unshielded Twisted Pair). The shielded variety is thicker because there is aluminum foil (the "shield") wrapped around the cables inside. The shielding protects your network cable from the harmful interference generated by fluorescent lights and electric mixers (if you happen to be near a kitchen). This shielded cable (a.k.a. STP—Shielded Twisted Pair) is also known as "Type 1" (no categories here) and is commonly used with token-ring networks.

The computers on your network are connected in an arrangement called *a topology*. The three basic network topologies are bus, ring, and star; they're not as similar as they might look. The *bus* topology uses short cables to connect computers to a central cable called the bus. If one of the short cables breaks, only one computer is affected; if the bus breaks, the network stops. The *ring* topology (usually called *token-ring*) requires that the connected computers pass information from one to another in a circle. (It never really looks like a ring because the wires coming into and going out of your computer are hidden in a single cable.) All the cables from the computers connect to a type of hub; if the cable breaks, the ring is still there, only smaller. With the *star* topology, the computers are connected to a central hub (the server itself, or another computer connected to the server). If one of the cables breaks, only one computer is affected. If the hub breaks, the whole network stops.

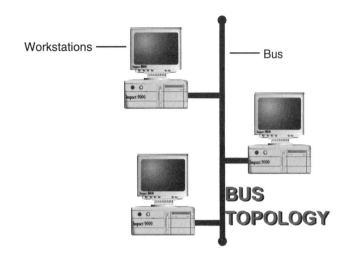

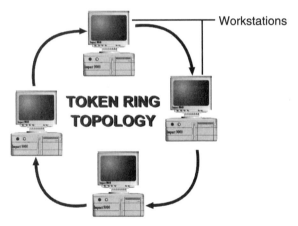

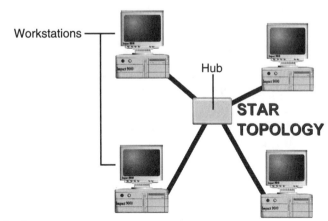

The three basic network topologies.

You may notice your LAN administrator speaking the strange network language. What on earth is this ten-base stuff? And how about eight-oh-two stuff? Pull up a chair and hear about Standards.

To help make networks work better, an important organization called the IEEE (Institute of Electrical and Electronic Engineers) got together and wrote some rules. They numbered them—802.3 for what resembles Ethernet, and 802.5 for token-ring. Some of you may be using 802.4 which is more commonly known as ARCnet. You can sleep better knowing someone can't arbitrarily change the rules of Ethernet tonight and have your network crash in the morning.

Cables have to be connected a certain way—and can't exceed certain distances—or else the cable poops out. The secret naming code for Ethernet cables is easier to figure out. The 10BASE-2 cable describes a *10*-megahertz (speed) *Base*band (type) network cable limited to *2* (actually 200) meters maximum length. 10BASE-5 can go 500 meters. 10BASE-T was thrown in to confuse you—it simply means twisted-pair, with a distance limit of less than 100 meters.

Wired for Action

Time to put your cable back. See how it connects to your NIC? Both ends of your patch cable usually have the same type of connector, but not always, so it's good to know the name for each end (in case you want to order one over the phone). Your network administrator is probably the best person to ask if you'd like to learn more about cables or connectors.

The Big WC (Wiring Closet)

What's behind that walljack? Usually it's a similar cable, like an extension cord, going back to a central location. Where's that? It's called the *wiring closet*. You probably have one on your floor, and from what you know about cabling, it can't be that far away. Usually it's much less than 100 meters.

Ask your network administrator where your wiring closet is, and if you have time to waste, ask if it's possible to visit. Three minutes is more than enough. What you'll find is a room with lots and lots of cabling. One cable coming in for each computer attached to the local network, one or two per office or cubicle. This is where it all happens, where you get connected to the rest of the network resources.

Here's the $66,000 question: Can you find *your* cable in there? The cable that goes all the way back to your walljack? In the best wiring closets, the answer is yes, and it's easy. Cables are routed to a big square switchboard (*patch panel*) with clearly labeled tags describing the other end, like "Room 217B." In the worst wiring closets there is no room to stand, no labels on anything, and human skeletons littering the floor.

If you have many floors in your building, you probably have many wiring closets. They're all wired together. Each is located in a central place so all the cables can reach it without exceeding their maximum distances.

Why should you care about the wiring closet? It's more background to help you solve problems later. Just think about it—if your computer says it can't find the file server, now you know the complete path it takes. The WC is also a great hiding place for your network administrator—and any spare patch cables you may need.

> **Hub** is a multi-port device used to connect many network cables, usually 10BASE-T. Hubs are connected using larger cables such as 10BASE-5 or 10BASE-2, or even fiber-optic cabling.
>
> **Concentrator** is another name for a hub.
>
> **Backbone** is the word used to describe the critical cabling between the wiring closets.

Just What Is a Hub, Bub?

In case you're wondering, all these twisted-pair cables coming together in your wiring closet are connected to a *concentrator*, or *hub*. Each hub can tie in eight or more individual cables, creating a little network! Once you connect a few hubs together, you have a big network! Now you know how to grow networks!

Hubs are fun to look at because they often have little lights that let you know that an individual cable (all the way back to your NIC) is working! If the light's out, it's broken. It's time for a light to come on inside of your head as you ponder this question: Where is the file server cable? Yes, the NIC in the file server is connected to a hub somewhere, if not in your own wiring closet. And printers? Yes, if they're the kind that attach directly to the network. As long as the hubs are cabled together, your computer and the file server (and the rest of the network) can communicate.

Drop Me a Line Sometime

So how did your cable come to find its way to your office? Do you think it was all neatly laid before the walls went up? Hardly. Quite often cabling goes in after a building is completed. Cable installers actually climb up into the ceiling and pull a cable from the wiring closet to your office wall, and connect the wire to your walljack, and hopefully clean up afterwards. This process is called *pulling a cable*, and the result is a new *cable drop*. You can guess what happens if they use the wrong type of cable or connectors. They don't usually exceed maximum distances because cable is expensive.

One other fact to be aware of: cables (especially twisted-pair) are sensitive to electrical interference. Such interference can come from fluorescent lighting, elevators, vacuum cleaners, and hair dryers. You can't do anything about the building cabling, but you may question your network administrator if you suspect a source of interference.

 If you ever damage your 10BASE-T patch cable, don't swap it out with a telephone cable! They may look the same, and it may fit, but it won't work reliably. Your telephone cable is flat, not twisted, and don't bother trying to twist it (11 turns per inch) because it won't stay.

The Least You Need to Know

You now know more about cables and cabling than your cable-TV repairman does. He doesn't know that:

➤ Your network cable is your lifeline to the network. Every e-mail, print job, file, and data request travels through your cable.

➤ Your network cable (also called a patch cable) connects the NIC in your machine to the wallplate.

➤ Your building cabling comes together in a room called the wiring closet.

➤ The backbone of your network is the cabling connecting all of your wiring closets.

➤ Cables are fragile and should not be yanked for any amount of money.

The Big NOS (Network Operating System)

Now that you understand hardware and cabling, you are ready to ask the big question: What makes that powerful computer a file server? It's the software that's loaded onto it. In this chapter you'll learn the basics about the most popular networking software from Novell called NetWare.

Normal Operating System Software (DOS and Windows)

First some review. What is DOS, anyway? This **Disk Operating System** doesn't do your work for you, but it helps you get it done. DOS can be called the "brains" of your computer because it controls almost everything you do with your machine. You use DOS when you format diskettes, copy files, use a word processor, and print, to name just a few activities. DOS is always there—waiting to see what you type in, figure out what it means, and go do it for you.

And Windows? It sits on top of DOS and looks pretty. For the most part, you don't have to know how to use a keyboard or type in Windows. You can use a mouse to point-and-click at what you want. Windows watches what you click on, and then tells DOS what to do. Windows is the beautiful skin over the bones of DOS.

These products are great for doing exactly what they are supposed to do—assist one person in using one computer at a time. This is great for home computers, really small businesses, and laptops.

But once you want to do something outside of your own computer, you're severely limited. The commands you type into DOS are received with a blank stare. "What's that?" your computer asks, when you request that it print your e-mail on the seventh-floor color laser printer.

Network Operating Systems Can Help

Welcome to the *NOS* (Network Operating System), here to help you with that exact problem. Before the NOS, no one dared to try talking to another computer or printer.

Novell NetWare is the most popular NOS. Its strength lies in the fact that it works with almost every type of hardware in existence. This really helps tie your business together, by connecting all of the various computers and gadgets that have accumulated over the years.

Novell's NetWare software.

NOS Services for You

If you consider all the events that could possibly happen on a network, they would fall into three general categories:

➤ **File support**—that is, the creation, sharing, storage, and retrieval of files—is essential, and the NOS specializes in providing a fast and secure method.

➤ **Communications** refers to everything that gets sent through your cable. You communicate when you log in to the network, copy a file, send an e-mail, or print, for example.

➤ **Equipment support services** includes all the special services that can be provided, such as printing, tape backups, network virus scanning, and so on.

Combining the power of DOS at your workstation with the power of NetWare on the network makes your machine a much more effective tool.

Extending the Power of Your Workstation

Once you have access to a file server, you can take advantage of all the features the network provides. Have you been assigned to a team that has to get a big report finished in a hurry? You can break the job into many different files and store them on the file server, in a common directory where everyone can get to them and they stay more organized and protected.

Don't have enough hard disk space to store several iterations of your presentation? Use the disk space on the file server. Everyone should be given their own personal space on the file server. Need to run the latest version of a drawing program but don't have enough space? Load it into your personal and private area on the network.

Want to save your strength, some energy, and a few trees delivering that report to your boss? Use your computer and attach the report to an e-mail, and never get out of your chair except to go to lunch. You can learn more about e-mail in Chapter 15.

Once on the network, you should have these capabilities. If you don't, contact your network administrator and find out when you will. Your network administrator is responsible for setting you up with the proper network security clearances to use the valuable network resources. To learn more about how access is granted and security is enforced, check out the details in Chapter 10.

How the NOS Helps You

How doth the network operating system help you? Let me count the ways. But just a few.

Reach Out and Touch a Resource

You want to get to the laser printer down the hall? You request it from the NOS (file server). Want to dial out on one of the network modems? The file server routes all your network traffic.

The NOS is responsible for keeping an eye on all the network resources out there. It knows when a printer is out of paper or off-line, and it can send a message informing the network administrator.

A Traffic Cop Keeping the Network Peaceful

What happens between 8:30 a.m. and 9:30 a.m. at work? Lots of people turn on their computers and log in to the network. Some do it at the very same instant as others. Ordinary computers would freak out at this sudden load, but the file server expects it, and excels at the challenge. All the requests come to the server and wait in line to be served (which takes less than a second). It's usually a very short wait, once your request reaches the file server (*millionths* of a second). Everyone gets an equal shot. Fairness reigns.

How about when someone prints their 100-page monthly review at 9:00 a.m.? Not a problem! That request comes in like any other, and when the server sees you want to print, it delegates that job to another part of itself.

What happens when two people print to the same server at the same time? Why don't the pages get intertwined? Because the NOS takes each print request and turns it into an official *print job* which stays together and is identified uniquely as yours.

Your Protector in Times of Trouble

When you store your files on the file server, you can be reasonably sure they will be there tomorrow. Your network administrator bets her career on it. The file server has lots of technical stuff used to protect your files, like double hard drives in case one fails, big Energizer-bunny batteries standing by in case the power goes out, and automatic tape backup equipment, all locked up in a room where animals can't get to them.

Your file server and its network operating system can take a licking and keep on ticking. It delivers come rain, snow, sleet, or shine. It… well, you get the idea. The NOS was specially designed to do things beyond the capabilities of ordinary computers. It has powers that are important to businesses, such as balancing workloads, maintaining proper security, continuing to run when a component fails, and most importantly, sharing the investment in valuable resources such as disk space, printers, databases, and whatever else can be networked.

Where Does the NOS Live?

Your NOS lives in two places at the same time. The bulk of it—the commands, the file system, and the protection devices—live inside the file server, stored on the hard drive. The other place it lives is in your own computer (and everyone's computer, if they are on the network). A small piece of software called the *requestor* lives on your computer's hard drive, and should run each time you start your computer. Once it runs, it tells the file server you are ready to participate on the network.

How Can I Get Connected to My File Server?

Sold on what a file server can do for you? Want to get started (if you aren't already)? As long as you have your NIC installed and a cable connected, you are ready to have your requestor installed.

Requestors, Shells, and VLMs

To allow your computer to talk on the network, it needs that part of the NOS that stays on your computer. This software comes in the same box with the NOS, on diskettes. You carry these diskettes to your computer and install the network requestor—which takes only a few minutes to do. Your grandparents might have called the same product the *shell*.

Requestor: The part of the network software that is loaded on your computer, talks to your NIC, and places your request on the network. Requestor software comes packaged with your network operating system

Node is another name for a fully-connected computer on the network.

Once the requestor is loaded, it acts like another personality inside your computer. Along with DOS, it watches the commands you type in. If it recognizes them as network commands, it jumps into action and does everything possible to carry out your network request.

The requestor performs something else just as important—it *listens* to the network! It acts as an open ear to everything passing by on the network cable. If it notices something with your name on it—like an important e-mail or maybe a message from the file server telling you that your print job completed successfully—

the requestor can interrupt what you are doing to provide the information. Lots of activity goes on back and forth between your requestor and the file server that you never know about. That's why broken cables cause so much pain and grief. Your requestor sits quietly in the background serving you. Trust it. It's looking out for your best interests.

Who installs the requestor software on my machine? Usually the network administrator installs the requestor software. Sometimes the contractors installing your network are responsible for loading it. It's no big deal; if you have the diskettes, it takes about three minutes to load, so you could do it yourself.

How can I get one? You only need one if you're not yet on the network. Ask your network administrator if you aren't sure.

Logging In to the Network

After the requestor software has been successfully loaded onto your workstation, you can log in to the network by changing to the network drive letter. From your DOS prompt, type **F:**. Then type **LOGIN** and press **Enter**. If you're in Windows, it's even easier. Start **File Manager** and look at the drive letters listed at the top. The first letter beyond your local drives should be your network login directory. Select it; then double-click on **LOGIN.EXE**. For either DOS or Windows, you will then be asked for your password. Type it in; then press **Enter** or click on **OK**. (Chapter 9 describes the details of logging in to the network.)

When you log in successfully to a NetWare file server, a few good things happen. Special drive mappings are created to assist you in getting around the network. Special printing assignments are set up that help direct and customize the print jobs you may be preparing for. Special software may be turned on to run automatically—for example, virus-scanning software. All these events are part of the *login script*.

Login script: Similar to an AUTOEXEC.BAT file for the network, this little program runs every time you log in. Login scripts contain the information needed to print, map network drives, provide greetings, and run special programs.

Logging Out at the End of a Day

When you have finished using the network at the end of the workday, it is a good habit to *log out* (also known as *logging off*) of the network. Just type **LOGOUT** at the DOS command prompt and press **Enter**. You can log out from anywhere on the network. The network will safely close all your files and release the access to your requested network resources.

The Least You Need to Know

Network Operating Systems are the brains behind the network. Here is a review of what you learned:

➤ DOS/Windows is a single-user operating system used to control your personal computer. Network operating systems like NetWare are designed to be used by *many* people at once.

➤ The bulk of NetWare lives on a machine called the file server.

➤ A small piece of NetWare lives on your machine, and it's called the requestor.

➤ The requestor software is the software that takes care of any network command you give it.

➤ To begin using a network, you need a login name (user ID) and a password.

➤ The network is a safer place to work because the file server has more ways to protect files than an ordinary computer has.

Chapter 6

Other NOSs

In This Chapter

➤ What are some advantages of other network operating systems?

➤ What benefits am I getting from a "File Server" network?

➤ What benefits can I get from a "peer-to-peer" network?

➤ Can I mix and get the best of both worlds?

So now you know about the most popular network operating system. It's called Novell NetWare. But what if you're using something else? Is that bad? Did you make the wrong choice?

Network operating systems come in a variety of shapes and sizes because businesses have different requirements. Novell is big, but as hard as it tries, it can't be all things to all people. Don't forget there's another 40% of the workforce using something else.

Some network operating systems perform very well in small networks. Others specialize in connecting many small networks together throughout the world. Some networks can help you when you don't really have a machine big enough to be a file server. Oh, and the big reason: some are even less expensive. The following are some of the other popular network operating systems you may run across.

Microsoft LAN Manager   The LAN Manager from Microsoft was an early challenge to NetWare, but never made much of a dent in the marketplace. It was installed on top of the operating system in a workstation running OS/2; the performance was nothing to write home about. Microsoft has announced the replacement for LAN Manager as Windows NT-Advanced Server.

IBM LAN Server   This NOS started out as IBM's version of the Microsoft LAN Manager with very few differences. Over the years the products diverged; IBM continued to improve its version. Built on top of the OS/2 operating system, the current product boasts speed and performance factors approaching those of NetWare, but marketplace acceptance has been minimal.

Windows NTAS   Microsoft Windows NTAS (New Technology, Advanced Server) is expected to gain a strong foothold in the NOS marketplace, especially with Microsoft marketing muscle behind it. It boasts strong security, high performance, and low cost because you pay only for the workstations you connect.

Banyan VINES   Banyan VINES (VIrtual NEtwork System) has been around a long time (since 1984). It's a very sophisticated NOS that provides a user with a view of the entire company's network resources, even if it's made up of hundreds of little networks! A single login to the network provides connection to all authorized file servers on the network. This feature (called VINES StreetTalk Services) stores user-information databases everywhere. The security system and printing are excellent.

Server or No Server, That Is the Question

Now that you're pretty comfortable with file servers, you're about to learn that not all networks *use* a file server. Instead, some spread out the function of the file server among all the ordinary computers on the network. These are called *peer* (or, if there's an echo in here, *peer-to-peer*) networks, because all computers act as peers to one another. Here's an analogy that compares how the two different types of networks behave.

Server-based networks   It's as if someone designated a particular machine to be king, locked it up in a castle, and left you to beg for scraps of information. The good news is that it spits the information at you at high speeds, and it's fair—everyone shares equally in what's available. You may recognize these castles by the products that represent them. The biggest castle is Novell NetWare. The smaller castles include Banyan VINES, Apple's AppleShare, Microsoft LAN Manager, Windows NTAS (New Technology Advanced Server), and IBM LAN Server.

Peer-to-peer network   The next village over started a democracy. They feel everyone is equal—peers—but each person has to work harder. You may recognize these villages by the products that represent them. Artisoft's LANtastic, Apple's built-in LocalTalk, Microsoft Windows for Workgroups, and even Novell's own Personal NetWare (formerly NetWare Lite).

Peer-to-Peer NOSs

With file server systems, the workstations on the network are either servers or clients. The servers control clients' access to their services, provide them with access to the files that are stored on them, manage the access of multiple clients, provide printing services, etc.

Peer-to-peer systems allow computers to be both clients and servers at the same time. Alternatively, each computer can be just one or the other. If you make one a server only, the system starts looking like a file server system. All computers can have a printer attached that is also available to all other computers.

Peer systems are less expensive to install than file server systems, but they are more restrictive, especially in the area of performance and total number of users. Peer systems usually consist of small *workgroups* that connect a small number of computers (2–20); file server systems often connect more than 100 computers. The following sections list the most popular peer-to-peer NOSs on the market.

LANtastic

One of the first and best peer networking systems is from Artisoft, and it's called LANtastic. They also offer a really basic product called Simply LANtastic. Either NOS is very simple to install, especially if you use the default naming convention. LANtastic operates on almost all hardware configurations.

One of the strengths of LANtastic is its optional security system, but you have to take time to set it up. Most people use the default security and do fine. It can support up to several hundred workstations.

You can access a NetWare file server on a LANtastic network, but you have to purchase additional software to do so. Standard LANtastic runs fine with a Windows workstation, but to obtain really impressive Windows versions of the utilities, you must buy LANtastic for Windows.

Windows for Workgroups

Microsoft's peer system is a great option when all computers are running Windows and Windows applications. Windows for Workgroups is an extension to Windows that provides all the functions necessary for an inexpensive peer network, except the hardware. If you already own Windows, you can purchase the Windows for Workgroups Add-on for about $60.00 per computer.

As an added bonus, this NOS includes genuine network applications free; they can make your network productive immediately. They include e-mail, fax software, a scheduling package, and network games! The only problem is relatively poor security, slower performance, and the inability to connect a plain old DOS workstation (a simple task for all the rest of the peer systems).

Part 4, "Building Your Own Empire" covers the entire installation and use of Windows for Workgroups, just in case you'd like to build your own peer-to-peer network.

Personal NetWare

Novell's third-generation peer NOS is called Personal NetWare, a full-functioning network operating system. It is a significant improvement over its predecessor, NetWare Lite, in the areas of security and performance. It's easy to set up, and integrates nicely into a network containing a traditional NetWare file server (it had better; they come from the same company). Add your own hardware; select from just about anything.

Personal NetWare works much like a file server system from a user's standpoint. The user has to log in to the network, and then sees all resources available. It's hard to think they all *aren't* coming from the same machine, like a file server. It's an attractive, seamless synthesis of all computers on the current network—and it works great with DOS or Windows workstations.

Apple

The makers of the Macintosh computer knew the importance of networking long before many other manufacturers. They built the capability right into their machines so you wouldn't have to purchase extra hardware, software, or cabling. Right out of the box, these computers could use LocalTalk to behave as peers on a productive network, using cables plugged into the printer port, sharing the Apple LaserWriter and NetModems. Eventually another application called PhoneNET became a more flexible Mac alternative to LocalTalk.

For those wanting a traditional file server system, the AppleShare NOS could be installed on a dedicated Macintosh. LocalTalk was, and is, much slower than the traditional Ethernet or token-ring networks, but it *was* free. Apple met the speed challenge by introducing EtherTalk and TokenTalk. Both work remarkably well (mainly with sharing files and printing services) when mixed into a NetWare environment.

To share services on a network of Macs, you access the desired resource through Finder. The display will show all of the shared objects available through the peer service. Just click on your selections; they will appear on your desktop as shared directories and printers.

So Which NOS Is for Me?

All this variety exists to meet the demands of the marketplace. Some people value speed more than security, or low-cost over reliability, so they have to decide whether to use a file server or a peer-to-peer network. Here are some of the current persuasions:

File Server	
Pro	**Con**
Good performance	Expensive when it's first going in
High speed	
Quick access to network resources	Complex to understand; you'll need (oh, no!) a geek to support it
Great security	
Superior management (someone else does it!)	
Easy expansion capabilities	

Peer Network	
Pro	**Con**
Cheaper—you don't need the file server machine	Slower performance overall
Easier for a small group to control	Sometimes you can't access something because the machine that has it is turned off
More flexible because you can pick up and drag parts around	Much less security than server-based networks
Simplicity—you can probably see everything on the network	Most are DOS-based; they can have the same problems DOS has (such as limited memory management)
	Who's responsible? Oh, no! The users!

Living Together in the Same Net

When networks were first getting started, they were simple arrangements of just a few computers in a single department. Many departments started acquiring networks, and they didn't follow any pattern except what suited them best. It was an ego thing.

Nowadays, it's not politically correct to be a lonesome network. All the departments should be interconnected and become one big LAN. But this is easier said than done. The many different networks each have their own rules and often don't mix with other systems. But it's too expensive to throw away all that investment in technology and replace everything with NetWare and a standard PC. So we try to co-exist.

QUESTION: Let's say I like Novell NetWare *and* Windows for Workgroups *and* Macintoshes running AppleTalk. Won't I need different cabling for each of them? If I hook them up to the same cabling system, won't the traffic snarl up with items crashing into each other, confuse the file servers, and cause other worries?

ANSWER: Not at all! Some cabling is so common, like 10BASE2 or 10BASET, that all of the major network operating systems support it. There's lots of room inside the cable, allowing everyone to travel through the same cable if necessary.

QUESTION: Okay, maybe the different departments could live with each other on the same cabling system, but could they really *communicate* with each other? Like sending mail and attached documents?

ANSWER: Once again, yes, but at times it's more difficult. For different types of networks to understand and exchange information with each other, special (and expensive) equipment is often needed. Most of the time this expense can be avoided by finding less expensive alternative forms of communication.

Advantages of Mixing

Having several network operating systems on the same cable gives you the best of both worlds. It's the ultimate in flexibility and cost control. It's a viable solution for maintaining the special investments of smaller departments that have already stabilized. It allows the remainder of a business to access the files of a previously isolated department. Also, these departments can often gain the advantage of new networking resources, such as printing and communication to the outside world.

Disadvantages of Mixing

There is bad with the good, however. Mixed environments are much more complicated to support, because the users want to do new things they never could before. They experiment more, sometimes causing problems on the network (printing, for example, can be a headache). It's much tougher to isolate problems. It's also tough for a single Help Desk to support all the possible hardware and application software associated with each operating system.

Allowing multiple network operating systems does take up some space on your cabling system. It's called *bandwidth*, and it's something you never want to run out of, or things will slow to a crawl. Network administrators worry about this stuff so that (hopefully) you won't have to.

Bandwidth A measure of how much information can be pumped through a cable system. E-mail requires only a small bandwidth. Capabilities such as multimedia and video require a very large bandwidth.

49

The Least You Need to Know

This chapter reviewed the roles of other network operating systems. You may be thinking about starting your own small network. At least now you realize:

➤ Other network operating systems exist and have advantages such as flexibility and cost.

➤ File server networks have great security and performance.

➤ Peer networks are more flexible.

➤ Sometimes it's possible to mix systems on a network.

➤ Starting your own new network on existing cable could cause a problem somewhere if you run out of bandwidth.

Chapter 7

So How Do DOS and Windows Fit In?

In This Chapter

➤ DOS and Windows remain basically the same on a network

➤ The network provides you with more commands to play with

➤ New drive letters mean new opportunities

➤ Some commands should not be run on a network

You may be pondering the world of operating systems (yeah, right!). If that super network operating system can do all those wonderful things, do we need DOS and Windows anymore? Absolutely! Remember that DOS (with or without Windows) is the operating system controlling your personal computer. It doesn't change drastically, but enough to warrant this chapter. These are hands-on exercises! Roll up your sleeves and let's get started!

Same Old Thing

To help understand how commands are used on the network, it's helpful to review the standard DOS environment and commands. This part will be review for most of you. If you're new to computing, you might want to pick up the *Complete Idiot's Guide to DOS*, which provides lots of this background information.

As Simple as A:, B:, C: You remember your drive letters, right? Drive A: is your diskette drive. Drive C: is your hard drive and drive D: could be your second hard drive (or CD-ROM if you have one). Where's the B: drive? Oh, yes, it's the same thing you were pointing to when you said A: (unless you have *two* diskette drives, then the B: drive is your *second* diskette drive). What's that? My B: drive is my A: drive? Yes, if you don't have a second diskette drive, your first is automatically A: *and* B:. Why am I belaboring this point? Because you'll find that network drives behave in ways just as silly.

Have you ever seen a computer with no drives? They're called *diskless workstations*, and they perform just fine on the network. Each of these machines has a special computer chip on its network board that tells the computer to connect to the network so it can boot up.

MD, CD, RD (or MKDIR, CHDIR, and RMDIR if you like)   These are the commands that tell the computer to create, change to, or remove directories on a diskette or hard drive. Good investment to have learned these, because they operate exactly the same way on a network. Use MD or MKDIR to create directories on the network. Use RD or RMDIR to remove them. The CD or CHDIR will change your current directory on the network.

DIR and Related Switches   Good old DIR works just fine on the network. Have you ever tried to find a file on your hard drive? If you know the name of the file, the DIR command with the switch /S helps you locate it. For example, to find a file called MYFILE.DOC use **CD** to change to the root directory; once there, type **DIR MYFILE.DOC /S** and press **Enter**. If the file is there, the command will find it, and display the entire path for your convenience. You can use the same strategy for finding files on the network, although it could take much longer because the drives are larger.

COPY & XCOPY   These DOS commands are used simply to copy files, and/or to copy files from one directory to another. They also work fine on the network. The XCOPY command is a bit faster, allowing you to copy subdirectories (and keep them intact) with the /S switch.

PRINT Simple text files in DOS can be printed easily with the PRINT command. It's not used much because most word processing software has a printing function built in. PRINT is still good, however, to print the README files. It works fine on the network.

HELP When in doubt about the use of a DOS command, try typing HELP. It won't help you with NetWare commands, but it will with DOS, which you will continue to use a lot on the network.

Windows and File Manager Many of you, in fact most of you, have migrated to the most common GUI: Microsoft Windows. It also runs fine on the network, with lots more added functions. File Manager (which performs all standard DOS commands for working with files and directories) functions the same on the network.

Brand New Network Things

Now we're ready to take a quantum leap into networking. The following commands are unique to networks, and are not available in plain old DOS. Fasten your seatbelt. Keep that same thought pattern: Easy. Simple.

As Simple as F:, H:, Z: New drive letters! Lots of them! Try some now, you'll probably find five or six letters that act just like a DOS hard drive. These drives are not in your machine, however—they're somewhere out there on the network. You don't have to know where; just be thankful you have them.

Ready for a brain-stretcher? All these new drive letters are probably pointing to the same hard drive out there. But not exactly the same place (or else why have them?). They are pointing to different *subdirectories* on that hard drive. So you don't have lots of different drives out there, just a lot of different drive *locations*.

What's the big deal, you ask? The big deal is keeping you calm in an emergency. It's important *not* to think of a particular drive letter as the *only* place you can find something.

Let's drive the point home with an example. Log in to the network. Type **Z:** and press **Enter**. This is called "changing to the Z Drive," of course. It may look like this:

```
Z:\PUBLIC\>_
```

In this case, the letter **Z** indicates the directory called "public." Now change to the F: drive (Boy, do you learn quickly!).

```
F:\LOGIN\>_
```

Drive F: identifies the directory called "login." Your brain may be telling you these are two different hard drives. Fight it! Prove otherwise! Change to the root directory:

```
F:\LOGIN\> CD\ (and press Enter)
F:\>_
```

And now change to the public directory:

```
F:\> CD\PUBLIC
F:\PUBLIC\>_
```

Now you can see for yourself that F and Z are pointing to the same directory, which must be the same hard drive. These multiple drive letters are simply a convenience to save you from having to type **CD** if you're trying to get to the most common directories.

NDIR   This command is the network version of DIR. It has a lot more power than regular DIR, but it takes time to learn the details. A plain old NDIR of your current network directory still shows lots of information.

Can't remember the switches that go along with your command? NetWare helps you out if you ask politely. Just use the question mark (**NDIR /?**) and you'll see all of the possible options. Then type your command again with the proper switch.

Two important discoveries can be made here. First, notice that all files have an "owner" associated with them. This name is the person who originally created or copied this file. It's a good way to determine who's been into the cookie jar playing with your files. Also, you can see files you don't normally see with DOS DIR. Some files, for example, can be hidden from your view on the network. These files don't show up in DOS. (You'll learn how to hide files in Chapter 10. For now, just remember NDIR shows you the owner of a file, along with interesting things like hidden files.)

CHKDIR   Ever wonder how much space is left in your directory on the network? CHKDIR lets you check out the maximum amount of space in your current directory, the amount of space in use, and the amount that's left available to you. Sometimes the network administrator limits the amount of disk space available to you. If so, you won't be able to use up the entire available disk space remaining. NetWare 4.x users can use NDIR /VOL to do the same thing.

LISTDIR   Have you ever wanted to see the layout of your directories? The LISTDIR utility draws a map of your file and directory system on your screen.

CHKVOL   Have you ever wondered how much space is left on your entire LAN? CHKVOL finds out what's out there, and reports back to you. Once again, NetWare 4.x users will find the same results using NDIR /VOL.

VOLINFO   Similar to CHKVOL, this command provides the same information about space on your network, displayed on an attractive blue screen.

NCOPY   This network copy command is an alternative to the DOS COPY command. NCOPY is faster than COPY for copying files between locations on the network. There's not much improvement if your local drive is the source or target, so either COPY or NCOPY is fine. On the network, NCOPY keeps special codes with the file it copies (for example, if it's a protected file). DOS COPY won't carry this information with the file.

NPRINT   Just like the DOS PRINT command, this standby works great for printing plain-text files on the network.

RENDIR   Here's a handy network command! It's REName DIRectory. Maybe you have a bug in your FISH program and you want to reload it without losing your old scores. Instead of making another directory and copying the contents over, you can simply rename the directory. Just type the command **RENDIR C:\FISH C:\FISH-OLD** and press **Enter**. All your Bingo files are now in the FISH-OLD directory for safekeeping. Now you can install FISH again, and it will create a new FISH directory. The only problem with RENDIR is that it won't work on your local C: drive.

Where are all these new commands stored? On the network, of course. But how did my machine find them, you ask? Because their location is now in your *path*. Try it. Type **PATH**:

If you typed it *before* logging in to the network, you get:

PATH=C:\,C:\DOS;C:\WINDOWS;C:\WP51

If you typed it *after* logging into the network, you get:

PATH=Z:;Y:;X:;C:\;C:\DOS;C:\WINDOWS;C:\WP51

When you logged in, the network adjusted your PATH so commands can be found automatically from the network. Most network commands live on the file server in a directory called Z:\PUBLIC.

Other Good Commands to Remember and Use

You don't have to remember every command to be a network wizard. You just have to find and remember those commands that make you happy. Here's a handful to get you started, along with reasons why you may want to remember them.

DOSKEY   If you plan to spend any time out in DOS, it's very helpful to load DOSKEY. I'm speaking especially to you hunt-and-peck artists out there. After DOSKEY is loaded, you can bring back any previously typed command by simply pressing the **up arrow** key. This can be helpful when you can't remember the exact switch on a command, just press the **up arrow** and change the switch. It's much faster than retyping the whole thing.

EXIT   If you're using the graphical DOS Shell or Windows, and you've just finished using a command prompt temporarily and want to leave, remember the EXIT command. EXIT will return you to the program in the primary window.

MOVE   Nothing too special about this command, except it erases the source—just like the mayhem in Windows File Manager when you click and drag a file from one place to another. This is the DOS version, and it also works on the network.

DELTREE   Tired of removing all of the little subdirectories when you are cleaning up your disk space? The DELTREE command does it quickly. It works great on the network, too. Just name the directory after the DELTREE command and you won't have to bother with CDs, RDs, or DELs. Unfortunately, this command is available only in DOS version 6.0 or later.

MSAV (or Any Good Virus Checker)   Always practice safe computing! Use a virus checker, and use it often. If you have MS-DOS 6.0, try **MSAV /N /L** and you'll live longer. If you don't have a virus checker, request one from your network administrator.

Networks are a really easy way to spread viruses because of all the sharing going on. Information, data, and files come in from many sources, such as diskettes or downloads from bulletin boards. If your computer catches a virus, or you suspect it has, *stop what you're doing* and call the help desk or network administrator. They'll want to find the source, and ask you lots of questions, but it's nothing personal; they're trying to stop the virus from being spread on the network.

Good Commands to Stay Away From!

Some commands are worth remembering just so you *don't* use them! Here's a few you should avoid, along with some ways they can get you in trouble.

DEL *.* or ERASE *.*   I don't know what the temptation is with these commands, but lots of people like to use them. It's kind of scary to do this on the network, and in that shared environment it's a good policy *never to delete a file you did not create.* If you do accidentally delete network files, you'll find that the UNDELETE command from DOS doesn't work. Try the SALVAGE command to bring them back (see Chapter 13 for more details on SALVAGE).

FORMAT   Don't worry—you can't format a network drive if you are using NetWare. But for those of you *not* using NetWare, an accidental FORMAT could wipe out something important. Buy formatted diskettes and you'll never have to use this command.

BACKUP   Yes, it's important to back up valuable files. It's another story to back up your entire hard drive to the network! It may sound like a good idea, but network space isn't that cheap, and you are likely to receive a nasty complaint from your network administrator. Imagine how much good space would disappear if *everyone* had that bright idea?

Use the BACKUP command for important things on your hard disk, but back up on diskettes, not the network.

XCOPY C:*.* F: /S   Oh, a wise guy! Yes, this does the same thing to a network that BACKUP does, except it's *worse* because the files aren't squished. Don't.

DEFRAG   The DEFRAG command cleans up the wasted space on a disk or diskette, kind of like squeezing the air out of a loaf of bread so it fits on the shelf. This command is great for your local drive C: and diskettes, but *stay away from the network drives with it*. They don't need this kind of help.

NDIR F:*.* /S   If you're interested in seeing just about every file on the file server, go ahead. This could take minutes or longer, and serves no purpose except to make you and your machine look real busy if your boss comes in.

You might be interested in searching the entire file server for a file, and it's okay to do this, but realize the command can take several minutes to complete.

The Least You Need to Know

This chapter provided information on computer commands you'll be using (and some you won't be using) on the network. We learned:

➤ DOS and Windows are still needed, and operate basically the same on a network.

➤ New drive letters on the network mean new locations for storing and retrieving files.

➤ New network commands are available to help you take advantage of the network's resources.

➤ Some commands can get you into trouble, and should not be run on a network.

Chapter 8

Peripheral Vision

In This Chapter

➤ What is a peripheral?

➤ How to take advantage of peripherals on a network

➤ How to tell whether a printer is available

➤ What a scanner and OCR are good for

➤ How to find out more about peripherals

Networking is a game of trade-offs; it demonstrates the laws of supply and demand quite well. In this chapter, you'll learn more about some of the supplies, and start demanding them.

What's the most common peripheral device? It's *disk storage*, usually connected directly to the file server. Disk storage is the real guts of your network, since just about everything that happens on a network passes through it. It's all hard drives, never floppy. They're usually like the kind in your computer—small, round and magnetic, and really huge in capacity, since this resource is shared by many network users.

This chapter is an introduction to all the other peripheral devices you may have on your network. Even more—lots more—exist than listed here, but this will give you an idea of what's possible.

Printers Galore

Printers can be attached directly to networks these days, but you can still find many connected to computers that act as traffic cops, or *print servers*, for incoming print jobs.

Peripheral Any device that adds value to your network. This is a geek term for printers, modems, and external storage.

Print job A memo, report, or other document that has been sent to a network printer, but hasn't printed yet. A print job also contains information defining the number of copies, special paper settings, and details regarding a cover page.

If you have your own personal printer, you probably use it much differently from the way you'd use your network printer. Network printers get no respect. They're like rental cars: Lots of fun to put through the grinder, but you'd never buy one used. Maybe this is why they have the reputation of letting you down when you need them most. It doesn't have to be that way. Your company should invest in a decent and appropriate-sized laser printer to handle your workload. After all, the majority of businesses today put out a single product—printed paper! Let's be kind to our printer.

Take a closer look at your printer. It often has many different paper trays, and each tray can hold a different type of paper. You could have plain paper in one, company letterhead in another, envelopes in a third, transparencies in a fourth, three-hole-punched in a fifth, and multi-colored paper in a sixth. Most printers only have two or three trays, so you have to fight over the contents.

An example of a laser printer.

The good news is that most software now takes advantage of printer capabilities today. For instance, you can select multiple paper-source trays for your project and save your choices with your file. When you send it to print, you can have letterhead on the first page, plain for the rest, and an envelope printed, all without leaving your desk!

Dos, Don'ts, and Etiquette for Network Printers

DO THIS WITH YOUR NETWORK PRINTERS:

➤ Print draft copies in lower resolution for faster printing.

➤ Print big jobs after hours when the printer is less busy. You can learn how to do this in Chapter 14.

➤ Recycle, when possible, both paper and toner cartridges. Save trees.

➤ Send test prints of a single page of a large print job before sending the whole thing.

➤ Be sure the paper tray you want to use is loaded before sending your print job.

➤ Refill the paper bin when it's running low—before it runs out.

DON'T DO THIS WITH YOUR NETWORK PRINTERS:

➤ Don't run multiple copies of a print job through the laser printer; use the office copier.

➤ Don't run away if the laser printer jams. Learn enough to clear the jam. If it jams often, see the system administrator or call a repairman.

Plan ahead! Make sure there is company letterhead loaded in your printer *before* requesting it with your print job. If that tray is empty, the network printer will stop dead in its tracks and wait until someone wanders by and fills it. Other print jobs will get backed up, and you'll get dirty looks from your friends.

For busy network printers, it's helpful to have colored paper used as separator pages. Users can quickly find the beginning of the next print job.

➤ Don't turn the power switch off. If it's printing garbage, take it off-line and go back and delete that print job. Then you can put the printer back online. If your printer has lots of memory, you may have to reset or power it off to clear the bad print job.

➤ Don't leave a printer off-line and forget about it.

➤ Don't send multiple test prints to a color printer. It's expensive.

➤ Don't connect your laptop directly to a parallel port on a network laser printer. You may confuse the printer and mess up your boss's network print job.

➤ Don't send special printer codes with your print job unless you are very smart and know how to reset it when you are finished.

Sometimes a printer can't understand what you want it to print, and prints garbage. This garbage is actually made up of special control characters not intended to be printed; they are supposed to tell your laser how to print the job. Somewhere the printer got confused and it has to be stopped manually.

Scanners—the Copier from Hell

It's as if a secret group of people know how to use the office scanner. There's something mysterious about it; the people who learn to use it start using it more and more. Actually, there's nothing mysterious about scanners at all. They're just another piece of equipment, ready for you to exploit!

Scanner
Used to convert printed copy into electronic image format.

The goal of scanning is to bring an interesting picture with you, along with a blank diskette, perform the magic, and leave with an electronic copy of your picture stored on your diskette.

Your first job is to find that scanner. Most companies have one. Scanners look like small copy machines; they can be difficult to locate because nobody really knows where to put them in the first place. Sometimes they are found lying out in an aisle next to a laser printer, or stored in the copier room, or stashed in a closet. You will usually find a computer close by, connected to the beast. Once you've found and identified it, you're halfway done. Next you stick your picture face-down onto the glass plate of the scanner and close the lid. Then you go sit at the attached computer and run the scanner software. It's usually Windows-based, and you should ask for help the first time. After a few seconds or minutes, you have a new file containing your scanned image.

A flatbed scanner.

Ideas for Using Your Scanner

Scanned images are great because you can use them in a variety of creative ways. You can add employees' pictures on the cover of performance reviews so you don't mix them up. You can add a classy company logo to your presentations. You can attach a picture of handwritten correspondence to an e-mail. How's that for moving into the next century?

Another powerful way to use a scanner is to scan in printed text for use in a word processor. Think of it! No more retyping of old speeches or addresses! But an extra step

OCR stands for Optical Character Recognition; it refers to the activity of converting images of text into actual editable text. For instance, a scanned image of the word CAT cannot be used by your word processor until it has been converted with OCR to become the letters C-A-T.

has to be taken for this real magic to occur. Once the text is scanned in, you have a plain image—a picture of the text, rather than the editable text itself. You must now run special software with this image to have it recognized as text. This is called *OCR*, and your scanner probably has a copy of it. If not, order it soon.

Dos, Don'ts, and Etiquette for Scanners

DO THIS WITH YOUR SCANNER:

➤ Keep the scanning area clean and free of clutter.

➤ Do make backups of your scanned file output.

➤ Clean the glass surface before you begin scanning.

➤ Report problems with the scanner to your network administrator immediately.

➤ Bring your own diskette to store your scanned images.

DON'T DO THIS WITH YOUR SCANNER:

➤ Never lay heavy objects on top of the scanner.

➤ Don't violate copyright or trademark laws.

➤ Don't use the controlling computer for other, non-scanning tasks.

➤ Don't touch the scanner glass. Oils are hard to remove.

➤ Don't eat or drink around a scanner.

➤ Don't leave your scanned files on the hard drive of the scanning computer, or on the network. The disk will quickly fill up and become unusable to anyone.

Can't find a particular file on your old diskettes, but happen to have a printed version of it? Scan it, apply OCR, and you're back in business!

Just the Fax, Ma'am

Fax machines were here before networks. They'll probably be here long after networks, too, because they excelled in the most important detail about communication. They perfected a standard that everyone in the world follows. You can buy the cheapest fax in the world, and it will still talk to every other fax machine, without having to touch anything on either end. Try that on your network.

Almost every company has a fax machine. It's connected to a phone line, just like a modem. People walk to it to drop off or pick up the few sheets of paper called a "fax." Many companies now have a *networked* fax machine, which means people can be lazy and never walk anywhere. Special fax software, once loaded on the network and your machine, allows you to direct your product to the network fax. Usually it's a few pages from your word processor.

Fax Short for "facsimile," a machine that converts printed copy into an electric signal which can be sent over standard phone lines, anywhere in the world, to another fax machine, which reverses the process and produces printed copy.

Ideas for Using Your Network Fax

Network faxing is a great alternative way to communicate with other people who aren't on your company e-mail system. This includes people who don't even have a computer. Faxing can also be used as cheap backup to your scanning device, since your document has to be converted and stored as an image before it's faxed.

Incoming network faxes are often not allowed, for a simple reason: They have to be delivered, which means someone has to read the scribble on the cover page. Fax software isn't that great yet, so don't hold your breath. You still need to walk to pick up your incoming faxes.

Dos, Don'ts, and Etiquette for Network Fax

DO THIS WITH YOUR NETWORK FAX:

➤ Always identify yourself on the cover page of a fax.

➤ Fax in moderation. It is often less expensive to use overnight mail.

➤ Take as long as you need to edit before you fax, just as you would if you had to fax manually.

Don't forget to send a *cover page* (identifying who you are, along with your personal phone number) with every fax! Fax machines receive large amounts on incoming material; without a cover sheet, it's difficult to determine who should get it.

➤ Understand your recipient's fax capabilities before you fax, especially for larger documents.

DON'T DO THIS WITH YOUR NETWORK FAX:

➤ Don't send 50-page documents; it's rude to the fax machines on both ends.

➤ Don't make excessive use of fax-back services; they often contain more material than you expect.

➤ Don't rely on a network fax machine for an incoming fax.

➤ Don't send anonymous faxes.

➤ Don't send multiple copies of faxes.

Modems to Mars

The age of electronic communication would not have been possible without the modem. They can connect directly to your computer and a phone line. By using communication software, your computer can dial another computer and breathe heavily. An electronic bulletin board (known as a BBS) is simply a computer with lots of disk space connected to a telephone.

Modem A device used to connect one computer to another using ordinary phone lines.

BBS (bulletin board system) A computer running a special communications package that acts as a kind of electronic bulletin board. A BBS allows many people to use it at the same time, in order to exchange ideas, download software, and converse with others.

It would be expensive to place a modem on the desk of everyone who needed one. That's why they are a popular network resource. Now the modems can be controlled and maintained in a central location.

Modems are habit-forming, especially once you've found an interesting BBS or data service. Take up yachting or polo instead—it will be cheaper. It's not uncommon for a moderately used modem to run up a $1000.00 phone bill in a month!

Ideas for Using Your Network Modem

Modems can be used to get out of your network and reach electronic database services like CompuServe or the Internet. They can also be used to get *into* your network. For example, if you had a modem at home, you could dial into your network at work and pretend you're at work!

It's more than likely that your company has several modems available for sharing on the network. "Pooling" this collection of modems makes it easy to share them equally among everyone on the network.

Dos, Don'ts, and Etiquette for Network Modems

DO THIS WITH NETWORKED MODEMS:

➤ Compress files before you send them. It's faster and cheaper.

➤ Always exit completely from the modem software when you are finished; it returns the modem resource to the network.

➤ Always use accurate identification with remote services.

➤ Always report problems immediately—they can get expensive quick!

➤ Notify management of access costs *before* using services.

DON'T DO THIS WITH NETWORKED MODEMS:

➤ Don't violate software copyright laws either by uploading or downloading software to electronic bulletin boards.

➤ Don't spend long hours downloading files during the day.

➤ Don't walk away from your computer with an active session.

➤ Don't try to connect to multiple services at once.

➤ Don't go exploring the Internet on company time.

Be careful not to change any of the software settings used by your network modem. The next person using the network modem may not be as smart as you, and the changed settings may not work as planned.

CD-ROMs

They look the same as your music CDs at home, but they hold 600 megabytes of important information. The *CD-ROM reader* is an ideal component to have on the network.

CD-ROM stands for Compact Disc—Read Only Memory— which means it's permanent; no one can change the contents. CD-ROMs can hold hundreds of megabytes of information—like entire encyclopedias or national phone listings or ZIP codes.

You may have a workstation with a CD-ROM reader built in. Those aren't the kind we're talking about here, but they can have the same benefits. Usually a networked CD-ROM reader is installed because the actual CD-ROMs are very expensive, and you buy them individually.

Some examples of popular CD-ROMs are complete encyclopedias, legal databases, national phone listings, news publications, statistical demographic material, and so on. Good stuff.

Many of these CDs aren't simply purchased, but subscribed to; a brand-new one comes several times a year to keep you in the latest data. Your network administrator makes sure the latest one is *mounted* and available.

Ideas for Using Your Network CD-ROM

CD-ROMs contain the information of many library shelves. Combine the wealth of information with the convenience of searching it at your desktop and you have a really valuable tool. Another advantage of CD-ROMs is they can be accessed by more than one person at a time.

Collecting CD-ROMs is like collecting baseball cards—you want them all. But a typical CD-ROM reader can play only one at a time. So the computer geniuses re-invented the jukebox (and borrowed the antique record-player's name for it): it's a machine made up of 4 or more readers stacked together in one box. Some have 16! And all can play at the same time.

Dos, Don'ts, and Etiquette for Network CD-ROMs

DO THIS WITH YOUR NETWORKED CD-ROM:

➤ Plan searches ahead of time to increase effectiveness and speed.

➤ Cut-and-paste information into your word processor, where it's much faster to manipulate.

DON'T DO THIS WITH YOUR NETWORKED CD-ROM:

➤ Don't print directly from a CD-ROM without understanding the size of the print job.

➤ Don't leave an online CD-ROM session unattended.

➤ Never open the CD-ROM drive door while it's on the network.

➤ Never reboot your machine in the middle of a CD-ROM session.

The Least You Need to Know

This chapter taught us that networked peripherals are our friends. Here are some ways they help us:

➤ They can print, scan, dial, search, and fax while you sit at your desk and sip coffee.

➤ Printers are available if they remain loaded with paper and toner, connected to the network, and are online.

➤ Scanners are good for getting pictures into your network activity.

➤ It's polite to share resources on the network. Don't be a resource hog.

Part 2
Being Productive

Who, me? Productive? I can't find it, keep it, share it, or print it. But I must be productive—I just spent four hours doing e-mail! And three hours trying to get that report to print out the way I like! And five hours looking for that file on the network! I'm already into overtime and I haven't done a lick of real work yet! I'm starting to sweat, my hands are shaking, and my computer is laughing at me! I've got the technology jitters and need a cure fast!

Relax. This section is just what the doctor ordered. You'll learn how to log in and navigate your way to successful storage, retrieval, printing, and e-mail. You'll be home in time for dinner.

JIM'S TURN TO FIX THE PRINTER.

Logging In and Exploring the Network

Logging In to the Network

At the command prompt, type **LOGIN** and press **Enter**. This is the Novell NetWare command that allows you to start talking on the network. If you see the **Bad command or filename** error, change to the network drive (usually by typing **F:** and pressing **Enter**) and try again. You should see the following:

```
F:\>LOGIN
Enter your login name: _
```

Now it's time to type in your network name. By typing **LOGIN**, you've asked your computer to ask for permission to get on the network, and the network is asking you to identify yourself. Your login name (commonly known as your *user ID*) is usually some form of your last name and an initial, like JSMITH. If you don't know your network name, Chapter 17 describes some of the people at your workplace who can help you, such as the network administrator. Ask them for help in obtaining a user ID and/or logging in.

After you've typed your network name, you should be asked to provide a password before you are allowed onto the network. Type in your password and press **Enter**.

```
F:\>LOGIN
Enter your login name: DBOBOLA
Enter your password: ******  (you won't see it being typed)


     Good morning, Dan
     H:\_
```

Congratulations! You have logged into the network! If Novell is not the product your company uses, try some commands from this listing of the most common networking products:

➤ If you are using LANtastic, try **STARTNET**.

➤ Maybe it's IBM LAN Server or Microsoft LAN Manager; if so, try **NET LOGON**.

➤ If you happen to be using Banyan VINES, try **BAN**.

➤ Windows for Workgroups would have already asked you to provide a LOGON name when your machine first started up.

➤ If you are using a Macintosh, double-click on **Chooser**. Then select what you desire on the network with your mouse.

If you were not successful in logging in just now, you might want to review the troubleshooting tips in Chapters 16–19.

Before and After Logging In

So now you've had the chance to log in to the network a few times. Does anything feel different? Maybe not to you, but your computer see things a whole lot differently. Why should you care? If you want to maximize your benefits from the network, you should see what it looks like from your computer's point of view. It may open your eyes to new sources of information.

Before logging in, your computer was content with your local drive C:, diskette drive A: and/or B:, and maybe a printer.

After logging in, your computer still has access to those local resources in the same way. In addition, it has access to the vast resources of the network. Let's explore it.

To Boldly Go Exploring the Network

First of all, for those of you with weak stomachs, this section is completely optional. The purpose is to satisfy any curiosity you might have about what happens when you log in to a network, and demonstrate some slick network commands for defining network drives.

For some of you reading this book, getting to a DOS prompt is no easy task. Relax. Success on the network does not depend on getting to a DOS prompt. It simply allows the freedom to run commands that may not be easy to find on your menu program, or on your Windows screen. If you can't get to DOS, and some of these commands look appealing to you, contact your network administrator and ask how you can get them put on your screen.

SaberMenus and Other Menu Systems

Saber is a company that makes a great menuing system for both DOS and Windows. If your company bought it, you can bet your company doesn't want you messing around in DOS, and that's okay. It forces everyone to work from the same starting point. It makes life so much easier for your support team to manage a hundred caffeine-driven Type A's thrashing new computers.

Many businesses employ creative geeks who design custom menu systems. Once again, it's not just to keep you from playing, but to make life simpler by providing fewer choices. If they didn't give you a way out, ask for one. If they say no, buy them lunch. If they still say no, threaten to boot from a system disk in drive A: and they'll start to sweat.

Finding Your Way Out to a DOS Prompt

If you found the DOS prompt, congratulations; skip this part.

To get *out*, you have to know what you're *in*. Stare at your screen for a moment. Do you see pretty little colorful pictures, or do you see only letters and lines? The latter means you have a character-based system (not Windows). To escape from such a system, look for menu options called Shell to DOS, Exit to DOS, or just plain DOS. Sometimes there's an Execute Program selection where you could type **COMMAND** and press **Enter**.

If you're in Windows, find the icon called **DOS Prompt** in the Main Group. Sometimes the icon has been removed, or moved by your support personnel. Don't panic. Use the **File Run** command in your Program Manager Menu Bar. Type in **COMMAND** and click **OK**.

Time for ALCS (A Little Common Sense)

Hold on for just a minute. Now that you're at the DOS prompt, you're in geek territory. If you aren't paying attention, you could do damage to your local C: drive by erasing things that shouldn't be erased. You could possibly erase network files that should also not be erased. Don't get too bold with your commands for now, especially the ERASE or DEL commands, and avoid the *.* (wildcards) syndrome. The network's just too big to ask for everything.

Not frightened enough? Or you're a terrorist-in-training? Okay, we'll be more specific. You, the average network user, could do the following damage:

YOUR LOCAL C: DRIVE: You might accidentally erase important files you need, like your AUTOEXEC.BAT or CONFIG.SYS file. You might erase important files your computer needs to get to the network. You could even erase the whole darned thing, for that matter.

IMPORTANT NETWORK DATA FILES: Your company may have set up locations on the network for you to store business files in. You can probably erase them, also. You can probably erase other people's files stored there, which is punishable by death in certain states. Be careful on network data drives.

IMPORTANT NETWORK APPLICATIONS: Relax. If the software was properly installed on your network by a real network administrator, then you can't harm these applications. You shouldn't be able to erase or change anything. You do, however, have control over your own personal profile files, which affect the way applications look to you. Like the Windows INI files. You could accidentally erase them or corrupt them—and an application like Word for Windows might not work for you anymore—but at least you didn't screw anyone else up.

How a MAP Can Help You Navigate

Just as a road map helps you find your way from city to city, the NetWare MAP command helps you find your way on the network. Instead of finding cities, we find applications and data files. Instead of driving, we change letters.

Let's go for a spin. Type **MAP** and press **Enter**. You get something that looks like this:

```
Drive  A:   maps to a local disk.
Drive  B:   maps to a local disk.
Drive  C:   maps to a local disk.
Drive  D:   maps to a local disk.
Drive  E:   maps to a local disk.
Drive  F: = IDIOT_SERVER\SYS:LOGIN
Drive  H: = IDIOT_SERVER\SYS:HOME\FRED
Drive  P: = IDIOT_SERVER\SYS:COMMON\ARCHIVE
Drive  T: = IDIOT_SERVER\SYS:APPS\WPWIN
        — —
SEARCH1:  = Z:. [IDIOT_SERVER\SYS:  \PUBLIC]
SEARCH2:  = c:\
SEARCH3:  = c:\dos
SEARCH4:  = c:\windows
```

Drive mappings The network term used to describe the drive-letter assignments that correspond to subdirectories located on the file server. For instance, my *drive mapping* for the Z: drive points to the network directory called PUBLIC.

This is the display of all computer storage locations currently available to you. Start simple. You know the old drives A:, B:, and C:. You may even remember the network drive F:, where you first logged in. Those were the only drives you had to work with before you logged in. After logging in, you were given several more. These are meant to make life simpler for you.

For example, look at Fred's drive mapping. He still has the F: drive, but now it seems to be in the LOGIN directory. He has been given an H: drive in the subdirectory SYS:HOME\FRED. We'll learn more about these private storage locations in Chapter 12. There's a T: drive pointing to the APPS\WPWIN directory. Even a Z: drive pointing to the PUBLIC directory. Yours will probably be different. You can change to any of these drive locations listed in the MAP command by typing the letter with a colon (:) and pressing **Enter**. If it's not listed in MAP, you can't change to it.

It's not too difficult to add new drive letters using the MAP command. The easiest way is to copy existing drive letters. If you currently have an F: drive and want to create a G: drive, you can type **MAP G:=F:** and press **Enter**. You will now have a G: drive available to do anything you want. Feel free to change directories on drives you create yourself.

Where Did All These New Drive Letters Come From?

You may wonder where these letters came from, why they picked these letters, and who's got the rest of them!

These letters were assigned when you logged in. During the login process, the network runs a set of commands for you called the LOGIN SCRIPT. This script runs several map commands and assigns a common set of drives for all users of the network. Some of the letters are assigned to everyone by NetWare, and everyone gets the same one, like drive Z:. The other (lower) letters were probably chosen at random by your network administrator. Their selection may have been on purpose, to help you find what you're looking for—such as W: for WordPerfect, S: for spreadsheet software, or H: for a "home" directory.

> **Login script** A small program like an AUTOEXEC.BAT file that runs when you log in to the network. It executes several MAP commands to allow you easier navigation on the network. It may also perform other activities like network printer assignments.

Most people will have the same or similar drive mappings, but not always. Secretaries may have different assignments than the managers or executives. A network administrator may have lots more letters. These are just different letters, not better letters.

Working on a network can be confusing. Suppose someone asks you to "Get that file that's stored on the P: drive," and you discover you don't have a P: drive—or maybe it's pointing to a different directory location. You may have difficulty finding the file if your P: drive is mapped differently. It's not your fault, it's their fault! They didn't tell you the *exact* location, only a shortcut drive letter that isn't always accurate. (It's always more precise to provide the *directory location as well as the drive letter* when describing where a file is located.) You can answer back, "You mean the file stored in COMMON ARCHIVE?"

Why Did My PATH Change and Why Should I Care?

Remember the PATH command from DOS 101? It's how your computer can find common commands that may not be in your current directory. Let's say you're in C:\GAMES and you want to run the XCOPY command. If you did a DIR, you wouldn't find XCOPY—but the command still works, because the directory where XCOPY lives is listed in the PATH statement. Before you logged in to the network, your PATH probably looked something like this:

```
PATH=C:;C:\DOS\;C:\WINDOWS;
```

Don't change directories if you are ever playing on the Z: drive. This drive letter should remain pointing to the PUBLIC directory, which holds all your important network commands like MAP, NDIR, and LOGOUT. If you executed the CD\ command on Z:\PUBLIC, your computer's first (and primary) search drive would be pointing to no directory at all—just the root of your network drive!—and things would go quickly downhill from there.

The network has its own version of searching for files; it's included in your PATH statement. After logging into the network, your PATH statement may look like this:

```
PATH=Z:;Y:;C:;C:\DOS;C:\WINDOWS;
```

By logging in to the network, you were assigned *search drives* that allow you to find common network commands, no matter what your location is, regardless of drive letter or directory.

Not all network drive letters are search drives; only the highest letters like Z. These search drives are called out in the MAP command so you can see them plainly. Every user on the network should have a Z: drive mapping that points to the PUBLIC directory. Some network users may have computers without hard drives at all. Where do they get DOS to run their computers? From the network, which assists them by setting up a search drive Y: that points to the complete DOS directory stored on the network.

You and Your Friends on the Network

Enough of the tough stuff. Let's have some fun before we leave behind the DOS prompt for good. A few commands are included with NetWare that can help identify who you are (for those *really* bad Monday mornings), and who those others are who may be lurking on the network. You probably won't need to use these commands much, but they hold an interest for some.

WHOAMI on This Network?

Once you're at the DOS prompt, you can prove you're logged in by executing (typing) the **WHOAMI** command (and pressing **Enter**). If it works, someone is logged in. Find out who. Look at the results:

```
You are user DAN attached to server IDIOT_SERVER, connection 2.
Server IDIOT_SERVER is running NetWare v3.12 (100 user).
Login time: Monday  March 15, 1995  11:16 am
```

Notice that the file server **IDIOT_SERVER** is listed. You may have several file servers listed here if you are logged into several of them.

Why is WHOAMI a big deal? It's the great identifier. You can walk up to a vacant machine, type **WHOAMI**, and find out who gets the security violation for leaving their computer logged in. If you ever find the user SUPERVISOR or ADMIN logged in, you hit the jackpot! These are the most powerful users on the network, and nobody should *ever* leave these user IDs logged in. Call the network administrator to report it, and log them out yourself by typing **LOGOUT** and pressing **Enter**.

What happens if you type **LOGIN** before you type **LOGOUT**? Don't worry, the network expects this all the time. Each time you execute the LOGIN command, the network secretly and automatically logs your computer out first. If you are unsuccessful in logging in, your computer will definitely be logged out of the network.

Who Else Is on the Network With You?

Care to find out who else is logged in at the moment? This may be of value once you've learned how to send short messages back and forth, and want to know who's available to bother. Chapter 12, "Easier Ways to Navigate in Windows and DOS," provides examples of sending messages.

Using the USERLIST Command (or NLIST USER /S)

Type **USERLIST /A** and press **Enter**. If you are using NetWare 4.X (Four Point Anything), try **CX /R** and then **NLIST USER /S**. See the results that follow:

```
User Information for Server IDIOT_SERVER

Connection  User Name    Network        Node Address   Login Time
_____   _____   _____       _____     _____

     1       HPIVSI       [      7] [ 8000994A441]  2-07-1995 10:50 am
     2     * DAN        [80220007] [  20AF19CC9E]  2-28-1995  5:16 pm
     3       FRED        [80220007] [  20AF19992C]  3-31-1995  8:01 am
     4       HEIDI      [80220007] [  20AF1907E4]  3-31-1995  9:33 am
     5       KIM        [80220007] [  20AF19CA23]  4-03-1995 10:42 am
```

6	SETA	[80220007]	[	20AF194B60]	4-03-1995	11:15 am
7	SUPERVISOR	[80220007]	[	20AF19EEC0]	4-03-1995	11:18 am
8	FRED	[80220007]	[	20AF194B0B]	4-03-1995	11:30 am
9	JSMITH	[80220007]	[	20AF190321]	4-03-1995	2:16 pm

Notice a couple of things. User FRED is logged in. Hey, FRED is logged in twice! How can that be? Our friend Fred has been sitting at more than one machine and logging into the network, since two different people can't have the same user ID. Unless Fred has very long arms, he's not sitting at both computers at the same time which means one of them might be considered a security violation (or maybe Fred forgot to log out before moving to another computer). Someone could sit down at Fred's computer and erase his stuff on the network. On the other hand, some companies allow many people to use the same user ID, for simplicity. These people are extra careful when it comes to storing and erasing files.

Also, look at the column on the right. It shows the time that user logged in. The first Fred logged in at 8:01 a.m., a whopping three days ago! That means Fred's machine was logged on all night, available for the cleaning crew to play on the network. Check your own network. Who's been on the longest?

The Least You Need to Know

This chapter helped remove some of the mysteries of networking by explaining:

➤ How to log in to the network.

➤ How you can see yourself (WHOAMI) and others (USERLIST) on the network.

➤ How the network is kept orderly through the use of shared and private directories.

➤ Knowing this order can help you find things, like software applications or data files.

➤ You can see much of this order with the MAP command.

Chapter 10

Security Basics

In This Chapter

➤ Why network security is good for us

➤ How network security protects our files and resources

➤ How users are given security clearances to use the network

➤ How to use network security commands

What's all the fuss about network security? Your files aren't the super-secret recipes of the diet-cola wars, so why should you care?

You should care because you have been granted access to valuable network resources, and it's your responsibility to protect those resources. You also have a bunch of personal files stored on the network that you should want to protect.

Network security describes anything that protects the resources of the network from harm. This includes protecting shared files, network software, and access to printers from unauthorized use.

This chapter explains what real network security is all about, from gaining access to making your files available to others.

Change That Password!

We've learned it's easy to get on the network now; you don't have to remember more than two things—your user ID and password. The user ID stays the same, but someone is always bugging me to change my password. Why?

Passwords are important. It's like the lock on your front door. Don't make it easy to guess (classic too-easy examples are the names on your mailbox, your spouse's or kid's name, or your phone number). Try something really hard to guess, but easy to remember. How about **SOTRSAB**, the acronym for Somewhere, Over The Rainbow, Skies Are Blue. Sing yourself into the network—it's much easier to remember. Just don't sing too loudly. (And make it some other song; you don't know who's been reading this tip.)

User IDs are intentionally easy to figure out; they aren't secret. Passwords are different. They tell the network you are who you say you are; on their say-so, it grants you access to your designated storage areas, printers, and privileges. Those things are valuable, and you should want to protect them. Anyone able to log in with your user ID (no matter where they're sitting) could have complete access to all your stuff. That thought scares most people (humans are such paranoid animals, with such good reason). So do yourself a favor and change your password at least once a month, if not more frequently.

It's tough to come up with a really good password, but it's worth the effort. The more unusual your password, the more difficult it will be for someone else to guess. Don't use names or addresses, or even any single word that can be found in the dictionary! Someone, somewhere, someday, might guess it. Try to use truly bizarre passwords like 6BOZO!STEW or UR2GEEKY.

Changing Your Password in DOS

Changing your password in DOS is easy if you pay attention. Just type **SETPASS** and press **Enter**. The tricky part is what comes first—your current password. This is to prevent some wiseguy from changing your password on you while you visit the restroom. (You wouldn't find out until the next time you tried to log in.)

After you enter your current password, you'll be asked to enter your *new* password, and then asked to enter the *same* new password again. Just to be sure you typed it correctly. Pay attention to those messages and they'll confirm the change. You have to start from scratch if you mess up.

Changing Your Password in Windows

Although you have many options, probably the best method of changing your network password in Windows is to use the icon called User Tools in your Network Group (if it's not there try File Run, type **NWUSER** and press **OK**). Select the button that has a picture of the file server. Click on the **Set Pass** button near the bottom of your screen. Enter your current password and a new password. Then retype your new password so there's no misunderstanding. The network will tell you whether it has been successful in changing your password.

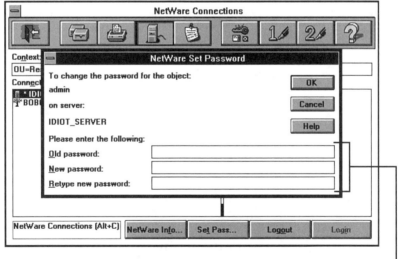

Enter your passwords here.

Changing your password with User Tools.

And security doesn't just end with name and password. Let's move into some details about the other two important security subjects: network file security and network user security.

How to Assess Your Power on the Network

Let's have some fun with a thought experiment. (It's much safer to perform experiments on your network inside your head; if something screws up, it's all in your mind.)

Remember drive Z:? Pointing to directory PUBLIC? That's where NetWare stores all its important files. What would happen if we changed to drive Z: and entered ERASE *.*? Would you be out of a job? Would all of the files get erased? I'm happy to report the answer is no, but it needs some explaining.

Finding Out What RIGHTS You Have on the Network

All users have certain privileges on the network. The network calls these privileges your *rights*; they are assigned to a user for a given directory. What's that again?

Try this for real. Go to one of the middle-of-the-road network letters, like F: or H:, type **RIGHTS** and press **Enter**. You'll see something similar to:

```
IDIOT_SERVER\SYS:\USERS\FRED
Your rights for this directory are:   [SRWCEMFA]
    Supervisor rights to directory.           (S)
    Read from a file in a directory.          (R)
    Write to a file in a directory.           (W)
    Create subdirectories and files.          (C)
    Erase directory and files.                (E)
    Modify directory and files.               (M)
    Scan for files and directories.           (F)
    Change access control.                    (A)
```

Impressive, yes? You can almost figure this out by reading it. In this example, drive H: is a personal directory where I store my own stuff. According to this RIGHTS listing, I can Read files, Write files, Create files, Erase files, and so on. This list is telling me I can do almost anything in this directory.

You probably have a similar drive, designed especially for you. It's purpose is to provide you with a place where you can store just about anything you want, since you have all security rights at this directory location. Find your home directory and start using it wisely. It's likely to be a drive letter between F: and H:.

The User Tools utility gives Windows users an easy way to see their rights. Chapter 12 will give you lots of details on this subject; for now, select the second button at the top. This is the *drive button*. By double-clicking on any drive letter, you will obtain the Windows version of the RIGHTS command for that drive. Time out for a quick look at a figure.

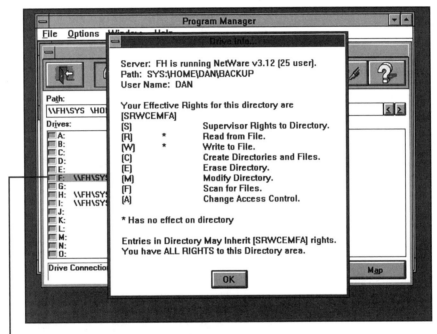

Double-click on any drive mapping to display your rights for that directory.

This user has full rights to his home directory.

RIGHTS aren't that difficult to understand once you get the hang of it. Here they are, for your learning pleasure:

Possible user rights for a given directory

File Scan (F)	The most basic right, needed to see files.
Read (R)	Another basic right, needed to open and read the contents of files.
Write (W)	The right needed to change the contents of files.
Create (C)	To start a new file from scratch, or to copy a file into a directory for the first time, you need this right.
Erase (E)	The right needed to erase a file (that was tough).
Modify (M)	Not as common; this right is needed to have the ability to change an attribute of a file (which we'll learn soon).
Access Control (A)	Also not as common; this right is used to give the same rights that you have in a directory to others.
Supervisory (S)	Also not common; this right means you are the king of the hill. By having this single letter, you have all the other letters automatically—even if you don't see them with the RIGHTS command. This means you can erase, create, rename, and modify to your heart's content; no network security will stop you. You probably have this right inside your own home directory.

Let's try to find out what rights we have on the Z: drive. Don't worry, the RIGHTS command doesn't change or hurt anything. It's just a reporter.

```
IDIOT_SERVER\SYS:\PUBLIC
Your rights for this directory are:  [ R    F ]
      Read from a file in a directory.            (R)
      Scan for files and directories.             (F)
```

Much different! I can't Erase, Write, or Create files here. If I tried, I would get the **Insufficient Rights** error message. That's good to remember—it explains that I don't have the security rights to do what I happen to be trying!

Let's collect the facts we've learned. We seem to have all control over all files stored on our local hard drive C: and all of our diskettes. After all, we are the kings of our own castles. But when we get to the network castle, we play by different rules. We have access to lots of directories on the network, but sometimes we find our power is limited inside them. We can't seem to copy a file into Z: or change any of the files already there. Someone powerful (like the network administrator) must have put them there. We do have the ability to copy files into other drive letters; in our example it was the H: drive. We have complete control over the file if it's stored in our H: drive.

If you ever have problems while storing a file, observe the directory location you are trying to store to. Ask yourself whether you have the rights to store it there. Listen to the answer. If it's "I don't know," then get out to DOS, change to that directory, and type **RIGHTS**. To store a file, you need at least the WRITE right—and the CREATE right if it's brand-new.

We could conclude something brilliant from this. As long as we have a directory on the network where we have some power to manipulate files, we can be productive. If my boss tells me to update a file stored in another directory, and I discover I don't have the proper rights to change files in that directory, all is not lost. If I can *see* a file somewhere, I can always copy it back to my own directory and change it here!

You may be wondering how these rights get assigned. After all, if they are assigned by user for each and every directory on the network, isn't that a ton of work? It turns out not to be a big deal. Right from the beginning of installation, nobody gets access to the major stuff like the NetWare utility directories. Someone has to sort out all the rest. Yes, the network administrator is responsible for making all the user-security assignments, but they often take a shortcut: They set up one good one, and copy it for everybody else. You become a member of a *group* that has the proper security clearance.

So the moral of this story is: All network users are given a set of basic rights that determine whether they can or can't copy (or change) files in a given directory. Some people have more rights than others, and life's not fair, but you knew that already.

How to See Important Information About Files

Time for another thought experiment (last one). Suppose the network administrator granted you absolutely all rights to that special directory PUBLIC that Z: points to. What havoc could you wreak by executing the ERASE *.* in there?

Terrifyingly little! No harm would be done; all you would see would be ACCESS DENIED errors. What gives? Didn't we just learn that having all rights means you can do anything in a network? How could we possibly get an ACCESS DENIED error? To best understand this complication, we need to learn about *file security*, we should start by learning more about files.

File Security

You're familiar with what a file is, right? Just a little package of stored bytes that contain your business letter, quarterly report, or a shopping list. That's the stuff *inside* the file. The file itself has a name (like MYREPORT.DOC), the date it was created, the size, and more—all of which you can see with the NDIR command. If you understand a bit more about these other *attributes* that control a file, you'll be more in control of your files.

File attributes define the state of a file. They include such descriptors as whether the file is read-only or read-write, and whether or not it's hidden, as well as the date it was created and who created it. More attributes are available to you, but these are the most common you are likely to run into.

It just so happens that these files we tried to erase on drive Z: are *protected* from people messing with them. They have been made *Read-Only*, which means they can't be changed or erased. Read-only describes one attribute of a file. All files have specific attributes that describe what can and can't be done to them.

Seeing File Attributes with the FLAG Command

One simple way to see file attributes is find the file location and run FLAG on it. Look at what happens when we change to the Z: drive, type **FLAG P*.EXE**, and press **Enter:**

```
Files         DOS Attr  NetWare Attr    Owner      Mode

PAN1080.PDF  [Ro——] [—ShDi—Ri——]SUPERVISOR N/A
PAN1091.PDF  [Ro——] [—ShDi—Ri——]SUPERVISOR N/A
PSTSCRPT.PDF [Ro——] [—ShDi—Ri——]SUPERVISOR N/A
PARTMGR.EXE  [Ro——] [—ShDi—Ri——]SUPERVISOR 0
PCONSOLE.EXE [Ro——] [—ShDi—Ri——]SUPERVISOR 0
PRINTCON.EXE [Ro——] [—ShDi—Ri——]SUPERVISOR 0
PRINTDEF.EXE [Ro——] [—ShDi—Ri——]SUPERVISOR 0
PSC.EXE      [Ro——] [—ShDi—Ri——]SUPERVISOR 0
PURGE.EXE    [Ro——] [—ShDi—Ri——]SUPERVISOR 0
PRINTDEF.DAT [Rw—A] [———————]ADMIN        N/A
```

The attributes are listed inside the brackets. You don't have to worry about most of these, but some are important. The **Ro** means these files are read-only, which means they are not changeable and not erasable in their current state. If we look at some files in other places, we might find something like this:

```
Files         DOS Attr  NetWare Attr    Owner      Mode

AUTOEXEC.BAT [Rw—A] [———————]FRED         N/A
```

Here we can see **Rw** (*Read-Write*), which means these files are not protected and can be updated, changed, and erased if... if... if...

Yes! These files can be changed *if you have the rights to do so!* What right do you need to change a file? The *write* right, but I'm starting to repeat myself. Now you can have lots of fun and explore files all over the network and see what you have control over.

To protect all of the official network files in the PUBLIC directory, no one (except the network administrator) has the right to Write or Erase in that directory. This restriction prevents anyone from accidentally changing or deleting any files. Some directories on the file server are so secret that most people don't even have the File Scan right—which means they can't even see the directory! Out of sight, out of harm's way.

How to Protect Files

That read-only thing looked pretty snazzy, didn't it? Wouldn't that be great to stick on files that you never want to accidentally erase or have other people change? You may have learned how to do it on your local drive C: with the DOS command ATTRIB. You can type **ATTRIB C:\CONFIG.SYS +RO** and press **Enter** and never have to worry about a program changing your CONFIG.SYS ever again. The network has a similar command to use on files stored in network directories. You've already been using it—it's called FLAG.

Using the FLAG Command to Change File Attributes

If you want to make our text file read-only, type **FLAG REPORT.TXT RO** and press **Enter**. The new attributes are displayed. Now, if you try to erase it with ERASE REPORT.TXT, you get the ACCESS DENIED error. This is good to remember. If you ever see the error message **ACCESS DENIED**, it simply means the file is flagged read-only. And now you know how to change it to Read-Write (RW) with the flag command.

Possible attributes for a given file	
Read-Only (RO)	A common attribute, used to protect a network file. Any file with this attribute cannot be written to, changed, or deleted.
Shareable (SH)	Another common attribute used to share a file. Any file with this attribute can be accessed by more than one user at a time. Most Shareable files are also Read-Only to prevent them from becoming corrupted.
Archive (A)	Don't worry about this one. It's only listed here because it's so commonly seen. It means the file has been changed since the last backup.
Hidden (H)	The secret file attribute. Any file with this attribute is invisible to network users, and to any programs that try to list, copy, or delete files.

Normal (N)	No, this isn't a real attribute, but it's listed here to help you understand how to remove any or all of the attributes in this table. To quickly remove RO, SH, and H from a file, type **FLAG** *FILENAME* **N** and the file's attributes will become non-shareable read-write.

If you want to share this file with others, you must flag it shareable. If it isn't flagged shareable and a second person tries to look at it while the first person is looking at it, the second person gets nasty error messages about the file being in use. Flag this file shareable by entering **FLAG REPORT.TXT SH**. The absolute easiest way to remove attributes like Shareable, Read-Only, and Hidden is to flag the file NORMAL. This returns the file to its default state (non-shareable, read-write).

We have to warn you, however, that to change the attributes on any files in a given directory requires you to have the rights to do such a thing. It's not READ, WRITE, ERASE, CREATE, or FILE SCAN. (Not much left, is there?) It's the MODIFY right! So if you ever get an error trying to flag a file, check your rights in that directory with the RIGHTS command and look for **Modify (M)**.

Another interesting attribute of files is the *Hidden (H)* attribute. A files can be flagged hidden with the command **FLAG REPORT.TXT H** and no one will see it with a normal DIR. You can, however, see all files—including hidden ones—with the NDIR command. It's another good reason to use NDIR instead of DIR on the network.

Another popular attribute of network files is *Shareable*. If a file is shareable, then multiple people can use it at the same time. You wouldn't want to risk file corruptions, however, so almost all Shareable files are also flagged read-only for protection. Shareable read-only is the popular flagged state of all files in the network directory Z:\PUBLIC.

What Your Network Would Be Like Without Security

Imagine a network where you don't need a user ID or a password. Anyone can walk up to any computer and get whatever they want. Company records would be available to everyone who had a network connection and wanted to look. Anyone could peek at or change your personal files, program settings, or calendar. The same important file could be opened and used by several people at once, each oblivious that their change could corrupt the file out of existence. Worst of all, anybody could erase anything—and everything—if they got too frustrated.

It's not exactly a nightmare, but you can bet the people responsible for your network lose sleep about security issues like this. We take security for granted. The next time you have a chance, take a look at how your rights have been set up around the network. The answer may surprise you. You may have much more (or much less) than you think!

So Don't Forget to LOGOUT Each Night

Lots of people like the convenience of leaving their computers turned on all the time. Even if it's your company's policy to turn off computers at night, many get a kick out of beating the system and turning off only their monitors. It looks like the whole computer's off, right?

After all, it saves several minutes in each morning not having to wait for the computer to boot up, check for viruses, login to the network, and start big programs like WordPerfect for Windows or DOOM II. Our time is expensive, right?

Your network support team sees things like time and expense a bit differently. When you type **LOGOUT** and press **Enter**, you break your network connection. That's good. Here's some good reasons to log out each night:

➤ To keep people out of your personal home directory.

➤ To protect your network files. They can't be backed up if your machine is holding them open.

➤ To allow the network administrators to perform scheduled after-hours maintenance on the file servers. They work later so you don't have to. If your machine is logged in, they think you are still there working, and might be waiting for you to finish.

➤ To prevent the late-night cleaning shift from breaking your all-time high-scoring record on World Champion 18-Hole Golf.

➤ To develop the habit of being security-conscious. Your company will thank you for it. (Well, maybe not, but they *should*.) Lots of international spies come to America looking for computers logged in to a network.

If you're convinced that it's good to log out, then you should also be convinced that there's not much point to leaving your computer turned on overnight. Turn it off and conserve energy.

The Least You Need to Know

Security puts the locks on all the doors and windows on our network. Some of the things we learned in this chapter were:

➤ Network security is good for us. It helps protect our files, valuable resources, and privacy.

➤ If you are having problems with a network file, sometimes it's because security is protecting it. Either the file is protected, or you don't have the security clearance to mess with it, or both.

➤ You can see security clearances of users with the **RIGHTS** command.

➤ You can see security protection on files with the **FLAG** command.

➤ Some files can be hidden from normal view. You can still see them with **NDIR**, if they really exist.

Chapter 11

Navigating the Network: Where Do You Want to Go?

In This Chapter

➤ Knowing where to look for shared data files on the network

➤ How and why to use private areas on the network

➤ How to find a file on the network

➤ How to use application software to find files

What good is a network if you can't find anything? If you're one of the millions who don't trust your network because...

The network ate your file...

The network must have erased your file; it was there yesterday...

The network is too complicated for you to find your file...

...then this chapter is for you!

Let's start by clearing up some misconceptions. First, the network does not eat files. It eats electricity. Maybe people think of files as food because it's easier to explain when they disappear. Think of them as rocks. (The files, not the people.) Rocks can't disappear or get eaten; they get misplaced or perhaps removed by a person intentionally, because the rock is no longer wanted.

No, the most likely way to lose a file is to forget where you last put it. Networks are complicated warehouses, with thousands of nooks and crannies to hide files in. We simply have to remember the aisle and shelf where our file is stored—just like our own car in a large parking lot.

Quick Overview of the Network Parking Lot

Our network parking lot is the file server's disk drive; as you can probably guess, it's made up of many directories. The major directories are right off of the root (just like your local C: drive) and there are lots of subdirectories under them.

File Server Directories

All NetWare file servers have four main directories off of the root of the primary hard drive. These aren't important to anyone except your network administrator. One interesting directory is called PUBLIC. This is the place where all of the networking commands and utilities are stored. Everyone has access to this area. It's so important that it's included in your PATH statement after you log in to the network.

In case you're interested, here are the four major directories on all NetWare file servers:

SYSTEM, where the important network administrative files are kept.

MAIL, used to store the user login scripts. Every user has one.

LOGIN, actually available to all network users *before* they log in. It contains only the files needed to log in (like LOGIN.EXE), and nothing more.

PUBLIC, where all the common commands and utilities are stored; it's made available to everyone.

Now the bad news. Your file server probably has many, many more directories that you *may* have to remember, especially if they are used for sharing files with others. NetWare stopped at four because it knew that businesses would have their own preferred names and places for directories.

Maybe some good news. If you had an anal-retentive type of network administrator who set up your remaining directory structure, you probably have a wonderfully organized parking lot where files rarely get lost.

Here's how a great directory structure might look:

\PUBLIC

\MAIL

\LOGIN

\SYSTEM

\USERS

\APPS

You can ignore the original four NetWare directories. Look at the USERS directory. Guess what's underneath it as subdirectories? All of the users! Even if it's hundreds of users, each would have an individual subdirectory under USER where they would store their personal files. Pretty cool, huh?

Next look at the APPS directory. Underneath APPS you would find a subdirectory for each and every software application loaded on the network!

You may also have a DATA directory, called by many different names, where many people can share the files they create. Sometimes this is stored inside the APPS directory as well.

That's it! That's all the main directories you need to know! And it's easy to understand. One place for users to store their stuff, and one place to go run applications!

Think of the file server's directories as only one of two things. It's either a place for you to store things (and usually find lost files), or a place to go to run software applications.

It's too bad that not all file servers are set up this way. Sometimes network administrators lack experience or training, or are simply too stressed out to set one up this *cleanly* (often they don't have the time). It's much easier for them to just throw the stuff in a directory right off the root with no rhyme or reason. Then it's really tough to find things. If you find yourself in this situation, it's best to ask this network administrator to re-install the applications you need, and place them in a proper directory.

Volumes to Remember

Now that you understand directories and subdirectories, think back to your first hard drive. What happened when you ran out of space? You added another drive (if you could afford it). Same with file servers. A common practice is to add more disk space to the server and call it a new *volume*. No need to get technical here—just think about a volume as another hard drive where files might be stored.

Volume is another name for a file server's hard drive. File servers can have multiple *volumes*.

All NetWare file servers call their first hard drive "volume SYS," and it's the common location for storing PUBLIC and other important directories. For most networks, the USER or HOME directory is also on this SYS: volume. The next volume is often called VOL1, but you could find any naming convention on yours. A volume name like APPS is sometimes used quite appropriately on a server.

You've seen this SYS: before, when we ran the MAP command. SYS simply refers to the first hard drive in the file server.

```
Drives A,B,C,D,E map to a local disk.
Drive F: = IDIOT_SERVER\SYS: \LOGIN
Drive H: = IDIOT_SERVER\SYS:USERS\FRED \TEST
Drive Q: = IDIOT_SERVER\SYS:APPS\GAMES \
Drive T: = IDIOT_SERVER\VOL1: \WINAPPS\WINWORD
```

```
            — —    Search Drives    — —
    S1: = Z:. [IDIOT_SERVER\SYS: \PUBLIC]
    S2: = Y:. [IDIOT_SERVER\SYS: \]
    S3: = C:\WINDOWS
    S4: = C:\DOS
    S5: = C:\
    S6: = C:\TOOLS
```

Notice the **T:** drive. Look closely. It is pointing to the same server, called IDIOT_SERVER; a new volume called VOL1 is probably the second hard drive in the file server. The directory WINAPPS\WINWORD exists on VOL1. You can see it's easy to mix and match different volumes in your drive mappings. You only have to remember this for the times that you map a drive yourself. You must include the volume name in your MAP command to be completely accurate.

Don't confuse *volumes* with *drive letters*! Drive letters are arbitrary; they can point to any volume, and can change easily with the MAP command. A volume is an actual hard drive in the file server—and the real storage place of directories. For example, the PUBLIC directory exists on the SYS volume. It doesn't matter what drive letter you map to it (Z:, Q:, or anything), PUBLIC will always be located on SYS.

You can use the volume name with the MAP command. The command **MAP R:=VOL1:WINAPPS\WINWORD** has to be typed carefully, remembering the colon after the volume label. It will result in drive R: pointing to the Word for Windows subdirectory on the server volume VOL1.

If you know the names of your other volumes, you can use this shortcut to change to them quickly. Let's say you're in any directory on the SYS volume (like drive F:), and you want to move to the VOL1 volume. Just type **CD VOL1:** and press **Enter**. Voilà!

The important thing to remember about volumes is that they are each a complete and different set of directories where files might be stored. So if you ever misplace a file, don't forget to look on all the possible volumes as appropriate.

Other Servers in the Neighborhood

Just when you think you have control over all of the possible locations for finding files, another big one pops up—other file servers! Many businesses have multiple servers because they've grown so large; often a user is connected to two or more at the same time.

You may have drive H: on a file server called SNO (Server Number One) and drive P: on SNT (you're quick!) which means you might have to worry about remembering file locations across two or more servers. The MAP command will display the names of the file servers. Usually you can store and find everything you need on a single server, but remember the possibility if you have more than one. If you have more than one file server, there is nothing to worry about. Just try to remember the name of the server that holds your home directory and data storage areas.

Finding Your Home Directory on the Network

Because it's so important, let's spend another few minutes on that USER directory on the file server. Once again, it's great to organize all users here. Common names for this directory are USER, USERS, USERDIRS, or (best of all) HOME. No matter what it's labeled, it's usually called the user's *home directory*.

Take a minute to look at your home directory. Use either DOS or Windows to select a network drive like F:. Change to the root of F: and look at the names. Do you recognize them now? Can you find something like USER or USERS or HOME? If so, change to it. Now look at the subdirectories. There's one with your name! And most likely it's the only one you see—and that's good. Remember learning about security in our last chapter? Here's a good example of proper security. You are the only user with the rights to see your directory. No one else can see your directory because they don't have the rights to, just as you can't see anyone else's directory. Neat, huh?

Navigating From Inside Software Applications

If you're trying to locate a file, it's often helpful to remember which software created it. Almost all files are created by either a word processor, a spreadsheet, or a database program. All of these products have standard locations for storing files created with them. Your challenge is to find them.

Setup, Backup, or Working Directories

These standard storage locations can be found for all software applications. They are designated during the installation of the product. It's not too difficult to scan through the menus or help screens of a program, looking for the location of the *working directory*. You may be surprised to discover that sometimes your network application points to a working directory on your local hard drive! Right under your nose!

And don't forget the *backup directory*. Most applications make use of them, and that can benefit you; it could be another place to look for a lost file if you are getting desperate.

WordPerfect, Word, and 1-2-3 Example

We can find the working directory in WordPerfect version 5.1 by holding down the **Shift** key and pressing the **F1** key. Next select **5** to show "paths and directories." You can see the working directory where created files will be stored by default.

```
Setup: Location of Files

    1 - Backup Files                 C:\WP51

    2 - Keyboard/Macro Files         C:\WP51

    3 - Thesaurus/Spell/Hyphenation
                        Main         C:\WP51
                        Supplementary C:\WP51

    4 - Printer Files                C:\WP51

    5 - Style Files                  C:\WP51
            Library Filename         C:\WP51\LIBRARY.STY

    6 - Graphic Files                C:\WP51

    7 - Documents                    H:\WP51\DOCS

    8 - Spreadsheet Files            C:\WP51\FILES



Selection: 7
```

This is where files will be stored if you do not specify a drive letter.

Sample default storage locations for WordPerfect

The working directory for Lotus 1-2-3 for Windows can be found by selecting Tools, User Setup, and fill in the appropriate Worksheet Directory as shown in the figure.

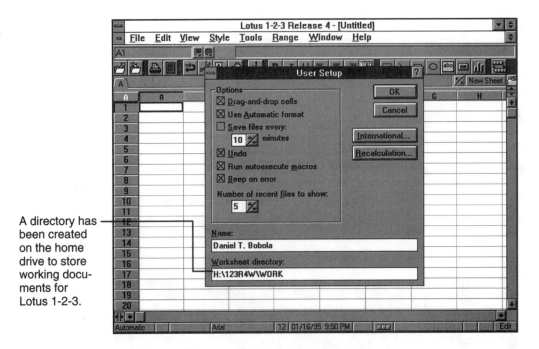

A directory has been created on the home drive to store working documents for Lotus 1-2-3.

Sample default storage locations for Lotus 1-2-3.

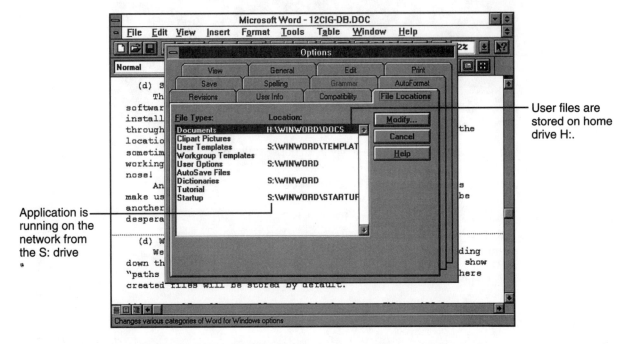

User files are stored on home drive H:.

Application is running on the network from the S: drive

Network file locations in Word.

Locating Network Files and Directories Using DOS

So now you understand all the possible hiding places for files—including home directories, application working directories, other volumes, and other servers. If you still can't find your file, don't give up hope. There's still the old standby called *global searching*.

Global search describes the method of searching all directories and subdirectories. DOS commands and Windows utilities can perform global searches on a single drive or volume.

How to Find That Lost File

To perform a global search, you have to remember *something* about the lost file. The best thing to remember is the file name and extension. Or at least the name. Or how about a few letters in the name? See a hypnotist for further details.

Good old DOS gives you the basic capability of searching with the DIR command. It's best to start in the subdirectory most likely to contain your file, since it's much faster. If you add the /S switch, the DIR command will search subdirectories below your current directory.

Don't forget the option to use *wildcards* like * and ? in your searching criteria! Wildcards can go a long way if you've forgotten only the extension or the spelling of a file name.

For example, if I need to find my manager's presentation and all I can remember is that it started with the letter "B" and was a Freelance Graphics file, probably stored on the SYS volume, I would start by selecting a drive letter on SYS, like **F:**, change to the root of F:, and type **DIR B*.FLW /S** and press **Enter**. The command might take awhile, but finally come back with:

```
[DOS output of DIR B*.FLW /S]
```

NDIR Versus DIR and the /S

DIR /S is a great command, but what if I don't remember the name or extension of the file? NetWare comes to the rescue with the NDIR /S command, and with lots of options. These include searching:

By owner (the first person to create the file). You can search throughout the file server for files created by a particular person if you know their network user ID. To find all files stored on volume VOL1 by the user whose ID is CBUTTS, enter the following:

```
NDIR VOL1:\*.* /OW=CBUTTS
```

By approximately when it was first created. Let's say the file you need is a Harvard Graphics file that was first created by you on the day after the project kickoff on January 1, 1995. It's most likely on your current volume SYS. Enter the following:

```
NDIR \*.HG3 /CR AFT 01-01-95
```

By approximately when it was last updated. Maybe it's that same type of file but was created years ago. At least you remember that you last saved it a few days ago. You could find it by entering the following:

```
NDIR \*.HG3 /UP=01-03-95
```

The only caveat to using NDIR or DIR on the file server is that if you start from the root, these searches will be long. Real long. I mean, scary long. Try to move around in at least one directory before using these global searches.

Locating Network Files and Directories Using Windows

It's not advisable to run the DOS DIR or NetWare NDIR from within Windows, simply because there is an easier tool to use in the Windows environment, and it's called *Search*.

1. From the Windows Program Manager, in the **Main Group**, start **File Manager**.

2. Before starting a search for any file, you must first select the drive letter. If the file is stored on the network you must select one of the network drives. To select a drive, click on the drive letter at the top of the File Manager screen.

3. Try to continue moving down into directories where the file is most likely to be found. Then you can begin the search. On the menu bar, select File and then Search.

4. Enter the filename and extension as best you can, using wildcards where necessary. Don't forget to select the option to Search All subdirectories.

5. Click on **OK**. The location of your file will be displayed if it is found. If not, you can start backing up one directory at a time until the search locates the file. The Windows search function is shown in the figure.

Select a drive to search.

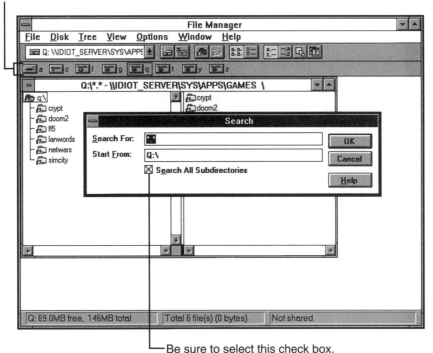

Be sure to select this check box.

Searching for files using File Manager.

The Least You Need to Know

Finding important things on the network is often frustrating. You learned how to make it easier on yourself by:

➤ Knowing where to look for shared data files on the network.

➤ Learning to organize your files in your private home directory so they can always be found.

➤ Determining which network drive is the most appropriate for searching with the NDIR /S command.

➤ Determining where applications have been set up to store their working files on the network, and where the default storage location is for your files.

Chapter 12

Easier Ways to Navigate in Windows and DOS

In This Chapter

➤ Finding and running Windows User Tools (NWUSER)

➤ Selecting file servers and printers

➤ Assigning drive mappings

➤ Selecting printers

➤ Doing all the same in DOS with NETUSER

Moving Around in Windows

Confused by those DOS commands for navigating on the network? Are you among those fortunate souls whose machines have been blessed with Windows? Then your life has been made easier. How much easier? Try 1000 times, as the saying goes, because you can now deal with pictures instead of words. This chapter deals with the utility called **User Tools**, considered a jack-of-all-trades, as far as network utilities go. With User Tools you can pick a server, assign a drive, grab a printer, and send a quick note to a friend, all before your first cup of coffee gets cold.

You don't always have to have User Tools running. You typically would use it at the beginning of your day, to set things up the way you

like. If you make these changes permanent, you won't have to use User
Tools until the next time you want to change something, which could
be weeks or months away.

To get started, make sure you've logged in to the network before
you started Windows (you should never log in to the network *after*
starting Windows, unless you like to live on the edge). Then start
Windows. Find the **NetWare Tools** group and double-click on the **User
Tools** icon. If you can't find the icon, you can also run it manually.
From your Windows Program Manager, select File **Run** and type
NWUSER in the **Command Line** box.

The User Tools icon.

You don't have to type a drive letter or directory, because this
utility will be found in your path. If everything goes right, you will see
something similar to the figure on the following page.

User Tools is the descriptive name for NWUSER.EXE that
actually resides in your local Windows directory on your hard
drive (C:\WINDOWS). It was placed there when your networking software was installed. If you don't have this icon on your
desktop and want to add it, create a new group (like **NetWare**) to store the
icon and select File **New** and click on **Program Item** and click on **OK**. Type
C:\WINDOWS\NWUSER.EXE in the command line and click **OK**.

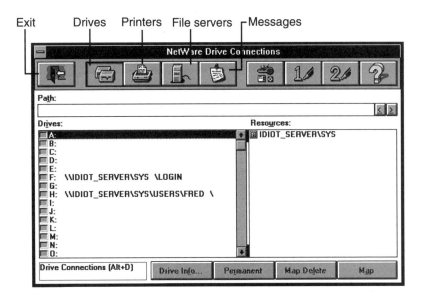

The User Tools utility.

Selecting a File Server with Windows User Tools

Click on **file server icon** (the picture of the taller box) at the top of the **NetWare Driver Connections** window. You will discover a listing of all file servers available to you on the right side of the window under **Resources**. On the left side of the screen you should see the **Drives** of the file server you are already attached to. If this is the only server you need, you're ready to move to the next section.

If your network has more than one file server, you will see them listed on the right side of the window under the Resources list. You can try to connect to any server on the right side of the window by double-clicking on your selection. You'll be asked to type your name and a password. You can have different names and different passwords on different servers, if you like to live that way. To keep things simple, they can all be the same. If login is successful, this server will now be added on the left side, and all servers listed will be available for your use.

Attaching Drives with Windows User Tools

Once you've attached to the file server(s) you desire, you can assign drive letters. You would do this to make it more convenient to find things on the server. In this example we will map a drive letter to the GAMES directory on the file server. Click on the **drive-mapping icon** (the two disk drives) at the top of the window. You are now viewing all of your drive mappings. For those who can't remember the entire alphabet, it is listed on the left. No kidding, these are all the drive letters you could possibly assign if you felt the need. If you have an entry for a given letter, then you have a drive assignment. Most people do just fine with five or six. Remember, the only reason to assign drive letters is to make it easier to find and use what's important to you on the network.

Let's look closer at the current drive mappings in the left column. Find the letter **F**, which typically has an entry. It may show something like **F: \\IDIOT_SERVER\SYS:LOGIN**. This means your drive F: is pointing to server IDIOT_SERVER at a directory called LOGIN on the SYS volume. So if I wanted to find the file **LOGIN.EXE** I would have no difficulty if I look on drive F:. Likewise, Z: points to the PUBLIC directory, where lots of network utilities hang out.

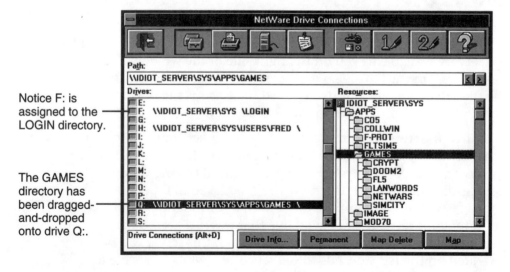

Notice F: is assigned to the LOGIN directory.

The GAMES directory has been dragged-and-dropped onto drive Q:.

Drive mappings.

Let's continue with our example, and assign an available letter (like Q) to the GAMES directory. First we have to find this directory. The right side of the screen displays the available volumes where directories are stored on our server. If we click twice on the **APPS** directory, it opens up into the many available subdirectories. Remembering our Windows techniques, we are about to try the old Click-and-Drag routine. We want to click on the directory **GAMES**, hold down the mouse button, and drag it over to the left side, aiming at the letter Q. If this is successful, the entry will now read **Q: \\IDIOT_SERVER\SYS:APPS\GAMES**. Rejoice at mastering another technique!

Don't remove any mappings that have already been made for you! Some of these are very important, like that Z: drive. If you get rid of Z:, you will have huge difficulties running utilities like this one. Play it safe and limit your fun to *adding* drive mappings.

If you like this drive mapping so much that you want it to appear automatically each time you log in, click on the **Permanent** button while this drive is selected. The next time you start Windows, this drive will be mapped like this. If it happens to reside on another file server, you'll be asked for a user ID and password to gain access to the directory location.

To get rid of any undesired drive mappings, simply click on the letter entry and drag it over to the right side, anywhere. The drive mapping is removed.

Sending Notes with Windows User Tools

Since the beginning of networking, one of the most entertaining activities has been sending notes. Foolish notes. When your friend least expects it. This is a good time to try it.

Click on the fifth icon at the top of the window, the one with a picture of a note tacked to the wall. You now see the NetWare Send Messages screen, displaying a list of file servers on the left, and users associated with the selected file server on the right. To send a note, simply click on the desired user (or group) on the right side. Then click on the **Message box** and type in your message. You are limited to this single line, so be terse. Or use lots of abbreviations. Finally, click on the **Send** button and your message will be delivered. Did I forget to mention that the receiver of your message will clearly see who sent this message?

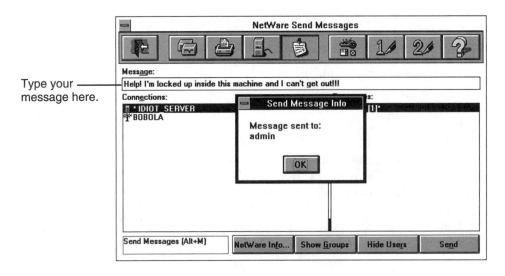

Type your message here.

An important business message sent to a friend.

What your friend sees on his or her computer screen.

Don't send the message "Hi, bozo!" to the group EVERYONE unless you want it—and your name as sender—to be seen by absolutely everyone logged in. Although you can send messages to groups of user IDs like EVERYONE, it's not recommended; it interrupts work. Who would do this? Well, for one, the network administrator—to warn everyone to log out before the file server is downed for maintenance. (But don't expect to see "Log out, bozos!")

If you don't see your friend's name, make sure you've selected the appropriate file server by clicking on it. If you still don't see your friend's name, it probably means that your friend is not currently logged in.

You can only send messages to people already logged in. After they read it and select OK, there is no trace of it. You probably don't want to send real business messages this way, but it can be an alternative method of informing your boss that you're on the way up, or to tell the front-desk secretary about an impending pizza delivery. If you want a permanent record of your message, you should use e-mail, which is discussed in detail in Chapter 16.

Selecting Printers with Windows User Tools

Probably the most useful function of NWUSER is assigning network printers (actually a printer queue, but you don't have to know the difference here) to a port on *your* computer, like LPT1 or LPT2. You can pick any of the available LPT numbers, even if you don't see them on your machine, because your print job will actually go out through your network cable! These assignments to LPT-whatevers is simply to remain consistent with the rest of your installed applications, which expect you to have a printer plugged in directly. Once you've assigned a printer like this, you can print from any application to a port LPT1; the network will pick up that request and send the job to the network printer.

Click on the **printer icon** at the top of the window. The NetWare Printer Connections screen is displayed. On the left you see the list of potential printer ports (LPT1, LPT2, LPT3, etc.). On the right is a listing of available print queues. Just as you did with the drive mappings, you can click-and-drag one of the print queues on the right, and drop it onto one of your LPTs on the left. You can make several assignments, but only one printer queue is allowed per LPT. Some people like to have several; for example, LPT1 is an actual local printer on their desktop, LPT2 is the network printer down the hall, and LPT3 is a special graphics or color network printer. Now you can easily control where you want to print by selecting your own LPT design.

Port usually means a connector on the back of your computer, used to plug in a resource such as printer.

If you like your new print assignments so much that you'd like to have them made automatically the next time you log in, click on the **Permanent** button. More details on printing configurations can be found in Chapter 14, "Printing Things on the Network."

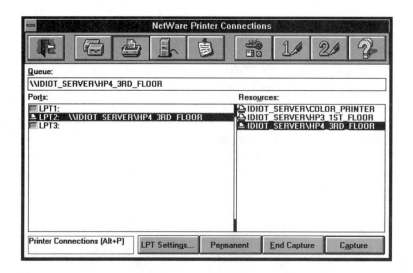

Connecting the network printer HP4_3RD_FLOOR to your LPT2.

Exiting From NWUSER

That's about it for this utility. Oh, you may have noticed a few additional buttons near the top and to the right. These can be customized by your network administrator to perform even more functions—like starting your favorite application. If they aren't programmed (and most are not), they won't do anything more than waste time if you click on them. You can easily exit NWUSER at any time by clicking on the picture of the **open door** at the top of the window.

The selections and assignments you have just made will remain in effect until you change them in the future, or log out. If you chose options to be permanent, they will remain even after you log out. Permanent drive mappings (and printers located on other servers) will be re-assigned the next time you log in, and you may be asked to provide a user ID and password while these assignments are made. All in the name of convenience.

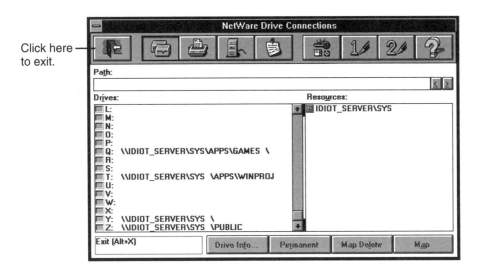

Click here
to exit.

Exiting the utility NWUSER.

Moving Around in DOS

It's almost as easy to move around in DOS with the NETUSER utility, which will be found in your path so you can execute it anywhere. This utility comes with NetWare 4.0, but the same function is provided in the earlier versions of NetWare with the SESSION and FILER commands. No matter which utility you select, you'll find screens very similar to these.

Running NETUSER

Just type NETUSER and you'll be up and running. NETUSER offers you the same basic choices of drive mappings, printer selections, and sending notes as the Windows utility.

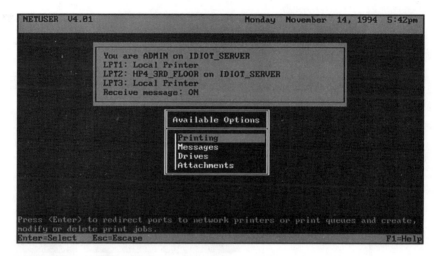

The NETUSER utility.

Mapping Drives with NETUSER

To map drive Q: to the GAMES directory as we did using the Windows User Tools, select **Drives** from the **Available Options** menu. You can see the current listing and notice that Q: has not yet been assigned. If you hit the **Insert** key, you will be asked for a drive letter. Simply type in **Q** and press **Enter**. You will be asked for a directory location. If you don't know it, keep hitting the **Insert** key. After finding APPS\GAMES, press **Enter**.

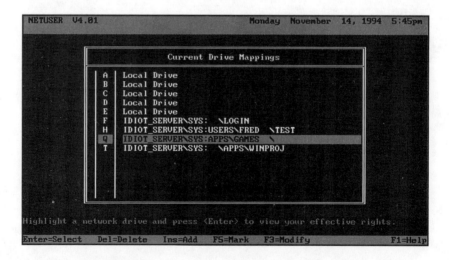

Mapping drives with NETUSER.

Selecting a Printer with NETUSER

Just as easily, select Printers from your main NETUSER menu. You will
see a list of your LPT ports available. For this example, let's pick **LPT2:**
and press **Enter**. In the screen called **Available Options**, select **Change
Printers** (since we haven't assigned one yet). First you have to select
the server your printer is attached to. Next select your desired printer
(actually a print queue) from this list and press **Enter**. The print assignment has been made.

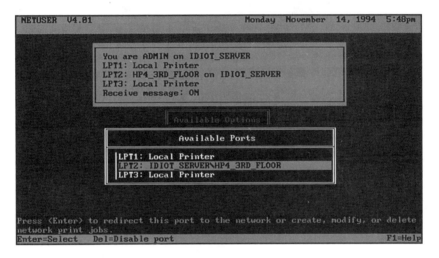

Choosing a printer in NETUSER.

Sending a Note with NETUSER

Sending short messages can be accomplished by selecting the Messages
option from the main NETUSER menu. You will be shown a listing of
all possible people you can send the message to. Select a user, type a
brief message, and press **Enter** to send it. When you receive messages
in DOS, they usually appear at the very top or bottom of your screen;
often they are difficult to see. Your machine is actually locked up until
you read the message and press the **Ctrl+Enter** key combination.

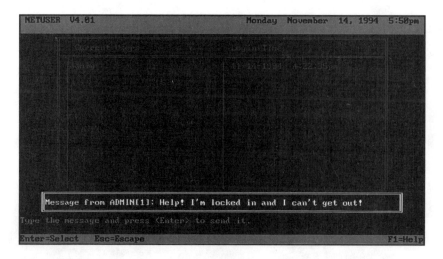

Short notes can easily be sent with NETUSER.

You can easily close the NETUSER utility by pressing the **Esc** key and pressing **Enter**.

The Least You Need to Know

Getting around on a network is tough enough without having to worry about details. This chapter described the utility that can make life a whole lot easier—User Tools and NETUSER.

➤ To assign a printer with User Tools, click on the **printer icon**. Drag-and-drop the desired printer on the right, with a port (like LPT2) on the left. Now print to that port in your application.

➤ To map a drive, click on the **drives icon** and find the desired directory on the right. Drag-and-drop that directory on any drive letter on the left, and the mapping is complete. Click on **Permanent** if you want to have this mapping created each time you log in.

➤ To change file servers, click on the **server icon**, double-click on the desired server, and enter the user ID and password for this server at the prompts.

120

Chapter 13

Storing and Filing Things on the Network

In This Chapter

➤ Controlling files by copying them where they're needed

➤ Problems associated with duplicate files

➤ Accidentally deleted files—how to bring them back!

Files are the excrement of computing. Some files are actually programs like Excel or SimCity. Other files are used to store data like your mailing list or office memo. All other files exist to support either of these two categories. On that somber note, let's go play with some files!

Using Those New Drive Letters!

First we'll recap the popular drive letters that help move you to your files:

Z:, Y:, and X: There is no need for you to play on these drives! These are called search drives; they are included in your path, so you can execute commands stored here without changing to these drives.

G: through W: These are the ones to remember. Relax—it's likely that you only have two or three of them. Find out which letters are used by your user ID. They will fall into one of two categories—either a place to store stuff or a place to find software applications to run.

F: This is usually the first network drive. Its purpose is to hold the LOGIN.EXE file so you can log in to the network. There is no need to use this drive after logging in, unless your business has mapped it to something useful like your home drive.

A: through E: These represent your local drives physically connected to your machine. You know A: and C:, and you might have a 5.25-inch floppy drive B:. You may also have a D: or E: which could be a local CD-ROM drive.

There's a Method to This Madness

Feeling overwhelmed by the 26 points of potential confusion? Don't be! Sit back and ponder this thought: *you only need **one** drive letter to store all of your stuff on the network!*

One? One? What are all the rest for, you ask? The rest of the letters are used to support you. Some of them are convenient place-markers for running applications; some are for holding utilities you may need; still others are used for storing other people's stuff. Eliminate all of the rest of these, and you are left with a single drive letter that always stays with you. It's your home directory, and a place where you are king of the hill (from the network perspective). You have all security rights here. That means you can do anything. In this directory.

Choose Your Personal Network Drive

The following examples are designed to be run from your home directory. Remember, this is the directory where you store your personal files. In our examples we'll be using the H: drive, mapped to SYS:\USERS\DAN—which certainly *looks* like a home drive.

If you store all of your personal files on a local drive like C:, you may be able to find a directory on the network where you can store files. You shouldn't be afraid of trying all your current network drive mappings. Contact your network administrator if you need help.

Sometimes your home directory is made to look like it's stored as a main directory off the root. This is done by using the MAP ROOT command, which tells your command prompt that it can't go back any further. The full path can still be seen in the MAP display.

Getting Your Home Directory in Order

Start by making your home drive your current drive. In our example we do this by typing **H:** and pressing **Enter**. The letter you use may be different; that's not important. What's important is finding the directory location where you (and you alone) have all rights to create, copy, and erase files. You probably don't have this capability on any of your other drive assignments.

Your home directory drive mapping should have been created for you as a convenience by your network administrator. (If you need help finding home directory, contact your network administrator.) To test your newfound powers, create a subdirectory called TEST by typing **MD TEST** and pressing **Enter**. You are allowed to make additional directories in your home directory; you have all rights here (you can prove this by entering the RIGHTS command we learned in Chapter 10). Now change into this directory with the **CD TEST** command. You also have all rights in here. Congratulations! You've just created our working area on the file server!

It's important to keep your home directory clean and organized. Since this is the place you will focus on storing files, it's a good idea to create subdirectories that make it easier to classify what you store. Nobody will see these; name them so it's easy to remember what's in them. You may want a directory called WPFILES, another called BOSSMEMO, perhaps a LOTTO or WISHLIST or MASTERS, maybe an ARCHIVE for older files you don't want to throw away yet. This sample TEST directory will be used for practice; then you can remove it with the **RD TEST** command.

Copying Files Using DOS

Quiz time. How many different commands can you use for copying files at the DOS command prompt? Time's up. Score a point for COPY and another for XCOPY. Two points for NCOPY, the NetWare command. Bonus points for you left-brainers who came up with MOVE. You can use any of these commands in these exercises.

Copying From the Network to Diskette

We'll start easy. First copy a file into your home directory. An easy file is AUTOEXEC.BAT. From your H:\TEST drive, type **COPY C:\AUTOEXEC.BAT** and press **Enter**. Now do an **NDIR** to display your creation:

```
IDIOT_SERVER/SYS:USERS\FRED\TEST\*.*
Files          Size    Last Update      Owner
——————         ———     ———————          —————————

AUTOEXEC.BAT   456     11-14-94 4:17p   DAN
```

Notice that your user ID is considered the owner, and the file is flagged as being non-shareable and read-write—which means it's available for you to change.

This is just a test file, but could as well be one of your important soon-to-be work files, like a business letter or graphics presentation. You'd want to back them up to diskette if they're really important. We can pretend this file is important and back it up to diskette. Stick a diskette in drive A:. Now type **COPY H:AUTOEXEC.BAT A:** and press **Enter**. Running a **DIR** on drive A: confirms that the file is safely stored on diskette.

Copying From Diskette to Network

It's simple enough to reverse the process and bring back files stored on diskette by typing **COPY A:AUTOEXEC.BAT H:\TEST** and pressing **Enter**. No problems here; you have all rights to your H: drive. But suppose you wanted to make this file available to your friend who's upstairs but also on the network. How do you go about it?

Your friend may have a home directory, and it's probably represented by the same drive letter as yours. But these are very different directories. Remember the whole path? Our example home directory is SYS:\USERS\DAN, while our friend's may be SYS:\USERS\KIM. There's no way I can get to \USERS\KIM because I have no rights there. I can't even see it! And she can't see mine! So home directories are not the best place to share files with others.

Well, any other bright letter ideas? How about the Z: drive? Didn't we just learn that everyone had the same drive Z:, and it points to a directory called PUBLIC? Would it make sense to store a file on Z: so another user could copy it back to their own home directory? No. Forget I mentioned it.

But you may have tried anyway. So here's the rationale. If you typed **COPY A:\AUTOEXEC.BAT Z:\PUBLIC**, you would get the error message **Insufficient Rights** because you don't have the security rights to copy a file to this directory. The network is protecting this area from clutter. You can't even make subdirectories here. So look elsewhere.

Copying My File for Someone Else on the Network...

If it's not your home directory and it's not the search drives X, Y, or Z, and it's not the login drive F:, then where can I copy a file so others can see it?

Many have pondered this question through countless rolls of two-ply. Some of the best solutions include a standard drive mapping for company-shared files, or workgroup directories. These are directories on the file server where many user IDs have security access for reading, writing, creating, and erasing files. In this example we've been told that a directory exists and it's called COMMON\DATA. That's all we need to know. We pick any unused letter, type **MAP P:=SYS:\COMMON\DATA**, and press **Enter** (or you can use the NETUSER utility or Windows User Tools we learned about in Chapter 12). Now we can type **COPY A:\AUTOEXEC.BAT P:** and it will be available to Kim if she looks in the directory COMMON\DATA.

What if you had to share files with just a few other people, and really wanted to use your home directory? Here's how (it's *not* recommended, but it can help explain security on the network). Remember that you have all rights to your home directory, and that includes the ability to give that right to other people. Create a subdirectory off your home directory. Call it SHARING. Put the files you want to share in it, and grant others access only to this subdirectory. For the user ID KIM, the command would be **GRANT ALL TO KIM FOR SHARING**. Kim will now be able to see this directory and share files in it. If Kim starts behaving badly and starts erasing your stuff, you can perform a **REVOKE ALL FROM KIM FOR SHARING** and lock her out again.

125

Who's Got the Latest Copy?

It's time to stop and think for a moment. How many copies of that AUTOEXEC.BAT file do you have right now? You can count 3—one on diskette, one on your C:\, and one in your TEST directory on the network. And your friend Kim might have copied your file to her test directory as well. What if this wasn't a mere batch file, but a real (and important) document?

Perhaps you all have some responsibility for this important document. Maybe you are in charge of the contents, Kim prepares graphics to place inside it, and a third person is responsible for formatting it. You are all working toward the same deadline.

It's unproductive for each person to maintain their own copy of the same file on their own diskette, because they won't see the updates from the other two. So the file is placed in a shared directory on the network, accessible to all three. But this brings up new problems. If all are making different changes to the file at the same time, how will they all be integrated? The nasty answer is, they won't. Only the last person saving the file will have control over the changes in the file. To prevent this *data concurrency* problem, always remember to have only one person working on a file at a time. Have that person save their changes before the next person is allowed to gain control over it.

A common question for shared files on a network is: *Who's got the latest version of this file?* This is a real problem on networks, and you should start thinking about it to prevent lost work in the future. Some solve it using file-naming conventions that increment with each save. Others purchase special software that controls access to files by allowing only one person to control and change a file at a time. Most depend on the application to have a capability that prevents multiple access to the same file.

Copying Files Using Windows (File Manager)

These same examples can be performed in Windows just as easily, if not more easily. From the Program Manager in **Main** group, select **File Manager**. Clicking on the network drive H: displays your home directory. If it's not already created, you can create the TEST directory by selecting File from the menu and then clicking on Create Directory. Type **TEST** and click on **OK**. The subdirectory is created.

In addition to H:\TEST on your screen, select **W**indow and then New Window, which will bring up C:\, where a sample file like AUTOEXEC.BAT is located. This is how to fit both H: and C: drives on the same screen so you can drag-and-drop files between them. Select the file with your mouse; copy it by clicking, dragging, and dropping the file into H:\TEST. The file copies without a problem.

Remember that you have to hold down the **Ctrl** key when dragging a file onto a directory to copy it. If you don't, the file will be moved instead of copied. The original copy won't exist anymore.

You can also select drive **A:** as the target, and then drag-and-drop the file onto your diskette for safe backup.

If you attempt to drag-and-drop the file onto drive Z:, you will be given the warning that you have Insufficient Rights to perform that operation. Is it all starting to make some sense?

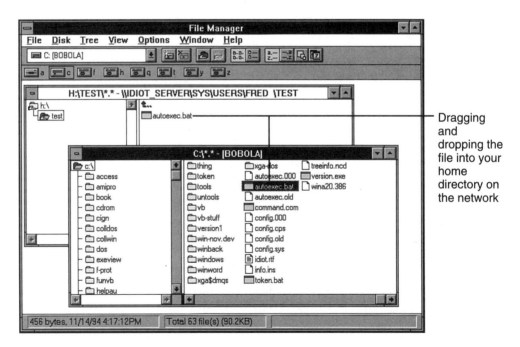

Using File Manager to copy and move files.

Erasing This Exercise...

One of the major problems with almost all file servers is that they run out of disk space. It's not from poor planning, it's just that people like to keep things. And lots of people keeping lots of files will chew up lots of disk space. Network administrators consider this a serious problem; a file server could shut itself down if space runs out. This is why you often hear complaints from your support people that people aren't cleaning up after themselves. Let's do everyone a favor and clean up after ourselves by removing our test files.

...in DOS

Remove the file AUTOEXEC.BAT from our home directory by typing **ERASE H:\TEST\AUTOEXEC.BAT** (or **DEL H:\TEST\ AUTOEXEC.BAT**, since these commands are equivalent). An **NDIR** shows the file has been removed.

You could also use wildcards like DEL H:\TEST*.* *if* you wanted to get rid of everything in that directory.

...in Windows

You can remove a file using Windows File Manager as well. Select the file **AUTOEXEC.BAT**, located in your home directory on drive **H:\TEST**. Press the **Del** key, or (from File Manager's File menu) choose **Del**. This brings up a Delete dialog box you can use to make sure that you really want to delete this file. Make sure you have the right file listed, and then choose **OK**. A Confirm File Delete dialog box will pop up. Choose Yes to delete the file.

Can I Salvage the File I Just Deleted?

Yes! One of the true miracles of networking is bringing a file back from the dead. How many times does it happen that you accidentally erase an important file along with other less important ones? Even once is too often, more often than your support staff deserves! Now you can salvage erased files yourself.

From inside the **TEST** directory, type **SALVAGE** and press **Enter**. Select the menu choice **Salvage Deleted Files**. If you are using NetWare 4.1, you will need to use the **Filer** command and select the

Salvage Deleted Files from the main menu. You will see a listing of all deleted files. This beats the DOS version because even the first letter is supplied for you! We can see the AUTOEXEC.BAT file which had been erased. By moving the arrow keys and selecting this entry, we can bring the file back. A confirmation is not provided, but you can assume our file has been safely returned to us.

Although SALVAGE is a DOS application, it can be run from within Windows. You may depend upon it enough to add it to one of your program groups.

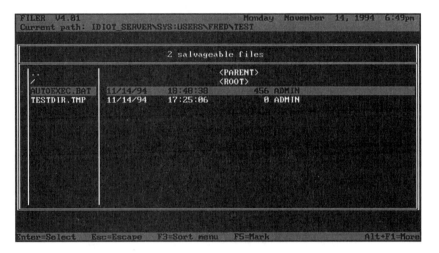

The NetWare SALVAGE utility can bring back erased files.

When to Use Salvage and When to Use Undelete

Many of you may be wondering why we didn't use the DOS command Undelete. The Undelete command functions just like Salvage—by selecting the likely file candidate from a list and providing the first letter. Undelete works great on local drives like your C: and A:, but is useless on network drives. So if it's a *network* drive, use SALVAGE.

The same goes for the reverse story. Salvage doesn't work on diskettes or your local hard drives.

Watch Out for PURGE!

Now that you've brought AUTOEXEC.BAT back into the TEST directory, erase it again. This time we will get rid of it permanently.

129

NetWare has a command called PURGE. It's one of those notorious utilities used to destroy evidence. Try it inside of this TEST directory. Type **PURGE** and press **Enter**. You may see a file or two flip by the screen. You will be left with a message saying something like **1 File Purged in Directory TEST**. This file is gone forever. It can't even be *salvaged*! Try it yourself.

So what good is PURGE? Your network administrator likes it because it recovers all of that wasted space holding erased files in the event that someone ever wants to salvage them. It's a way to clean up shop.

The next time you have a file you really need to get rid of, you can ERASE it and then PURGE—and it will never be seen or heard from again. (Unless it was stored long enough to have been backed up to tape, that is.)

Sometimes entire directories are set to be *purge directories*, which means erased files are immediately purged. This is often used for printing directories and common shared areas where files accumulate.

Who Cleans Up if I Die?

Ever wonder who would miss you at work if you happened to disappear one day? We can't speak for your peers, but the network would sure miss you! For about a day. Then it would want to reclaim your storage space since it's so precious.

Businesses are dynamic places. People come and go for various reasons. When they leave permanently, it's the responsibility of the network administrator to clean things up.

Your Real Estate Bequest

The tangible stuff you've left behind is your disk space. Ironically, it's not what's in the files that matters, it's the space the files take up. Your diskettes can be recycled, your local hard drive formatted. But how do you untangle the network-storage end? If the network is somewhat organized, the majority of files should be found in the user's home directory. It's a simple matter to delete the home directory of the late user ID, and purge it from existence.

To prevent you from ever coming back (or more likely to prevent someone else from using your account), the network administrator should quickly remove your user ID and password. They can also leave the user ID, but *disable* the account to prevent it from being used by others. This is often done while administrators spend time reviewing the late user's directory contents to determine whether anything should be archived.

When it's time to actually remove the user from the guts of the NOS, it's anticlimactic. It's nothing more than selecting the user ID and pressing the **Delete** key. Lots of people are inspired to become network administrators so they can do stuff like that.

The Least You Need to Know

We learned in this chapter the basics of file management on a network. Some good ideas like:

➤ Files can be copied easily on the network, using either DOS or Windows.

➤ It's always a good habit to make a backup copy before changing any files on the network.

➤ Sharing files on a network is not always easy; only one person can access the file at a time.

➤ If you ever accidentally erase a file on the network, it can often be brought back with the SALVAGE command.

Chapter 14

Printing Things on the Network

In This Chapter

➤ How the network helps you print reliably

➤ What is a network print queue, and how does it help you print?

➤ How to connect to a network print queue

➤ How to check the status of a print job

➤ How to kill a print job that's out of control

You have to learn how to print on a network. It's the fashion statement that says you've arrived. It's proof that you've triumphed over technology. Beyond that, it wastes paper.

How to Print Anything, Anywhere, Anytime

Carry a portable printer with you at all times. You know, those fancy new portable laser printers. Also carry a printer cable. Now you can walk up to any computer, plug into LPT1, and print without a hitch to the connected printer. If you want to print on a network it's not as easy.

A Word About Your Ports

You understand LPT1, right? It's the physical connector on the back of your computer, also called your *parallel* port where you connect most printers. While you're on the network you can forget about these physical ports. The network lets you do crazy things like picking ports that aren't really there. You can't see them. They're inside your network cable.

Yes, the network lets you arbitrarily pick LPT1 through LPT9, and assign them to print to any printer on the network. You can have all nine assigned at once! (Yours have probably already been selected and assigned by your network administrator.) By convention, most administrators reserve your LPT1 for a locally-attached printer (but you get that without doing anything—big deal)—whether you have one or not. The LPT2 port is assigned to the closest network printer. Possibly LPT3 is assigned to a backup network printer, or a different type of network printer.

What the Heck Is a Queue, Anyway?

Question: A Klingon, Martian, and Killer Tomato are locked in a room with only three computers, a network, and a single laser printer. The computers are exactly the same, and all cables are exactly the same length. They each pick a computer. They all hit the print button at exactly the same instant. Which one prints?

Before we answer, let's leave out one element. Leave out the network. Connect all computers directly to the printer. Now hit print at the same time. You get a mess. Each sheet of paper may contain bits and pieces of all three jobs munched into incomprehensible garbage, even though the Tomato would claim it to be his. That's because print devices, like tomatoes, are basically dumb. They do exactly what they are told, which is to print the first thing they see at their connector.

You can't live like that on a network! Lots of people are likely to print at the exact same time as someone else to the very same printer. We need a way for all print jobs coming into a printer to *line up and wait their turn*. We need a *queue*.

Where should the print jobs wait? Not at the user's computer; that should be freed up for doing more work. Not at the printer either, because you'd have to stuff every printer with tons of expensive memory and disk space to cover the busiest days. It's best to store the jobs in some unlimited disk space available for everyone to share on the network, until it's their turn to print. This space is called a *print queue*.

Answer: They all do!

Printing in DOS

Almost all DOS applications expect you to have a local printer. That's fine from the network's perspective. Your requestor (remember Chapter 6?) fools your programs into thinking you have printers attached directly to your computer. To print in a DOS application, select the **Print Setup** or **Print To** options, and choose the LPT port that points to a network queue. This print port assignment will stay put and work for all applications, for as long as you stay logged into the network. Your application won't know the difference. How do you know what LPT port is pointing to a network queue? An easy way is to use the **CAPTURE** command provided by NetWare.

Queue A fancy word to describe the single-file line your in, patiently waiting for something to happen.

Print queue Disk space on a server used to hold print jobs as they line up and wait to be released one-at-a-time to the designated printer. Print jobs are processed on a first-in-first-out (FIFO) basis.

Print job The complete contents of a user's print request, containing not only the original document, but also cover pages, form feeds, paper requests and other pertinent information relating to the complete request.

Are You Captured (or Set Free?)

This is the network command that displays or creates a connection between your local port and a network queue. It can even control up to nine ports, even if you don't have them!

Start easy by simply viewing if you have any ports connected to a network queue. At the DOS prompt type **CAPTURE SHOW** and press **Enter**. You may see something like this:

```
LPT1:  Capturing is not currently active.
```

```
LPT2:  Capturing data to server IDIOT_SERVER print queue
HP4_3RD_FLOOR
   Notify:            Disabled
   Automatic end:     Enabled
   Timeout count:     Disabled
   Name:              FRED
   Form feed:         Enabled
   Banner:            LPT2:
   Keep:              Disabled
   Copies:            1
   Tabs:              No conversion
   Form:              0

LPT3:  Capturing is not currently active.
```

This means the LPT2 is *captured* to the **HP4_3RD_FLOOR** print queue.

When you run CAPTURE SHOW, you may see all of them as "not currently active"; this means none of your ports are currently captured, and you will not be able to print on the network. LPT1 is not captured, and it works fine when you really have a printer on your desktop connected directly to your computer.

LPT1 can *also* be captured, but then it gets confusing if you really do have a locally-attached printer. Jobs sent to LPT1 would be routed across the network to the queue, which is probably a different printer. You wouldn't be able to print anything at your own printer! Typically, your first network printer is your captured LPT2.

If Not, Here's How

If none of your ports displayed in CAPTURE SHOW are captured, it's time to capture one of them! Remember the rules, and there's only one: You have to know the name of your queue. Okay, that may be too much to ask. But at least know where your job will print out if you capture to a particular queue.

FOUR GUIDELINES FOR PRINTING ON THE NETWORK:

➤ Find the printer you want.

➤ Learn what queue attaches to that printer.

➤ Capture your port to that queue.

➤ Print to that port.

So how do we capture a port? There are three ways: real easy, easy, medium, and hard.

Real easy is getting somebody else to do it for you. Most good networks are set up this way. Your local ports are captured the minute your login script runs when you log in to the network.

> You may have heard of the *login script*. That's the file that can run a bunch of commands automatically when you log in. The two most popular things to stick in a login script are (1) a drive mapping and (2) a capture command. If you don't have a login script, or aren't sure yours is working properly, ask for help from your support team.

Easy is doing it in Windows. It's described in detail in the next few pages.

Medium is doing it with our DOS utility **NETUSER**. It's easier because you don't have to type the name of the queue. At the command prompt, type **NETUSER** once again and press **Enter**; then select **Printing**. In this example, no port is currently captured.

Hard is doing it at the command prompt. It's harder because you have to remember the name of your queue and type it in correctly. Want to try? For example, the command for capturing your LPT2 to the HP4-3L print queue is:

```
CAPTURE  /Q=HP4-3L  /P=2
```

137

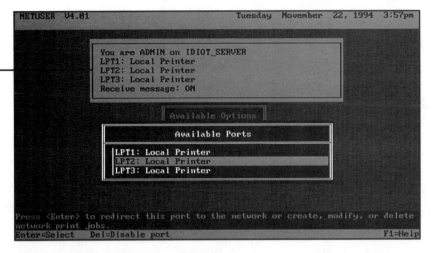

Notice that there are no currently-captured ports.

The NETUSER utility again. First select a port.

Selecting the port brings up the **Available Options** menu. Select **Change Printers**.

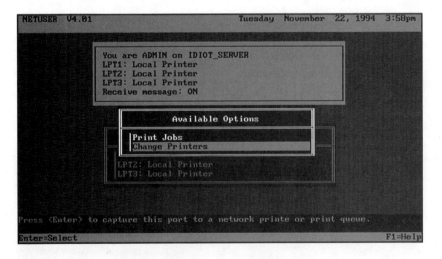

Preparing to look for a network queue.

Remember that print queues are nothing more than disk space on a file server. So it makes sense that you have to select a file server first, even if you only have one. Press **Enter** once you've selected your file server.

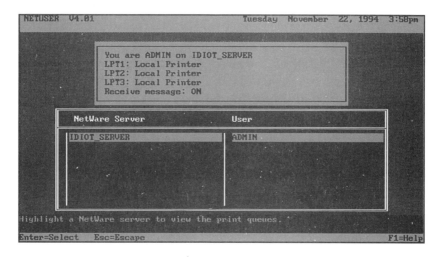

Before you pick a queue, you have to know what server it is located on.

Now you can see all the available print queues and choose one. Make sure you know which printer is attached to the queue, so you have an idea of where to look for your printed jobs.

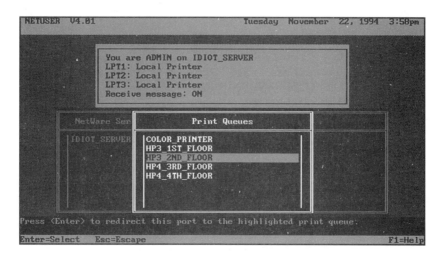

Available print queues to attach to our LPT2 port.

Once you select the queue, your port will be automatically captured to print there until you change it (or log out from the network).

Printing in Windows

You don't have to use any of the DOS utilities to print in Windows, but they are available if you find them easier to use. Most people find the Windows User Tools much easier, but the new Print Manager in Windows for Workgroups much harder.

Windows printing can be complicated to understand because Windows has its own print queue, in addition to your network queue. By default it's turned on; if you'd prefer to deal with only one print queue instead of two, you can turn it off in the Control Panel by selecting the **Printers** icon and clearing out the checkbox at the bottom of the dialog box labeled **Use Print Manager**.

Capturing a port to print to a network queue can be done in either DOS or Windows, and they do exactly the same thing. Use the one that's easiest for you.

A quick review from Chapter 12 reminds us how to use the Windows utility from NetWare called User Tools. In Chapter 12 we hadn't learned about queues yet, so everything should be much clearer now. The printer icon you select in User Tools is actually the listing of all available *print queues*! By dragging and dropping a print queue onto your LPT port, you are *capturing* a port to a queue. You can remove captured ports by dragging the queue off the port and dropping it outside the menu.

You can use this main printing menu to customize print jobs by selecting the button near the bottom labeled **LPT Settings....**

Customizing Your Print Jobs

Banner Computer print job cover sheets that are used to identify the owner of individual print jobs.

Form feed A blank piece of paper inserted after a print job as a separator.

Have you ever wanted to tell the world how wonderful you are? You can publicize yourself at the printer! You can have an attractive cover sheet (called the *banner*) customized to include your name, and maybe a location or even a phone number (or someone else's, if you don't like the attention). The real purpose of the banner is to identify print jobs at the printer. Without them, your job is likely to end up in the back of someone else's print job, never to be seen again.

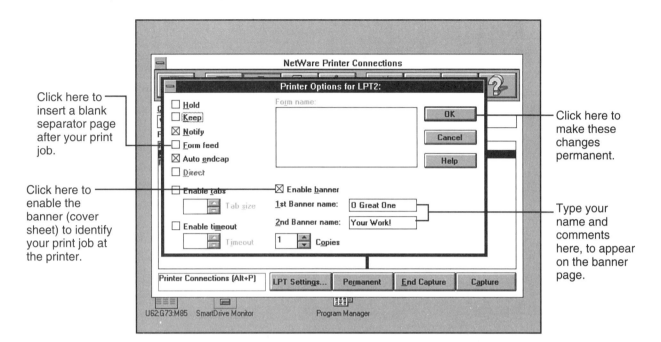

Click here to insert a blank separator page after your print job.

Click here to enable the banner (cover sheet) to identify your print job at the printer.

Click here to make these changes permanent.

Type your name and comments here, to appear on the banner page.

Options for customizing your print jobs in Windows User Tools.

Making Your Selections Permanent

After you have made your desired changes, you may want to make them *permanent*, which means these selections will be here even after you log out and reboot your machine. Simply select the **Permanent** button at the bottom of the screen.

Notice that the Permanent button is really a toggle switch. When a drive mapping is permanent, it will have an icon of a drive just to the left of the drive letter. If it is not declared permanent, there will be no icon. If you had accidentally clicked Permanent twice, the icon may have disappeared. Click it again and you will see the icon return. Incidentally, making either a drive mapping or a print queue "permanent" does not add any statements to your login script. This function is built into Windows; it creates the connection when you start Windows.

141

Q-Tips

There isn't much you have to know or understand about print queues to make them work for you. But you can be more productive if you know how to look at the correct queue and see whether your job is really in there (or did the Tomato eat it)?

Beginners should use NETUSER (or Print Manager in WFW) to view their print queue(s), because it only displays the currently attached print queue(s). Your network administrator might prefer to use PCONSOLE because these demigods are responsible for hanky-panky in **all** the available print queues.

Your company probably has lots of printers, and (if you're lucky) a decent naming convention to go with them. Typically it's a combination printer-type-and-location code. In this example, such a queue is the one named **HP4-3F**. Translation: "The HP4 printer located on the third floor." Are yours labeled this clearly?

Once you know the names of your queues, you can start observing them. Let's say you've printed a big job and it hasn't come out yet. Send it again? No! Go look in the queue!

There are several ways to look inside a print queue. Two are DOS utilities (which can also be run from an icon in Windows); the other is the new Print Manager provided with Windows for Workgroups. The first DOS utility is called **PCONSOLE** (Printer Console), a utility that shows *all* print queues. The second is a more personal viewer called **NETUSER**. Since most users care only about the print queues they are attached to, we will focus on **NETUSER**. If you have Windows for Workgroups, you will also be able to view your print jobs (only) using the standard Print Manager icon, which will display the names of all attached queues.

It's time to take a peek at what's inside a print queue. We will start with the DOS utility. Get out to a DOS prompt, type **NETUSER**, and press **Enter**. You see the opening NETUSER SCREEN:

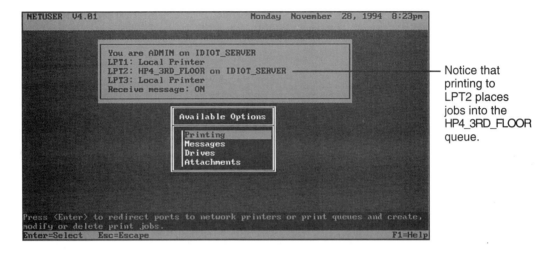

Notice that printing to LPT2 places jobs into the HP4_3RD_FLOOR queue.

The NetWare NETUSER Utility.

Select **Printing** on the **Available Options** menu, and then use the **up** or **down arrow** key to select the LPT port/queue to observe.

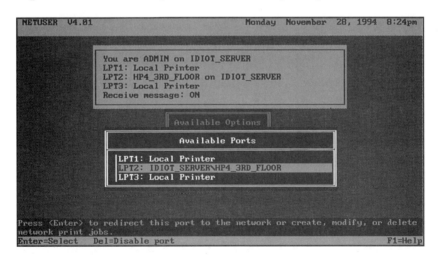

The available print queue to view.

When you press **Enter** on your selection, you will see the print jobs waiting to be printed. The queue is likely to be empty; print queues process jobs quickly. But you might find entries sitting in the queue, like this example:

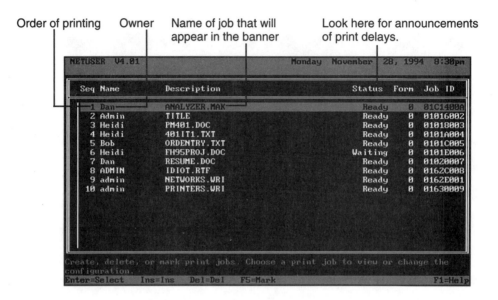

Order of printing　Owner　Name of job that will
　　　　　　　　　　　　appear in the banner

Look here for announcements
of print delays.

Print jobs lined up in a queue.

Dan's job is set to print first. Heidi's two jobs will print after the Admins job. Large print jobs may take a while to add to the queue. While they do you will see the Status column read **Adding...** during this process. All other jobs have to wait for it to finish. It's a first-in, first-out arrangement.

Also notice job sequence number 6. The Status column describes this job as waiting. Using the **down arrow**, we can move to that selection and press **Enter**. This is how you can see and change details of any print job already in the queue (see next figure).

Possible print job status entries.

Active	The job is being printed.
Adding	Print output is still being received from computer.
Held	The user has put an indefinite hold on the print job.
Ready	The job is ready to print, waiting for the printer.
Waiting	The user has specified a future time to print this job.

144

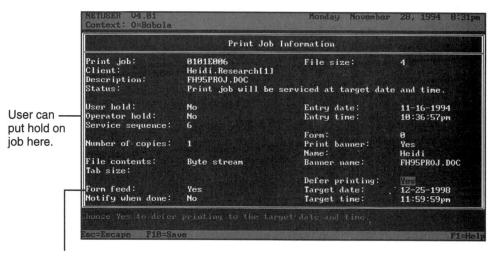

User can put hold on job here.

Form Feed turned on, print job deferred until a future date.

Changing the print jobs settings.

When the Network Eats Your Print Job

Now that you know all the different places a print job can be hiding, it's easier to find the problem when your print job never comes out.

Start at your own computer. Did you really capture that port? Do a **CAPTURE SHOW** just to be sure.

Next think about that application. Did you really select the proper LPT number? Printing to a port that isn't captured often makes a job disappear without a trace. If you are using Windows, be sure to check the Print Manager. This is where you will find incorrect ports with jobs sitting in them.

Still no luck? Time to check the print queue with either NETUSER or User Tools. Find the right queue, and observe the status column. Look for any *holds* or *waiting* messages which were intentionally placed. Also look to see whether the job stuck while *adding*—which can mean a printer-memory error, or a corrupt print job. Don't forget that the queue operates in the order of first-in, first-out, and you may be waiting behind several large jobs.

Kill Word commonly used to describe the act of removing a print job from the queue.

If you still haven't located your print job, go look at the printer itself. Look at others along the way. Maybe your job is popping out somewhere else. This happens on rare occasions when your LAN administrator routes all jobs from one queue to another, in order to service a printer. They really should tell you first. While you are at the printer look for signs of trouble. Does it have enough paper? Is the toner running low? Is it asking to feed a different form type, like letterhead? Is it off-line?

If you still haven't found it, call 911 (or the network equivalent— you *do* have that help desk number, don't you?).

How to Kill a Print Job with PCONSOLE

It often happens that you send something to the printer you wish you hadn't, like something fifty times bigger than you thought, or maybe 10 copies printed in frustration. What's the fastest way to kill the print job?

Use either NETUSER or PCONSOLE and select the print queue where the job has been sent. Either of these commands can be entered at the DOS prompt, or in a DOS-prompt window inside Windows. Use the **arrow** keys to locate the dastardly print-job entry, and press the **Delete** key. You will be asked to confirm that you really want to delete this thing. Say yes quickly, before it starts printing. If the print job has already started to print, you will be asked again to confirm killing a job that is currently printing. Once again say yes. The print job will be gone forever, and not even salvage will bring it back.

Don't ever turn off a printer that is currently printing; the paper will jam, and it will be very difficult to get it started again. Always make sure a printer has completely stopped printing before turning it off.

Some of you will still be screaming, "IT'S STILL PRINTING!" and that's true, especially if you have lots of memory in your printer. Maybe the whole job made it into memory. The best way to stop it is to take the printer off-line and wait for the print buffer to clear. Once it's clear, turn off the printer to make sure any trace of the job is gone. Turn it back on. The next job in the print queue will start printing.

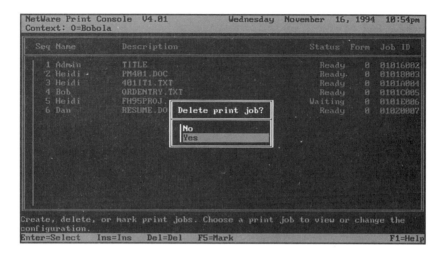

```
NetWare Print Console  V4.01          Wednesday  November  16, 1994  10:54pm
Context: O=Bobola

 Seq Name         Description                      Status  Form  Job ID
    1 Admin        TITLE                            Ready    0   01016002
    2 Heidi        PM401.DOC                        Ready.   0   01018003
    3 Heidi        401IT1.TXT                       Ready    0   0101A004
    4 Bob          ORDENTRY.TXT                     Ready    0   0101C005
    5 Heidi        FH95PROJ.        Delete print job?      0   0101E006
    6 Dan          RESUME.DO  ┌─────────────────┐   Ready    0   01020007
                              │ No              │
                              │ Yes             │
                              └─────────────────┘


Create, delete, or mark print jobs. Choose a print job to view or change the
configuration.
Enter=Select    Ins=Ins    Del=Del    F5=Mark                      F1=Help
```

Requesting confirmation to kill your job.

The Least You Need to Know

Many chapters could have been written about printing. You were lucky; we only had to learn the basics, like:

➤ The network forces zillions of print jobs to stand in line and wait their turn until they get complete attention for their needs. This waiting line is called a *queue*.

➤ Users can connect a real or invisible LPT port on their computer to a network queue by using the CAPTURE command, NETUSER in DOS, or the User Tools icon in Windows.

➤ You can find the status of a print job by observing the Status column in the print queue screen of either NETUSER or User Tools.

➤ I can also use NETUSER in DOS or User Tools in Windows to kill one of my wacky print jobs—simply by selecting its entry in the queue and pressing the **Delete** key.

Communicating on the Network (E-mail)

Messages From Outer Space

Electronic mail is like sleeping—we spend a third of our life doing it, and have nothing to show for it.

People have been sending live messages to each other on computers since the invention of the network. Remember the quick notes we sent in Chapter 12? Have you guessed what the two big problems are with this type of messaging?

Quick notes are limited to 234 characters, and don't last long.

Problem 1: Meaning could be lost if you can't fit the message into 234 letters and spaces.

Problem 2: No permanent record remains.

Is this really that bad? Some experts believe over 90% of all e-mail messages are intended for a single addressee, and contain no more than two sentences of real information. The rest is extraneous words and copies to impress other people.

So these short-lived messages are the perfect match for our lifestyle! Unfortunately, most companies have stifled this capability; they fear time might be lost with computers talking behind their backs (and no record of it). Our loss.

To solve the problems of message size and permanence, the first electronic mail programs were invented. These first albatrosses were pretty crude, but they got the job done. Users were still limited to a paragraph or two, and had to know the user ID of the addressee. Novell NetWare used to ship one called MAIL free with their NOS, but full-featured products quickly took over.

E-mail—the Communicating Frontier

Electronic mail (*e-mail*) is the term that describes the composing, sending, and receiving of written messages on a computer network. E-mail packages make it easy to create and edit messages, then select names from an electronic book to "mail" the message. E-mail is the silent killer of time; it's easy to get caught up in long notes on the subject of the big game, lunch plans, religion, sex, and politics! It's also quite a vocal killer of disk space. It started out with good intentions, stopping the paper trail of interoffice memos and buckslips. This new technology replaces them with small bytes of electronic notes stored and delivered on the network. A few years ago, people complained that the paper trails wasted an hour or more per day. Now, with e-mail, we waste two or more hours per day.

Are we communicating more? Are we communicating better? No judgments have to be made here. All that has to be made is you—more productive! Let's learn some lessons in harnessing and focusing the e-mail power of our network.

What You Have to Know to E-mail

Almost all e-mail is constructed the same way, attempting an analogue to postal mail. Everybody has a name and address, and a post office that is closest for them to use. Most e-mail packages require a user to enter this information before gaining access to the e-mail system. To send mail to someone, you only have to know their name and address. You don't care what post office they use.

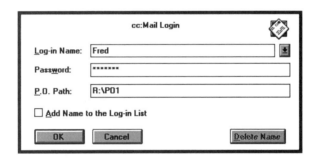

E-mail requires a name, password, and "post office."

RULES FOR EFFECTIVE E-MAILING:

➤ Don't use capital letters, or people will think you're yelling at them.

➤ Be polite; don't start any argument in e-mail.

➤ Keep it short, or people won't read it all. Two short sentences (20 words) will cover 90% of your messages.

➤ Convey most of the meaning in the Subject line, so your recipient can pick and choose the most important notes quickly.

151

➤ Don't print your e-mail as a backup. You don't need it. Only print the e-mail messages you *have* to have in hard copy.

➤ Be selective in reading your e-mail. Respond to only those messages that help your business move ahead.

Which Brand Do You Use?

It really doesn't matter; the major brands of e-mail are all about the same price, and have about the same function. Most have helpful features like a spell checker.

I've listed some of the most common e-mail packages on the market in the following sections. This is not a product review; features will change with each release. The purpose here is to prepare you for the coming bombardment when all e-mails will be tied together. At least you will have heard of the other products that will be creating the stuff in your in-basket.

FirstMail   I mention this program because it comes free with the Novell NetWare NOS, and it's an acceptable place to try out the concept of e-mail. Once you start, however, you'll know why it's named FirstMail, and why it's free, so don't criticize too harshly.

cc:Mail   Lotus Development Corp.'s cc:Mail is the most popular electronic mail package for businesses. It's not the easiest to learn, but once it's mastered, the program has almost all the power any user could want—including rules for managing messages automatically. These is also a remote-client package you could use at home; it connects to your office with a modem. It looks and operates the same as if you were in the office. The only feature it currently lacks is the capability of calling back mail you didn't mean to send. This seems to happen often.

Microsoft Mail   The behemoth Microsoft also puts out a solid e-mail package, the first completely designed for the Windows environment. It also has a great Windows remote program for getting your mail at home. You'll get a first-hand look at a form of this product in Chapter 23, when you install Mail in Windows for Workgroups.

GroupWise (WordPerfect Office)   This product from Novell, the creators of NetWare, is the same product previously known as WordPerfect Office. It has a popular following among WordPerfect fans. It is also more tightly integrated into the Windows environment than cc:Mail. Other notable strengths are its combination of e-mail with group scheduling, built-in rules-and-forms capability, and ease of learning. It makes great use of dialog boxes to provide a wealth of information for incoming e-mails.

BeyondMail for Windows   From Banyon Systems, Inc., BeyondMail is another full-functioning e-mail alternative. Its strength lies in its rules feature, probably the most powerful around. For instance, you can set up your mail so your computer beeps when you receive an urgent message from your friends, or even your boss, while you are working in another application such as a word processor or spreadsheet. BeyondMail is also very easy for first-time e-mailers.

DaVinci eMail   This product has a dedicated following; it's considered a solid, middle-of-the-road offering. DaVinci eMail offers all the basic functions needed to send and receive mail.

The Internet   What do you think people are doing on the information highway? They're sending e-mail to each other! And they have access to the entire world. If you have access to the Internet, you will know about the universal e-mail system known as simply "mail." It's built into the UNIX operating system, and it's a bear to learn and use, but the reality of communicating to anyone on earth more than makes up for it.

Sending Mail to Friends Using Another Brand

A common need among businesses is to communicate directly with customers and other businesses using e-mail. The problem is that different businesses often use different e-mail products. These products don't often work well together, and require the use of a dedicated computer that converts the e-mail back and forth.

The growing solution is to communicate through the Internet. It makes sense for each user to have a global e-mail address. The makers of the products mentioned above will have to figure out how to make this happen. Until it does, you have to find out from your support team who outside your business you can e-mail.

Receiving an E-mail

All e-mail packages operate in basically the same way. You just have to get used to the sightly different menu options or commands that differentiate the products. For the examples in this section, we are demonstrating the functions of cc:Mail, one of the most popular e-mail packages.

Another name and password to remember!

These aren't the same as your network user ID and network password, but you can sometimes make them the same. Then it's easier to remember.

After entering our name and password (and sometimes the post office name if we have more than one), we come to the first screen of our e-mail program. Usually this screen is also the display of your current in-basket, displaying all the e-mail waiting for your disposition. Take a peek at a typical morning's e-mail:

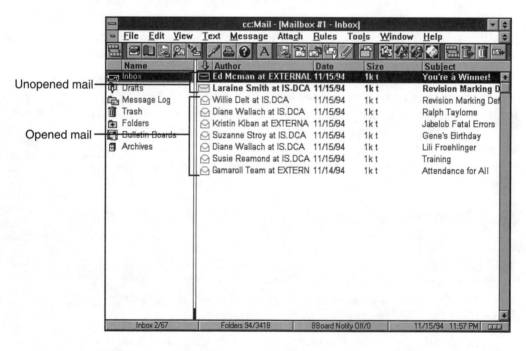

Fifteen items of mail in my in-basket; two have not yet been opened.

There is both opened and unopened mail in this in-basket. The unopened mail is at the top, in bold. If we double-click on the piece of mail from Ed with the subject "You're a Winner," it opens up and fills the screen with its contents.

If we take a closer look at the e-mail, we see it's constructed of basic parts. The figure shows how you can learn more about your mail by understanding who it came from, who else received a copy, when it was sent, whether there are any attachments, and so on.

In-basket The screen displaying your e-mail awaiting your disposition. You can delete what's in it, store the stuff elsewhere, or just leave it here forever. But why?

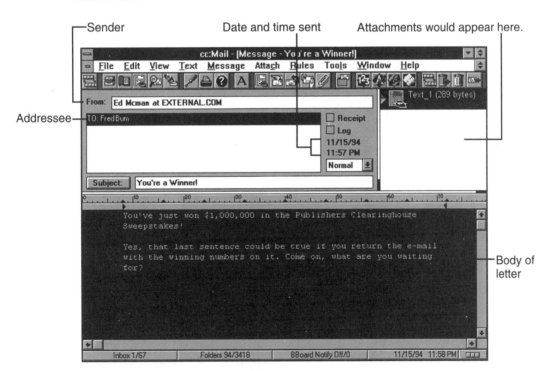

Anatomy of an e-mail.

If an e-mail ever offends you, fear not. Simply throw it in the garbage can. With cc:Mail you even have an icon of a garbage can. From the in-basket screen, it's easy to drag-and-drop the individual letters onto the garbage-can icon for removal. Use it often to keep your mailbox clean.

Sending an E-mail

Opening and reading e-mail wasn't so bad, right? It's time to send some now. Usually you start from scratch and have to remember the name and address of your audience, but here's an easier way to start. You can *reply* to an existing message more easily than you can create a new one. Fewer steps are involved; the name and address are automatically filled out for you, and there's no mistake who will get it. In this example Ed's e-mail is still open on the screen. We simply click on the **Reply** button.

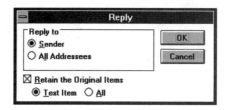

The easiest way to send new mail is to reply to existing mail...

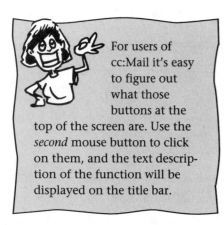

For users of cc:Mail it's easy to figure out what those buttons at the top of the screen are. Use the *second* mouse button to click on them, and the text description of the function will be displayed on the title bar.

When the reply dialog box pops up, we are asked whether we want to reply to just the sender, or all the addressees. Try to reply to only the sender whenever possible, to reduce excess e-mail. Once you click on **OK**, you are at the necessary screen, ready to type your own e-mail. Notice that the address is already filled out, and a copy of the previous e-mail is included at the bottom of your note. When you've typed your letter, click on the **Send** button; the electronic mailman picks it up and delivers it.

Address is already filled out.   Ready to start typing

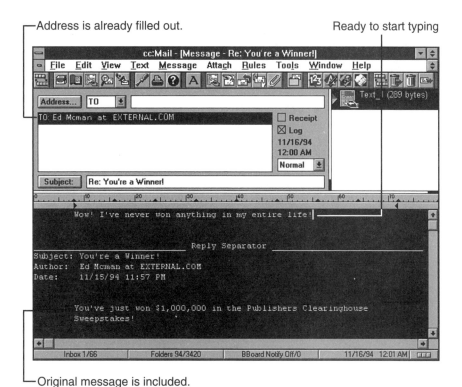

—Original message is included.

...because it's already filled out.

The e-mail system is fast. It usually takes only a few minutes to be delivered (on larger systems, your e-mail might have to be routed through different post offices, with greater delays).

To send new mail at any time, click on the **Create** button. You'll get an empty message screen, ready and waiting for you to type your very important message (or the office pool results). Our first task is to type in the name of the person we want to send to. Hardly anyone ever does this. It's so much easier (and less prone to errors) to select the name from the address book, which is often available at the click of a button. Here we click on **Address** and get to select from the alphabetical listing. Next, we type in our message in the body of the e-mail. Most packages include editing features such as font and color changes to help you create a more effective message.

Finally, to send our mail, we simply click on the **Send icon**—the picture of the postal letter with wings attached.

Click here to open the address book.

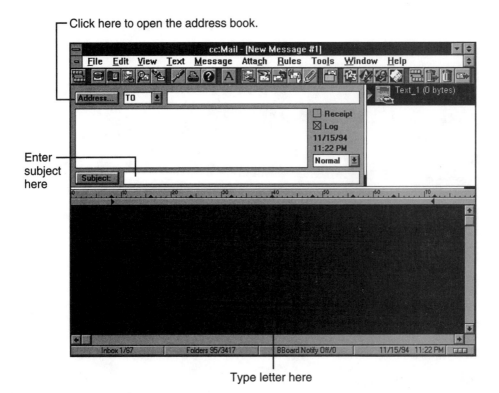

Enter subject here

Type letter here

Creating a new e-mail to send to a friend.

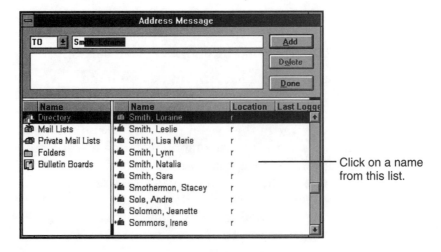

Click on a name from this list.

Select the name from the opened address book.

Losing, Finding, and Organizing E-mail

It's a bad habit to let your in-basket grow out of control. If you can't delete the mail, at least organize it into directories or folders. Almost all e-mail packages have this function. For instance, Ed's note to me might be considered junk mail, and I could make a folder called JUNK, and then drag-and-drop junk e-mail from my in-basket onto the JUNK folder. If I want to see my JUNK mail, I simply double-click on the JUNK folder and I get a screen similar to my in-basket, containing my junk mail. On second thought, why waste storage space on junk mail? Delete both the junk e-mail and the JUNK folder by dragging-and-dropping them onto the garbage can.

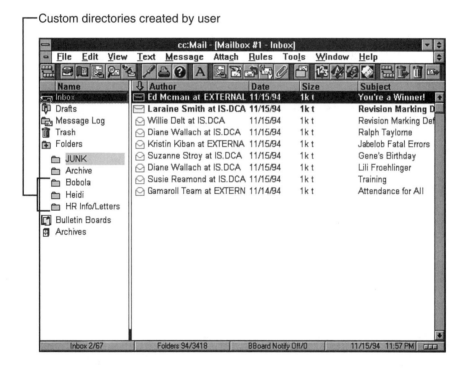

┌─Custom directories created by user

Organize your mail by creating custom storage baskets.

Other Forms of Electronic Communication

E-mail isn't the only way we communicate over the network. Productive businesses also effectively implement some form of network *calendaring*, *scheduling*, and *faxing* (bet you didn't know "calendar" was a verb).

Personal Information Managers

This category of software is often found on stand-alone computers, and can also be used on the network. *PIMs*, as they are called (for *personal information manager*), help an individual organize his or her time by providing an electronic calendar capable of entering and displaying a personal schedule. The only drawback to a PIM on a network is that they don't usually allow others to see your personal schedule. They remain personal.

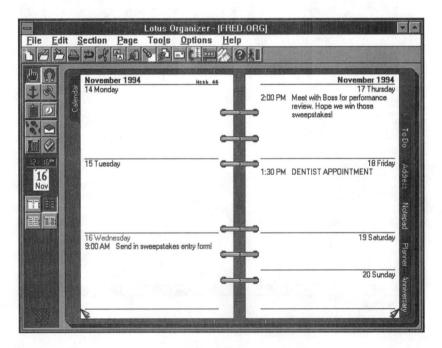

Simple calendar and reminder functions in a PIM.

Schedulers and Calendars

To make up for networked shortcomings of PIMs, software developers invented the network calendaring and scheduling programs to add productivity to our lives. These calendars are open to everyone on the network, either by making a master available to all, or allowing individual ones to be seen by others.

Calendaring really becomes effective when it's combined with the power of a scheduling program. With scheduling, it is possible to determine the best time to arrange a 10-person meeting without ever having to call anyone. These packages review all personal calendars stored on the network, and determine when the fewest conflicts arise. Of course, this is only effective when people keep their calendars up-to-date.

Scheduling appointments across a network using GroupWise.

Network Faxing

The faxing craze has hit the network world like a storm. It's no longer necessary to print out a document (which usually gets thrown out shortly after) from your word processor and carry it over to the fax machine. Many packages exist that tie directly into your word processor, enabling you to send the document over the network to a fax machine connected to the network. Often it's as simple to select a fax machine as it is to select a printer. A dialog box pops up and asks you for the fax-related information. You may need some new information—such as the phone number of your destination fax, and perhaps one or two accounting codes—to process the transaction. Network faxing is still in its infancy as far as *incoming* faxes are concerned. It's really difficult for a fax machine to figure out how to route pizza ads.

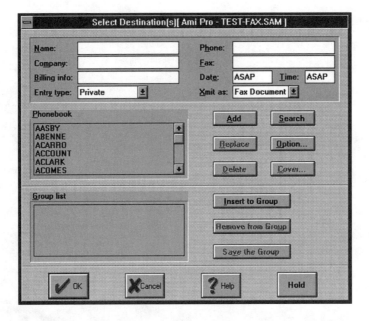

Fax prepared to be sent over a network modem.

We Never Have to See Each Other

It's sad but true. In the quest for increased productivity, we are becoming more and more isolated. You can battle this plague by using electronic communication in moderation. Don't e-mail your office partner for a lunch date. Turn around and ask.

The Least You Need to Know

Your computer is a great tool for communication, especially when using electronic mail. Instead of paying first-class postage, you learned:

➤ The network can be used to send immediate messages that disappear after they're read, or formal messages called e-mail that are controlled and managed.

➤ How to use e-mail to create a sample letter, address it, send it, and receive a reply back.

➤ The easiest way to send mail is usually to reply to an existing note.

➤ It helps to organize a growing e-mail basket by creating additional directories that categorize the most common types.

➤ Faxing, calendaring, and scheduling are popular methods of communicating, available on many networks.

Part 3
Staying Connected

What did the server say to the client? Nothing! The LAN was down!

How many computers does it take to make a network? Two—as long as one of them is broken!

How long does a network cable have to be to prevent interference on your computer? Long enough to reach the bottom of the lake!

Our network is so slow we have to fax our e-mail!

Our printer is so slow the paper has already been recycled!

Tired of these corny jokes? Frustrated with your network? It's not working the way they said it would? And you don't know who to call? Read on and learn the common-sense methods of staying connected to your network.

Chapter 16

Solving Your Own Network Problems (Columbo Cigar Optional)

Is It a Real Problem?

A real problem is something that prevents you from doing productive business work. Not hearing the chainsaw ripping through the ghoul in Doom II because your SoundBlaster isn't configured properly is *not* a real problem. Having your boss yell at you for not being able to print the latest sales figures—that's a *real* problem!

Let's also clarify the difference between an annoyance and a real problem. An annoyance is something that may slow you down, whereas a real problem stops you dead in your tracks. Examples of annoyances are a printer that jams often, e-mail passwords that aren't changed with the login password, or a network not being available when you come in on a weekend to catch up. Annoyances can be handled or tolerated, but they're usually beyond your control so don't worry about them.

Define What You Can't Do

If you think you have a real problem, the most important thing to do first is *describe* it. Put it in writing if you can; then you can stare at it and contemplate solutions. Here are some examples of good and bad descriptions of real network problems:

Good Descriptions of a Problem:

➤ When I turned my machine on this morning, an error message on my screen said **A file server could not be found**.

➤ I'm not able to save my file! When I try to save it to drive Z:, I get the error **Access Denied**, and nothing gets saved to Z:.

➤ I'm not getting any error messages, but when I print to the HP4Si on the network, nothing comes out. The printer seems to be working fine; it's online and has plenty of paper. Also, other people seem to be printing to it fine.

Bad Descriptions of a Problem:

➤ The #%@&$ thing doesn't work!

➤ What does it matter? It never works for me!

➤ I get an error message. I don't remember what it said exactly. Something about being denied something or other.

Notice that you can start working immediately to solve problems that are described well. So can your support staff. Lesson learned.

Gather Evidence

Once you have a good description, try to come up with additional information that can help you solve it. When was the last time you successfully performed this activity? Can anyone else do what you are trying to do? Will they try if you ask them? Are you trying something new, and maybe finding bugs that haven't yet been solved? Is your machine doing anything else strange?

You can put on your Columbo trench coat and gather even more evidence if your heart desires. It can help solve the really tough problems. Think like a detective. Are you missing anything you used to have? Have any key files changed? Have you tried to do this same activity at another computer? Can you print to another printer? Could your machine possibly have a virus? a cold? the plague?

Think paranoid. Are there signs that someone else may have been using your machine? Are there cigarette butts in your disk drive? Do you hear strange voices coming from your computer telling you it's time to upgrade?

If It's a Real Network Problem, Can You Work Around It?

Working around a problem means staying productive with the required tasks of your business. You don't always have to have your computer and network operating to perform your work.

Staying Productive Without the Network

Toss aside your computer for a moment. How did you do this work before you had a computer? Lots of people say they used a typewriter, did it by hand or by calculator, or even broke out the colored pens and pencils. The result was the same, even if it didn't look as beautiful; the result was the *information.*

Keep this in mind before spending hours trying to solve a network problem. Be flexible enough to consider non-computer alternatives to your problems. Most companies keep a typewriter or two hidden away, so consider it if you're trying to create a simple letter in a network emergency. Do the same with graph paper and calculators if you can't get to the network spreadsheet.

Most will complain that they only have one source for their secure network data; if the network is down, they simply can't do their work. Ingenious and effective employees will know this is not the case, and call the human relations department (or any department) and ask for other temporary sources for specific data. You will often find it, in many forms and in many places.

Creating Alternative Solutions for Yourself

Now that you are flexible enough to remain productive with a network problem, why not go one step further and plan for future problems (not causing them, preparing for them!). All you have to remember is *what's* important and *where* it is.

If you are working with important master spreadsheets on a regular basis, you would consider them important. They may be located on the network so everyone can easily get to them. You know the *what* and *where*. Stick a copy of the *what* in a place *where* you know you can always get it—your local C: drive! Don't actually use it from C:, just have it there as a backup in case the network is ever down. Remember to keep these emergency backup files up-to-date if the masters on the network are ever changed.

Disaster recovery
A plan that describes the detailed steps necessary to restore technology to its previous state before the disaster. Disasters can be anything from a brownout to a hurricane.

With a little creative thinking, you'll find that almost all network resources can be made available to you in an emergency situation. Your network administrator and management team call this *disaster planning*, but typical users never get to see this valuable planning. That's too bad; these plans often contain creative solutions for coping when the lights go out and users can't get to their data. If you continue to experience network problems, create your own disaster plan! After all, you are the best person to describe what files and resources are most critical to you.

If You Can't Work Around It, Can You Solve It?

Sometimes there's no way around a network problem. Using a particular computer, network, and printer may be the only solution (imagine, for example, a critical secure report that requires a special printer)—and if something isn't working, it has to be fixed.

As a general rule, if the problem is inside your office or cubicle, there is a chance that you can fix it yourself. Follow the guidelines for simple problems below. If the problem is beyond that—in the walls, wiring closet, or file server—you need to get the network administrator involved.

Find Out What Changed (You? or Something Else?)

The biggest cause of network problems is changing something. Anything. Change a cable here or some software there, and you're likely to hear screams from somewhere.

If someone else (like the network administrator) changes a printer without telling you, you may experience frustration until you know where the printer is and how to use it.

If you change things yourself, be prepared to fix things yourself. Loading that new software may change your AUTOEXEC.BAT or CONFIG.SYS files; have you thought about backing them up first? Then if something doesn't work, you can copy the old ones *back*. Moving your desk and computer closer to the window may sound refreshing, but the move can place stress on your network cable (leading to problems later); ask for a longer one instead of stretching it.

Isolating Tactics

Here are some simple things you can try before calling in the big guns:

Wiggling loose things   If that connection of your network cable to the wall jack seems loose, take it out and push it back in firmly. All cable connections should be secure, including your keyboard cable, display cable, and printer cable. If you wiggle them and something starts working, you've identified the likely source of error. Report the defect to your support group and get a replacement.

Substitution   This can be the fastest way to cure your problem. If you suspect a cable or component and have access to another similar part, try substituting it and see if it works. Be careful of your source for substitutes, you don't want to use "known defective" parts that may be laying around your wiring closet (but should instead be in the garbage).

Location, location, location   Where you sit has lots to do with cabling. If you're experiencing network problems try to sit at another computer temporarily and see if it works here. You may not have isolated the problem as cabling, but at least you've found a temporary place to work. Then call the network administrator and give the details of your problem situation.

Divide and Conquer

Two types of games that relate to solving network problems—the lottery and twenty questions. Picking the correct number is like solving the network problem. The lottery is quick and easy, but you have to be able to pick *exactly* the correct answer. In twenty questions you can have a strategy for winning every time, but it takes more effort to narrow down the options to the correct solution. No one can always pick the right number for the lottery, but we all can learn how to win at twenty questions every time.

The object to winning this game is to think in categories—categories of computer types, information paths, even error messages. Once you're in the right category, divide it in half and throw half out! Continue dividing and throwing halves off until you are left with the remaining piece containing the problem. Try following along with these categories to find the problem:

➤ **Distance** For instance, the cable distance between your computer and the server. This path is made up of several smaller paths connected together. Can you isolate the failing piece?

➤ **Process** A process like printing is made up of smaller processes that happen in sequence. Any one of them can fail. Can you find out which sub-process holds the problem?

➤ **Association** Network activities can often be done by anyone and everyone, so find out who can and can't perform the activity that's giving you trouble. Can anyone else do it? Who and why? It may have to do with security and network rights.

Fix It or Report It!

Network administrators can only solve problems if they know about them. All network problems should be reported. All reported problems should be fixed. Ignored problems will certainly haunt you at the worst possible moment, so bring them to the attention of your network administrator.

Don't Throw Gasoline on the Fire

Lots of problems cannot and should not be handled by yourself. If you don't have a clue how to solve a problem, leave it alone and just report it. By trying to fix it yourself you could do much more damage, and be responsible for lost data. Nobody ever wants to be responsible for that! So if you walk by the file server one day and see smoke coming out the back, it's best to simply report it and not try to put it out with your cup of coffee.

Escalation Procedures That Work

If you've reported a problem and it hasn't been fixed yet, do something about it. Often a simple note to the network administrator with a copy to both your managers is all it takes. The important thing to remember is: Describe the problem in terms of real business impact.

As an example, which note do you think is most effective at repairing a defective print server?

A. Lanny, you have to fix this print server immediately!

B. Mr. Ministrator, please assist us in repairing the print server. In the meantime, please provide an alternate method for printing the third-quarter sales figures, since our VP will be presenting them the day after tomorrow. Thank you for your help.

C. Hey Bozo, what gives? You couldn't fix that stinking print server if your lunch depended on it. Your momma wears army boots!

Also, don't cry wolf. Your support staff is handling several emergencies, and yours may not be the most important in the wider realm of things. So if your VP really doesn't need this report ASAP, wait your turn patiently.

The Least You Need to Know

Taking control of our life is satisfying—particularly on the network. In this chapter we learned how to start solving network problems on our own:

➤ How to recognize a problem from a non-problem.

➤ How to recognize problems that you can fix.

➤ Using the divide-and-conquer technique to solve problems.

➤ How to escalate the urgency of network problems and get them solved.

Chapter 17

How and When to Use Your Network Support Team

In This Chapter

➤ Discover people employed to help you with the network

➤ Get the most out of your technical support staff

No one expects you to do it all, no matter what they tell you. A medium-sized business of 500 employees will maintain a staff of five to ten people responsible for "information service and support." These are people employed to help you use technology. Managers and supervisors are included in this number, but it's mostly an assortment of trainers, help-desk crew, analysts, and LAN and network administrators. Finding out who they are and how they can help you can make you a happier person with more time on your hands and less worry in your face. This chapter will outline what their duties are, and how they can help you solve your problems.

The Help Desk

Most companies with more than 100 networked PCs will have some form of a *help desk*. This poor, abused group is designed to help you solve everyday technical problems by phone. You have a problem, you call the help desk, and they put you on hold until you hang up.

You can use your help desk most efficiently if you take a few minutes to gather and organize some information before you call. They're going to need it anyway. Write down a good description of the error message; include what you were doing just before the error occurred. They'll like that.

Help desk Small group of people who provide in-house technical phone support for computer network users.

Good help desks make a company more productive. A call comes in, information is exchanged quickly, a solution is provided within minutes. You, the user, become happier with the technology solution and use it to your company's advantage. That's the plan.

So why do many help desks have such a notorious reputation? Sometimes they get off to a bad start, without proper training or planning. Sometimes they are understaffed (you can tell by the stress in their voices). But don't give up on yours! You can help them help you! Ask them next time, and they'll let you know the subjects they are experts in, best times to call, and escalation procedures. You can tell them what subject you need them to be expert in, and they can tell their supervisor.

Unless you've been told otherwise, expect to use your help desk for the following purposes:

➤ to learn how to use a function inside a software package

➤ to get more information on using any network resource

➤ to report problems with any network software

➤ to find out status on connections to other resources (like mainframes, minicomputers, and database servers)

The help desk is an excellent place to call if you've just noticed a change in performance and want to know what's up.

Sometimes the people you reach at your help desk aren't all that technical, but don't give up. Exceptional skills in communications and finding solutions outweigh an immediate narrow answer from a geek. They should get all the information from you, and respond shortly with an accurate resolution.

Don't forget to thank them. These are people who rarely answer a phone to find a happy person on the other end. If they've done their job and helped you to be more productive, let them know. It inspires them to repeat the performance next time.

Trainers

Good trainers are worth their weight in gold. They are responsible for teaching others the best way to use software—in far less time than it would take individual users to learn by reading the manuals.

Training is a big business these days. It's typical to spend over $300 *per day* for instruction on how to use a software application package (like WordPerfect or Excel) at a training center. And that's cost per person, so imagine the expense to your company to train all 50 of your company assistants in Word for Windows or Lotus 1-2-3. And think about what you'd learn! Nothing more than the basics, probably right out of the manuals you already have! These expenses are another reason why companies are getting fed up with numerous software upgrades (new function doesn't justify the expense of learning it).

Your company may be fortunate to have its own trainers. These are people who have been trained in training, usually technical subjects. They are required to learn new products and teach them to others.

The advantage of having your own trainer is that they can customize the content to keep it appropriate. No wasted time learning features that don't apply, or hearing sales pitches you don't care about.

Effective trainers sometimes sit at the help desk and learn some of the current problems so they can incorporate them into the training material for future sessions.

Your LAN Administrator(s)

Almost all computer networks, no matter what size, have an individual designated as the LAN administrator. In the smallest networks, this is a part-time job performed by the most technical (or interested) person of the group. (Sometimes coercion and bodily threats are involved.) In larger networks, it's more than a full-time job for several people, and the level of required expertise is high.

Backups, Upgrades, Security, and Technobabbling

No matter what size, some basic responsibilities await the LAN administrator. First is to get everything set up and running. Software is loaded and users are added. Printers are set up. Working directories are designed and created. What happens next depends on how important your network is to your company.

Security is the key to protecting an important network. LAN administrators spend much of their time establishing, monitoring, and enforcing security policy. This includes setting all the appropriate flags on shared programs and giving correct rights to all who use the network.

LAN administrators want everything to run smoothly, so if they hear about an improved NIC driver that prevents a certain problem from occurring, you can bet that they will download it from the manufacturer's BBS and schedule a file-server-maintenance period to install it.

Your network administrator is also your friend. When they have to take the network down in the middle of the day (or even at the end of a day), it's not simply to aggravate users; it's for a good reason. Be understanding and patient.

Finally, your LAN administrator should keep on top of industry knowledge concerning networks to give your business the competitive edge it needs. They attend geeky conferences to learn the latest performance enhancers and bring back yo-yos that whistle and glow in the dark.

The I/S Department

You may know them as Information Systems, I/T (Information Technology), MIS (Management Information Systems), System Operations,

Data Processing, Technical Support, Computer Support, Network Support, or the Three Stooges. These are the white-shirted busybodies responsible for the data of your business. Important data like payroll, customer records, and human resource information. Your business would stop dead in its tracks without this data; someone has to be responsible for its safekeeping.

I/S is the corps of people responsible for the larger minicomputers, mainframe computers, and critical databases used by your business. Typically, all this equipment is placed in a room with large windows for showing off (the "glass house") and their offices are nearby. They dress more formally than any other group mentioned in this chapter. They take their job seriously.

You can also find the *analysts* in this group. These are people who do nothing more than make sure your networks and larger systems are running at top speed. Don't you wish you would see them standing at the network laser printer with a stopwatch?

There are also *planners* in I/S whose job it is to order 50% fewer disk drives than you need. They get yelled at much of the time.

You can also find *database administrators* in this group. They're in charge of the larger databases you might have, trying to make them faster and keep them secure. It's sometimes good to make friends with at least one of these people if your job requires lots of access to these databases (especially if you ever need data during a network crunch).

Getting to the Mainframe in One Piece

Some of us use our networked computer to get to the mainframe or minicomputer. We use a piece of software called an *emulator* that provides us with a logon screen to our *host*. These host sessions can be really confusing; they require a different logon, user ID, and password, as well as a completely different way to print (*What You See Is Never What You Get*). Because of these common problems, someone in your organization is usually responsible for assisting users with this subject. Often it's the LAN

Emulator Software that makes your computer pretend to be an old-fashioned terminal connected to a mainframe or minicomputer.

Host Another name for a mainframe or minicomputer.

administrator again. If you are having problems using a host computer on the network, don't feel embarrassed. Demand help and good service from your I/S staff, and don't be afraid of complaining to your management if you aren't getting the help you deserve.

How Local Geeks and Nerds Can Help

About one in twenty individuals qualifies as a network nerd, geek, or guru, and the ratio is growing. These are simply people who enjoy computers a lot. Because they spend lots of time with them, they've already learned the little nuances that make everything work just right. They have a regular job like you, so they're not part of normal technical support. Often they know more than your normal support staff.

Since support is not their normal job, they aren't obligated to help you with your computer problem. But there's nothing better than a healthy geek to solve that glitch. They know what works and what doesn't. They've already invested their time learning, so you don't have to. Their expertise is usually vast, so don't be afraid to ask about anything (software programs, host connections, using network gadgets, loading printer paper).

What to Use for Bait

Local geeks are often in great demand around computer networks, so it may be difficult to get their attention. Make it worth their while by supplying what they need. Junk food (salty and crunchy), caffeine-laden drinks, computer and science fiction magazines, zipped computer games from a BBS, or a pocket protector (just kidding) can be all it takes. They like the challenge of an interesting problem, so state your problem in that fashion ("I've never seen anything like it…").

1-800 Numbers and Those Old Manuals

Don't forget the obvious. Most software applications now come with online tutorials and extensive help material. You can usually move your cursor to the thing you don't quite understand and press the **F1** key for help. The manuals are also stuffed in a closet somewhere. Most employers expect you to make some effort at learning what is needed to perform your job.

What's next if you've stumbled across problems trying to use a feature of a product, and your help desk and geeks simply don't know? You can often contact the creators of the product by phone. Sometimes it's free, but often you must pay for it. Businesses can purchase support contracts that allow users like yourself to call and not be charged directly. Your help desk or LAN administrator can tell you what numbers to call, or you can look them up in the manuals that came with the software. You can also try 1-800-555-1212, and ask for the 1-800 number for your software company. If it's listed, you'll have a free shot getting some information.

Many software support companies now use what's known as a *fax-back* system for answering problems. These are usually free except for the phone call. A recorded voice steps you through subject categories until you pinpoint your problem area. Request the number identifying a short printed solution to your problem. It will be sent to you via fax. You select the problem number, enter your own fax number (including your name and personal phone number if using the LAN fax), and hang up. The machine will call your fax machine and send your request.

Be careful of support numbers that charge by the minute. It's best not to call until you have every bit of information in front of you to avoid any wasted time. Demand good service, and ask to speak to a supervisor if you aren't getting it. All charges can be removed for unsatisfied customers, as long as they ask for it.

Who You Gonna Call? NETBUSTERS!

Your Support Team—and who among them to call for these problems:

➤ **Hardware: Your Computer Doesn't Work**

Hardware Maintenance Support, possibly Help Desk, Vendor Support

➤ **Network: Can't Connect to the Network**

Network Administrator, LGF (Local Geek Friend)

➤ **Network: The Performance Stinks!**

LAN analyst or network administrator, I/S department, your friendly management team.

➤ **Printing: How Do I Do It?**

LGF, Help Desk, Network Administrator

➤ **Software: How to Do Something in an Application**

Press **F1** (Help Key), help tutorials provided with software, the manuals, Help Desk, checking electronic bulletin boards, calling the vendor at 1-800 numbers.

The Least You Need to Know

It's good to let go and let others help you. Especially when it's their job to help you. You learned you could improve your technical support system by:

➤ Discovering people employed to help us with the network; who they are and what they do.

➤ Learning what to expect from your Help Desk.

➤ Discovering the LAN Administrator and what he does.

Chapter 18

Problems You Didn't Cause (Don't Worry) but Which May Bug You

If you've ever caught yourself cursing the network because it's slower than a dead racehorse, this chapter might help to explain what killed it.

Geez, This Network Is Slow! What Can We Do?

Networks can be slow in two ways. Either some of the time, or all of the time. Which is it for you?

If it's all the time, there's not much you can do, except to make sure you aren't the only one experiencing the slowness. Just watch a couple of your office friends (or enemies), and get a feel for their network speed doing similar kinds of work. Anyone using a similar computer should experience roughly the same speed at network activities, like opening e-mail. If you are significantly slower, notify anyone who will listen. Send an official e-mail to your network administrator.

It's dangerous to put up with poor performance from your network. It's a sign that something is getting ready to break or is already broken. It has to be fixed.

If your network is slow only part of the time, that's normal. Typical networks have daily and weekly cycles of slowness. Pay attention to your network cycle, and you can benefit from it, instead of putting up with it.

Why Does a Network Slow Down?

A network slows down when too many people use it at the same instant. All networks are designed to perform well when used randomly, but few businesses operate in total randomness. You probably have a scheduled starting time early in the morning. You probably take time off for lunch around noon. You hopefully pack up and are home by the late afternoon or early evening. If you multiply these scheduled activities by all your fellow employees, you can imagine the impact on your network. A daily breakdown might look like this:

DAILY NETWORK ACTIVITY:

➤ **Midnight to 8:00 a.m.:**   Almost no activity

➤ **8:00 a.m. to 9:30 a.m.:**   *Heavy* activity as users login, start day

➤ **9:30 a.m. to 11:30 a.m.:**   Moderate activity, lots of e-mail

➤ **11:30 a.m. to 1:30 p.m.:**   Very *light* activity during lunch

➤ **1:30 p.m. to 4:30 p.m.:**   Moderate activity of all types

➤ **4:30 p.m. to 5:30 p.m.:**   *Heavy* activity for printing and saving

➤ **6:30 p.m. to 10:30 p.m.:**   Very light activity

➤ **11:00 p.m. to 12:00 a.m.:**   Very *heavy* as backups are taken

We can draw some simple conclusions from this breakdown. We might choose to do e-mail in the late morning, if possible. Lunch time may be the best time to get the best performance on the network, unless you want to come in and work after midnight (oh, yes!). You can expect print delays as backlogs build up near the end of the day, so do them at 10:00 a.m. or 2:00 p.m. instead. Technically, you'll be *compensating* for a network shortcoming.

Networks also slow down when important file server activity is happening. This could be a tape backup, a tuning issue, or a real emergency.

Networks may not even be available during a scheduled maintenance of your file server. This usually happens several times per year, for no more than a few hours each time.

HOW YOU CAN BENEFIT FROM THIS WISDOM:

➤ Do network-intensive activity in off-peak hours, like lunch.

➤ Expect delays doing e-mail first thing in the morning.

➤ Do heavy network activity on Monday or Friday.

➤ Don't always count on catching up around midnight or on weekends—you may get stuck during a backup or server down time.

How Scheduled Maintenance Helps You

If you're angry with your network support staff, skip this part.

Hello, this is a commercial from your network support staff. We want to let you know how we are making life more wonderful for you and your children. It's that time of year again, and our wonderful network needs its flu shot. Want to keep it healthy for everybody, right? This time we are going to:

➤ **Get rid of the old** (old user IDs, olds apps, old data)

➤ **Make room for the new** (cleaned disk space, new drives and applications, new hardware)

➤ **Shake, rattle and roll** (file server tuning, upgrading the NOS, improving security, updating hardware)

As soon as it's finished, we'll let you know. You'll enjoy the benefits of more disk space, better performance, newer and better functions, and a safer environment to network in. Thanks!

How to Survive Backups, Bottlenecks, and Bugs

Play along with the support game. Don't fight the fact that a tape backup has to take place, and the more often the better. Don't fight scheduled maintenance. Better safe than sorry. Your network staff tries to cooperate with work schedules and policies. Listen to their announcements for scheduled maintenance and server down time; plan your work accordingly.

Networks also slow down when being used heavily during a normal tape backup. Tape backups are good because your network files get copied to a small cassette tape that gets stuffed in a safe place. When a server crashes, your files can be recovered from this tape.

A tape backup tries to copy every stinking file from all file servers onto tape, and it's a relatively slow process. It may take an hour or more per file server. During that time you can still use the network, but you are asked not to.

Users are asked not to use the network during a backup because it slows down the tape backup. The goal is to get the backup finished ASAP, but if users ask the file server for other services at the same time, both will suffer. Once a tape backup starts ("kicks off"), it should not be stopped. It's best to let the server focus all its energy on finishing the tape backup.

You may run into network *bottlenecks*. This refers to a part of the network running much slower than you think it should. A bottleneck could be a heavily-used laser printer that just can't keep up with demand, or a cable carrying too much traffic. Let your support staff know about such besieged resources, then take action to avoid them. Find another printer, even if it's a farther walk. (With all this automation, you need the exercise.) If your network segment is too busy, find another available computer elsewhere to work temporarily. Your boss will get the point, and so will the support staff.

Another big network killer is the virus. A virus can attack your machine alone, or it can spread through the network like wildfire. A typical symptom is to notice your computer running awfully slow. Always, always, always protect yourself from viruses by running virus-checking software often—or better yet, use the proactive type that's always in the background waiting to pounce on the first sign of bad germs.

The Network Is Down (Can We Go Home?)

Let's dance! Yes, even the best network plans often go awry. It might happen once a year, or less often, but the odds are that it will happen. A severe situation can be caused by an important component suddenly breaking, power outages, and natural disasters (but if that happens, who cares about the network?)

Typical network policy is to inform users of any emergency activity with at least an hour's notice. Right.

Word should spread quickly regarding how long it's going to take before it's up again. It's true that the announced restart time is designed to be beaten. But don't count on it. (Even so, it's bad manners to quadruple the estimate and spread it to co-workers.)

Hey, It Happens

Most network crashes come and go like an earthquake. These are nightmares for everyone involved. It only *seems* you're the only one who just lost the meaning of life. Maintain your composure and think about that summer getaway near the beach.

If you've been paying attention, you'll have a recent backup copy of your important work stored locally on your c: drive. You may be able work just fine without the network for a while. You could set an example for everyone. Wouldn't that be a gas?

They're Bringing the Server Down in 15 Minutes!

This sounds like an emergency waiting to happen, and it is. Lots of major disasters can be seen coming minutes or hours before they reach the breaking point of known failure. Important network values tick away at the server console where the mood of your support staff resembles a wake. This is the time to check the underarm deodorant claims of brands purchased by your network administrators.

Believe it or not, it's better to beat certain death to the punch. If your support staff knows the server is going to lock up in a few minutes, they will *intentionally* bring it down so they can control it. By doing this they can make sure everyone's files are properly closed to prevent corruption. Deciding to "down" a file server is a big event. It has a real impact on the way your business is run, so support people are usually required to give warnings to everyone logged in—*before* they take the server down. It's usually fifteen minutes before, but can be as little as two or three.

Hey! That's long enough to save all the files you are working with, and even *copy them down locally*, where you can continue to work! When the file server has safely returned following the disaster, just copy your work back up. Aren't you the productive one?

IMPORTANT RULES FOR DISASTERS:

➤ Don't worry, it's almost never your fault.

➤ Relax and think clearly. You've prepared yourself by reading this chapter.

➤ Be flexible. Work locally or find something else to work on.

➤ Find another computer to work on if needed. Sometimes other file servers or network segments are available for use.

➤ Don't bother the support people once they've told you when the network will be available again.

We're Running Out of Disk Space

File servers need disk space to live. If you've ever witnessed a file server running out of disk space, you'll know that it's not a pretty sight. Besides the terror of guessing how many pieces the network administrator will be chopped into, there's the gut-wrenching pain of knowing that every single user with an open file has a chance of losing it.

Because of this interesting factoid, your support staff runs around in circles trying to get people to erase network files they no longer need. No matter how hard they try, and how many new drives they buy, the users fill them up with files. Fast.

Another interesting factoid is that printing can be the straw that breaks the proverbial server's back. Until printed, all print jobs are stored temporarily as files on the server—usually (and unfortunately) on the SYS volume. They get erased immediately after printing, but they could mean trouble if you're down to a few remaining megs on your server. Graphic print jobs can be several megabytes, and a few at the critical moment can stop the server dead in its cables.

Are You Completely Innocent?

But who cares about file servers? We are the users! And we demand disk space! And this is an appropriate request, as long as we are reasonable in our use.

What's reasonable? Anything in your home directory you can justify with a business reason. It's reasonable to ask you to get rid of other files you (or your company) don't need. You don't need to keep a copy of every single file you've ever created. You don't need sixteen versions of a report. You don't need duplicates of your local directories on the network. Get rid of them and do everyone a favor.

If your work consists mainly of word processing, a few megabytes may be all you need. Heavy graphics might need more, maybe 5 megabytes. Typical users don't need more than that. If you've got 30 megabytes of network storage—guilty.

You may have good intentions but still be taking tens of megabytes more than you think. Most people look only in their home directory. Look for your files wherever they may be kept, especially common storage areas on the network, and directories pointed to by applications. Look for redundant copies of files; get rid of all except the latest. Personal application software might be better stored on your local computer.

In businesses where disk storage gets out of hand they start *allocating* (and limiting) disk space. All users are allocated perhaps 5MB of maximum storage. It may sound like good business policy, but it can be the start of a bleeding ulcer for someone exceeding the limit during the saving of a 100-page business proposal.

Where Did Our Thing Go? It Was Here Yesterday!

Another problem that might bug you are things that disappear in the night. Perfectly good printers are replaced or swapped with more complicated ones that you don't know how to use. Fax software you finally learned how to use is replaced with another brand. A favorite drive letter or directory you got to know because lots of older files were stored there suddenly disappears.

Realities: In with the New, Out with the Old

Stuff gets replaced for a reason. And it usually happens at night to disturb the fewest number of users. Some good reasons may seem strange to you, but are important to your company. Often the older equipment becomes very expensive to maintain, eats too much electricity, or requires more expensive supplies like toner. Sometimes the software company becomes difficult to work with, or the product selection changes.

How can you cope? Accept the change. Trust that it's in your best interest (or prepare a business case for changing it back). Go look for the new thing and get familiar with it. Find someone (or call the help desk) and ask what it can and can't do. Find out whether those old files went to tape. Get your fair share of this new investment.

The Least You Need to Know

Networks are almost human—they break down once in a while. They need care and nurturing, and aren't we glad *we* don't have to do it? This chapter showed you how to accept the necessary evils of network maintenance:

➤ Networks need to be properly maintained because (like any machine) they can get worn out and break if neglected.

➤ Maintenance affects the network users when it occurs during scheduled work hours. The network often runs slower, or not at all, during this maintenance activity.

➤ Users can avoid the inconvenience of network emergencies by being flexible and planning ahead.

Problems That Lots of Us Have, and How to Fix Them

You can call them the *Top Ten Network Problems*. Almost all problems for beginning network users fall into one of a small number of categories, so relax and find your answers here.

Solving problems begins when you recognize you have a problem. Something doesn't work that should. Something you've done before can't be done now. These are problems. This chapter is about solving common problems.

You have to observe messages that come from the network. It tries to help you understand why it can't do something for you, and it talks

If error messages are flying by on-screen too quickly for you to read, try holding down the **Ctrl** key and pressing the **S** key. This combination of keys represents the *scroll locking* feature of DOS. To let them fly by again, press **Ctrl+Q**.

to you in the form of error messages. Sometimes they zoom by on your screen, and you barely have time to read them.

Things to remember for solving common network problems:

➤ **Record the error.** Write it down on a piece of paper.

➤ **Find the error and solution in this chapter**—and do what it says. Success will be yours.

➤ **If the error isn't listed here,** call your network administrator for help.

"A File Server Cannot Be Found"

You know it must be around here somewhere. Just how hard did your computer try to find it? If your office partner's computer can see it, it's there!

SOLUTION: Check your patch cable.

You know—that cable attaching your computer NIC adapter to the connector on the wall. Sometimes they come loose, especially if you move things around on top of your desk. Sometimes your furniture gets moved slightly by the evening cleaning crew. Anything grabbing that cable can cause it to go flaky. The message is usually discovered in the morning, when users are first turning on their machines. After any large network change or update—like dropping new lines to the offices of new users—several users can expect to get these until any wiring errors are completely corrected.

The good news is that you know your NIC is okay, and so is your networking software (except when your driver IRQ doesn't match your NIC IRQ, but who would have messed with that?). Life would be great if you had a spare patch cable. You could replace yours and see if that does the trick. Your patch cable may be okay, too; then you need to get someone else to help you, because the cable problem may be somewhere else.

In rare instances (or maybe not so rare), perhaps your file server isn't available. It might be down from an accident or scheduled maintenance. If this is the case, your machine has to wait until the server is back up before it can see it. When the server is back up, just reboot your machine, since it's the easiest way to reconnect.

The NetWare Shell Has Not Been Loaded (Windows)

This is a real bummer. You get this error if you start Windows before logging in to the network. Many of us have automated startup procedures on our computers to make things easier. Too easy, that is. If we incorrectly type our password (without even noticing), the AUTOEXEC.BAT file starts Windows, even though we aren't logged in yet. You should always be logged into the network *before* starting Windows.

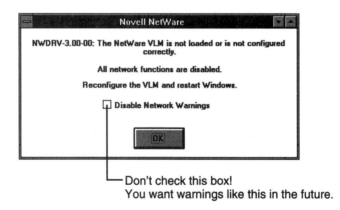

Don't check this box!
You want warnings like this in the future.

Starting Windows before the network software has been properly loaded.

SOLUTION: *Finish loading Windows and then exit from Windows. Load the networking software (for NetWare, change to the directory C:\NWCLIENT, type **STARTNET**, and press Enter) and log in completely to the network. Then start Windows again.*

Everything should be cool again. If it still didn't work, maybe your password has expired. Or else your Windows INI files may have been messed up somehow. If you continue to get this message, call for help.

I Can't Log In!

More common than people like to admit, this plea for help often comes just after new users are added to the network, or after a major network upgrade, like going from NetWare 3.12 to 4.10. See if you can find comfort in these explanations.

I Can't Even Remember How To!

SOLUTION: Ask for help in automating the process.

Everyone should have an AUTOEXEC.BAT file that connects them to the network at the start of each day. This should automatically load the NIC drivers, the VLMs or shell software, change to the network drive, and execute the LOGIN command. If your computer doesn't connect to the network automatically, and you want it to, contact your network administrator.

Once this is working, all you have to remember is your user ID and network password. The user ID should resemble your last or first name, so check your driver's license if you need a hint. The password is another story. It's *supposed* to be difficult for others to guess.

It Doesn't Like My Password

SOLUTION: Type in the correct password. If you've forgotten it, contact your network administrator and ask for a new one.

If you have to worry about multiple passwords, make it easy on yourself and change them all to the same thing. When one of them expires, change all of them at the same time.

Don't feel bad. Lots of people forget their passwords, especially when your company forces you to have multiple passwords (like one for e-mail, one for the host access, one for remote access, and one for the network in general). Do your best to keep them all in sync, or the same.

Your password may also have expired. You should have received warnings from the network, and maybe you ignored them. Security-conscious businesses usually set an expiration date for passwords of all user accounts at 30 or 60 days. Use the SETPASS command we learned in Chapter 11 to change your password before it expires.

Using NetWare 4.0 or Later

SOLUTION: Change to the proper context to log in.

More brain power is needed to log in to the latest versions of NetWare. User accounts can now be stored in different areas called *contexts*. You have to be in the right context to log in successfully. It's kind of like a directory, but you don't see it. Your network staff can automate this process so your machine starts in the proper context for you.

Context A location where a network object lives. User IDs are stored in a context. So are print queues, file servers, and software applications. You only care about this if you use NetWare 4.0 or later.

To log in every time without error in NetWare 4.0 or later, you have to remember your *complete context*. These strange beasts look like Internet IDs, using periods as separators. My complete context might be entered like this:

```
LOGIN .DBOBOLA.SALES.HQ.MYCOMPANY
```

Your support team can tell you what your exact context is.

"Bad Command or Filename"

This error plagues users on the network just as it does users of plain DOS and Windows. Here are the more popular categories, so try to best describe what you were doing at the time.

When Trying to Remember a Command

SOLUTION: Retype the command correctly.

This is the easiest error to stumble upon. Any user typing his or her own name at the DOS command prompt and hitting the Enter key will see this familiar nuisance, unless your name happens to be, for example, "COPY," "XCOPY," or "NCOPY" (or any internal DOS command, external DOS command, and NetWare command, respectively).

Basically, any command not recognized by DOS, Windows, or NetWare will generate this error. It means your computer doesn't know what to do with what you have just typed, so it does nothing more than show you this message. If you happen to misspell a proper DOS,

Windows, or NetWare command, you will also get this message, for the same reason. If you add symbols or spaces when you shouldn't, or leave them out when you need them, you can also get this message.

When You Know It's Spelled Correctly

SOLUTION: Change to the directory where the file is located.

If you are certain you are typing the command correctly, and you are certain this command exists somewhere inside your computer or the file server, but you still get this error, you then most likely have a problem related to your searching capability. If it's a network command, make sure you are logged in and your Z: is pointing to the PUBLIC directory.

Your machine first looks in the current directory, then in each network search directory, which includes the local drives in your PATH. If it doesn't find it anywhere, you get the **Bad command or filename** error message.

Normally, you can run only commands existing in your current directory, for example, C:\WINDOWS. The network search drives and path statement simply tell your computer where to go looking for commands if it doesn't find them in the current directory.

You may be asking yourself why we don't simply create a path or search drive to every single directory, so we always find our files and never get this error message. Well, the limiting factor is called the *environment space*, a portion of memory you can use to fit important reminders for your computer. You can see your environment settings if you type the SET command. You will see PATH as one of your entries (if you have a path). If your path statement and number of search drives grows too large, your environment space may run out of space without warning you, leaving you in a bad state. Another reason against the all-encompassing path is performance. It takes a while for your computer to go searching through every directory to find a command each time. Longer paths can translate into overall sluggish performance. Things near the end of your path take longer to find than things near the front. Also, in some cases, different files with the same name exist in different directories within your computer, but your PATH will use only the first entry it happens to find.

"Access Denied"

You tried to modify the file attributes of, delete, rename, or copy a file for which you lack rights. This is one of the error messages that warns you (too late) that you cannot do something. It most often appears when a user is trying to save changes to a file that is protected from change.

While Trying to Save Protected Files

*SOLUTION: Do a **Save As...** and temporarily put in another name.*

Remembering from Chapter 10, files can be protected from change through the use of attributes, and this particular attribute is called Read-Only. A file (or even directory) can have attributes assigned in two ways. DOS uses the ATTRIB command; NetWare uses the FLAG command. Protecting files is important, especially ones like the customer database file. Many of our accountants need to see that file, but we don't want them accidentally changing it, so the copy available to them is flagged Read-Only. Some salespeople may need to often update parameters pertaining to their customers, so the portion in their control has the attribute of Normal, or Read-Write.

Trying to Erase Protected Files

*SOLUTION: Flag the files **RW** (Read-Write), or **N** (meaning Normal, same as RW except it's one less keystroke), and erase the files. Do this only if the files are yours.*

This is another error message that you don't have to get worried over. It is telling you that a scenario is in place for your protection, or for the protection of the network. For example, you will get this message if you try to erase the NetWare files in the PUBLIC directory. Same with the login files in the LOGIN directory, before and after you log in.

Sometimes this message is self-inflicted, if you've flagged a file yourself to prevent yourself from accidentally erasing it.

If the file really is important, don't worry, you probably won't have the Modify right (which you'd need to change the attribute to Read-Write) anyway.

Trying to Open a File Already Opened by Someone Else

SOLUTION: Wait until they're done with it.

If you need to change the file in any way, you have to wait until the first person releases it. If you just want to look at it, and your application allows this, continue opening it in the Read-Only mode. No harm will come to this file.

"IPXODI Not Loaded"

SOLUTION: Reconfigure your network adapter for the correct IRQ.

You may get this error if you just installed any type of adapter card into your computer. Adapter cards need things called "interrupts," and if another card takes the interrupt needed by your NIC, you may get this error message.

A quick way to look at the specific information of an IPX file is to type **IPX I** (the **I** stands for information) and read it directly. It will read out the brand and type of the intended NIC. Then you confirm which NIC you have. If the information does match up, but IPC still does not load, check for other adapter cards that may be temporarily interfering. Sometimes the selected interrupt should be modified so it can coexist with other adapters.

A less likely reason for the message is an actual cable, or a NIC problem. If the integrity of an IPX.COM file is ever in doubt, it is very easy to just generate another using the appropriate shell-generation diskette from the NetWare software.

"Insufficient Disk Space" or "Disk Full"

This error usually rears its ugly head when you least expect it. If you're lucky, your software application will give you another chance to save your work. Here are your choices:

While Trying to Save a File

*SOLUTION: Do a **Save As...** and select another directory or drive location.*

Don't panic! In almost all cases, this message is actually describing the *network* drive, not a local drive. And it's *not* out of space; it just seems to be, because you are attempting to store to a drive or directory where you have no rights. The network lets you see the drive, but without the required rights to store files, your application interprets the problem as a full disk. You should be able to solve the immediate crisis by providing a drive letter in which you have full access. Use a local drive if you can't find a network one (even a diskette drive if necessary). Don't try to get out of the application until you have safely saved your files.

You may have a bigger problem on your hands if there is an Account Restrictions feature for disk space on your network. You may not be allowed to save any more files until you clean out some others. Don't worry about that now, save your file locally! Then clean up.

When You Really Are Out of Disk Space

*SOLUTION: Do a **Save As...** and select a local drive or diskette.*

In the rare case when a drive is actually full, you do have a big problem. A local diskette drive is usually the best alternative. If your local hard drive C: is full, save to diskette—and then start cleaning off your hard drive! If the network drive is truly full, your network administrator may have to start updating the ol' résumé. Viruses (and simple batch programs) can also be designed to chew up your most precious resource, so it's a good idea be aware of your computing state of health at all times.

My Print Job Is Stuck!

Sorry, but this takes a little more thinking on your part. It helps to narrow down the possibilities if you describe where you think your print job is stuck. If you don't want to think, then just do all of the following suggestions. As always with printing—good luck!

Stuck in the Application

SOLUTION: Make sure the correct printer is selected in the application, and that the printer is displayed in Print Manager.

This is when nothing is coming out from your app. It's the rarest form of stuckage, but it can happen after you've added or changed print drivers, or when you're playing with early versions of new software.

Stuck in Windows Print Manager

Check the Print Manager. If you see a print job entry in one of the LPT ports, but it's not doing anything that looks productive, then the job is scientifically considered "stuck."

SOLUTION: Check the status of the job in Print Manager. If the printer is "Paused," change it to "Online." If it already is, then your LPT port is not captured (or you have lost your network connection).

The Print Manager has a button (leftmost at the top) used for holding (pausing) print jobs, which you would do if you wanted to hold up many jobs to print all at once. Press this button again to release the job.

You should also see the name of the print queue listed next to the printer. If you do not, then you must capture a port to the desired queue as described in Chapter 15. The new Print Manager allows you quick access to NetWare User Tools; you just click on the **Connect Network Printer** button.

Stuck in NetWare Print Queue

SOLUTION: Make sure the printer is turned on and online; also look at jobs before it. Maybe just wait. Also check printer for jams, an empty paper tray, or messages to load a different paper type.

Stuck at the Printer

SOLUTION: Make sure the printer is not jammed, out of paper, or asking for a different paper load.

Printers can refuse to print for a number of reasons. First check the obvious. Is it turned on, online, and full of paper? Are there any error messages on the printer display panel? It may be a defective printer or network cable, the print server may not be up, or the network administrator may even have stopped the queue.

The Printer Is Printing Garbage!

SOLUTION: Do not turn the printer off (the paper will jam). Take the printer off-line. Delete the job from the queue ASAP. Wait until the printing stops, then turn the printer off, which will kill the rest of the job in printer memory. Don't print again until you fix your job.

Printers are dumb; they print what you tell them to print. Garbage in, garbage out. Most of the time garbage is caused by print instructions being confused. Your presentation may have PostScript graphics in it, but you forgot (it's easy) to tell that to the printer when you sent the job! Instead of printing in the new language, it prints what appears as garbage in the old.

Graphics are usually the killer, so check your document for clip art or scanned images that require PostScript, and find a printer capable of printing it. Even simple graphics are often made up of common symbols that can throw off an otherwise smart printer.

Even when jobs print correctly, they can leave the printer in a bad state for the next job. To gather clues, take a look at what printed just before your garbage.

My Computer Died

SOLUTION: Bury it!

Okay, I apologize for that one. Computers die every day. Here are some of the common solutions to bring them back to life:

➤ Is the power button turned on?

➤ Is it plugged in?

➤ Does your machine plug into a power strip? Is the power strip turned on and plugged in? Has it blown a fuse?

➤ Is the power out on that outlet? Can you plug anything else in to check it, like a pencil sharpener or GameBoy?

➤ Is your monitor turned on?

➤ Is the brightness turned all the way down on your monitor? (The computer may look like it's snoozing when it's not.)

➤ Are all the cables plugged in and secure?

Or Is It Simply Frozen?

SOLUTION: Thaw it out!

Now I'm getting carried away. Most people describe their computer as "frozen" when it completely locks up, doing nothing more than beeping as they bang away at the keyboard, if that. Usually there's an important file up on the screen that hasn't been saved for the last half-hour.

The best thing to do is write down as many facts as you can—especially what is on the screen—and then turn the computer off. Wait a few seconds and turn it back on again. This scares away almost all problems like this, every time. (Sure it works, *this* time...) Sometimes the problem happens only once and we never, ever see it again.

If your machine continues to lock up for no apparent reason, call your support staff and demand that it be replaced. Computers are difficult enough without having a sick one bother you.

The Least You Need to Know

Some network problems can be explained, even solved! This chapter reviewed some of the simpler ones, like:

➤ How to save your work to a local disk, diskette, or another drive or directory before attempting to solve network problems.

➤ Continuing to be productive by understanding and fixing common network problems.

➤ Solving the most frequent printing problems that plague even experienced network users.

Part 4
Building Your Own Empire

Can't get no satisfaction? Think it's absolutely crazy to build your own network? Think again—and put on your propeller cap and pocket protector! Using software you probably already have, and some components you can easily get, you can start your own electronic mini-highway (or at least an off-ramp). Included in these pages are the complete instructions from start to finish, including where to buy stuff, how much money you'll need, and how long each step will take. You don't even need a building permit!

Chapter 20

Planning Your Own Successful Network

> **In This Chapter**
>
> ➤ How planning can save you money and time
>
> ➤ Where to buy network components
>
> ➤ How much you can expect to spend

You can't just throw a network together without planning! How would you know when you were finished? When would you celebrate? How would you know when it's time to start complaining that it's not fast enough, big enough, or just plain better?

Let's Plan for Just a Moment

It's apparent that you want, need, or have a network, which is why you purchased this book. If you're creating your own network from scratch, it's helpful to understand the primary reasons for this behavior so you can be on target with your purchases. And remember, it's possible to gain the benefits of a network by connecting as few as two computers.

GOOD REASONS TO SET UP YOUR OWN NETWORK:

➤ To share that fancy new color laser printer; to print files that currently have to be saved to diskette and loaded onto the computer attached to the printer.

➤ To allow convenient access for multiple people, so that no matter whose machine a file might reside on, everybody can get at multiple files.

➤ To start official e-mail in our office, as we move to a cleaner and more efficient "paperless" office.

➤ To try a better way of scheduling meetings and appointments through software installed on a network and available to all.

➤ To share that fax machine. We can save time and paper by sending the document over the network directly to the fax.

Once you've focused on a few of these primary reasons, you can decide which type of network is best for you. To make the explanation of setting up a network easy, I'll set up an example. In this example, we have a branch office of six employees who want a simple network to automate the office. Our large headquarters operates using Novell NetWare, but they're too busy to help us for now. We do understand the need to connect with them in the future. They've given us permission to set up a simple small network, on the condition that we pay for it. Big deal, huh?

Our Plan

One of the first decisions to make is which network operating system to use. We don't have any computers to spare in our office, so it would be difficult to create a dedicated file server. Since our humble office probably won't grow beyond ten computers, we decide that a peer-to-peer network is the best choice. We have several good products to choose from—including Personal NetWare, LANtastic, and Windows for Workgroups. We select Windows for Workgroups primarily because of cost. It came pre-installed on our computers when we purchased them, so as far as we're concerned, it's already paid for. WFW also has a reputation for being relatively easy to use; it's integrated into what we already know (for example, File Manager and Print Manager), and it comes with a nice selection of networking applications such as e-mail and fax. WFW supports all the major network adapters and cabling, so it should give us no problem with standard Ethernet adapters, 10BASE2, or 10BASET cabling systems.

After setting priorities and reviewing the budget, our branch office comes up with our plan. We really only need five of our computers networked, since two part-time employees can share one, and two of our old computers aren't worth upgrading, so we will donate them to charity or let employees take them home. This means we will need five network interface cards (NICs) and enough cables to connect them all together. Because of the distance between our desks in the office, two of the cables need to be longer, and two can be real short. The priorities are as follows: Kim and Dan should be set up first. Kim will have the shared printer on her desktop. Heidi and Bob come later. Mike's last, but if things go well, everyone will be up and running the very first day!

We have two old ArcNet cards that headquarters sent us, but decide not to use them since they're old and dusty, slower than our desired Ethernet, and we don't want to mix types. No cables can be found, so we'll have to buy them new as well. One machine has only DOS loaded, so we need a single copy of Windows for Workgroups.

Stuff You Will Need (and Where to Find It)

We're happy to discover that we can do one-stop shopping for almost everything we need—except for the money to buy it with. (Chances are you're also within 50 miles of the new generation computer super-markets.) It's best to call ahead and ask for the available selections and stock levels, in addition to what's on sale (especially RAM). Don't overlook competitive alternatives like warehouses or mail-order companies. As long as the equipment is name brand and can be returned if it doesn't work, you won't get into too much trouble.

Money—How Much and Where to Find It

Good computer stuff costs money. So does bad computer stuff. It's always best to check out what your company already owns before you go out and buy anything new. Your purchasing department may also have special buying contracts that can provide steep discounts if you use them.

Once you are certain that you have to go outside and buy it yourself, how much will it cost? In very rough ballpark terms, it will range from $100 to $200 per machine, but could be much more if you have special requirements. You'd get mad if I didn't give you all the caveats first. Can we assume you already have the computers? Look closely at this list for *each* computer you want to network:

COMPUTER CHECKLIST FOR PREPARING TO NETWORK

➤ Does the computer work?

➤ Does each one have a processor powerful enough to run Windows (Intel 386 or better)?

➤ Does each one have enough memory to run Windows well (6MB)?

➤ Does each one have an available card slot to fit a NIC?

➤ Does each one have enough disk space remaining to load the necessary software and drivers (1 to 2MB if WFW is already loaded, much more if not)?

➤ Are they all within a reasonable cable distance from each other (50 meters or less)?

Computers, Printers, and More of the Obvious

You may have to purchase memory or disk upgrades for some of the computers. New computers are so powerful and cheap that it's often worth it to simply buy a new one, rather than upgrade an older computer. If you need to add something to one or more of your computers, some rough guidelines are provided here. It's best to get someone knowledgeable involved when upgrading a computer.

For several hundred dollars, you can purchase a processor upgrade that converts a 386 to something bigger; these are okay. Stay away from 286 machines and their upgrades if you want to use Windows.

Memory prices fluctuate daily, so shop around and take advantage when you can. It might run between $30–$60 per megabyte, depending on the size you choose. Purchase memory guaranteed to work with the type of computer you have. Make sure you have room on the motherboard, or you'll have to purchase a memory adapter board (or *replace* the motherboard memory with larger memory).

Disk drives can be purchased for low prices ($200 for 500MB), but first make sure you have enough physical room inside your computer, in addition to having the proper adapter card and power to drive it.

Whew! Well, we're over the bad part! We hope you didn't have to spend a single dollar on your computer hardware. Let's start now with the actual *networking* expenses.

Network Adapters, Cables, and Hubs

Each computer requires a NIC. The least expensive and best choice all around is the Ethernet card. Remember the cabling when selecting your NICs because the connectors have to match. You may not even need a hub if your computers are within throwing distance of each other.

The average Ethernet NIC can be purchased for about $100. Cabling costs between $10 and $20 per unit, and you will need one for each computer. Some cabling needs terminators at each end (remember Chapter 4?). Panic sets in. Until we stumble across the ultimate solution.

Here's what we've decided to do for the example: purchase a *network starter kit*. These kits are available everywhere now, and come with:

➤ 2, 3, 5, or more NICs, all the same, guaranteed to work

➤ enough cables to connect the NICs together

➤ some brand of networking software

The great news is that the package deal costs much less than the individual parts! Even if you purchase a package with one too many NICs (leaving you room to grow, or a spare part), the price is still less than what we would have normally paid.

Our package deal is a box about the size of a Lionel Train set. It says it's a complete package of 5 NICs, 5 cables (each 20 feet long, 2 terminators), and some network software. Let's say the price was $498.00 (on sale), almost $200 less than buying the individual hardware parts. We're happy with the deal, and carry it to the cashier.

209

Network Software and Applications

Our kit comes with some very good network software, which we choose to set aside. (In effect, it's free, since the hardware was still less expensive with this bundle.) The reason we are setting the software aside is that we already own Windows for Workgroups, and nobody wants to volunteer to learn the new stuff.

Windows for Workgroups came already installed on our machines. It's great because it has the networking software already built in, even though the computer didn't have a NIC yet. One of our machines is a leftover, so we have to purchase one copy of Windows for Workgroups for it. It is important to purchase WFW 3.11, and *not* just Windows 3.11. Be sure to look for the word *workgroups* if you are going to network.

Stick With Name Brands

We could have saved even more money purchasing a bundle from another manufacturer, but none of us had heard of them before. It's a good rule to avoid the least expensive choice, along with the most expensive.

Our total time spent planning and shopping for network parts comes to 2.5 hours; that includes browsing in the music section, buying some nylons, and getting a snack.

The Least You Need to Know

Simple networks aren't just born; they're planned! This chapter reminded us of the importance of planning for our Windows for Workgroups network, including:

➤ It takes money to network—money for NICs, cables, and software!

➤ Proper planning can help us save money building our network!

➤ All the pieces we need to build our own network can be found in a typical computer supermarket.

➤ Generics might be good for medicine and shampoo, but not network components. It's best to stick with quality brand names with guarantees and warranties.

Chapter 21

Installing the Network Hardware and WFW

In This Chapter

➤ Installing and configuring a NIC (Network Interface Card)

➤ What WFW (Windows for Workgroups) is all about

➤ Making WFW work using the network hardware we've chosen

Following our plan makes it easier. We don't want to bite off more than we can chew, so we decide to work on one computer at a time. We start with the computer that we could possibly spare (in case something goes wrong). If we run into any problems, we'll stop and completely solve them before touching another computer. We also got permission from our boss to use her computer while she's out to lunch.

Installing the Network Cards

Opening the networking boxes and taking inventory is a good place to begin. No sense in building a network if you don't have the terminators in hand. Or enough cabling. Or cabling that is really long enough to go where you want it to go. If you have any of these problems, this is a good place to stop and solve them before proceeding.

Before You Start

We want you to live through this adventure. Please unplug the power cord from your computer before you take the lid off. Also, make sure you have enough room to work. Disconnect the monitor; move it to a sturdy and safe area on your desk or the floor. Properly disconnect any other cabling that may get in the way of taking the cover off your computer.

An easy way to remember where all cables go is to label them first! Tape similar cables and connectors lightly to each other and label them while they are together. Then you simply match them up when it's time to put everything back together again.

Opening Your Computer and Installing Your NIC

You will need a screwdriver (not magnetic) to open up your computer unless it has thumbscrews you can twist with your fingers. If it's a desktop computer, look in the back for several screws holding the cover. Floor-standing models will have these screws on the side or in the back. Take them out and don't lose them.

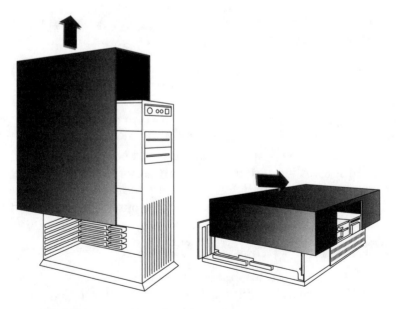

Opening your computer to install your NIC.

Static electricity can destroy your computer parts! The tiny little spark you feel when you rub your feet on carpeting and then touch metal contains enough voltage to fry computer chips! Take special precautions before installing your NIC:

➤ Before handling any components or touching anything inside the system unit, discharge your body's static electric charge by touching a large piece of metal, like a window frame or file cabinet.

➤ Do not remove cards or memory chips from their antistatic containers or bags until you are ready to install them.

➤ When handling your NIC, hold it by the edges, and avoid touching the circuitry.

➤ Do not slide the adapter cards over any surface.

➤ Avoid having plastic, vinyl, and Styrofoam in your working area during this part of the project.

➤ Limit your body movements during installation. This will reduce additional static electricity.

Once you're inside, don't play. Resist the urge to look for small animals, food, or the pink bunny. Find where the adapters are plugged in, and understand how your NIC is going to fit in there. Vacant slots are usually covered with a thin metal or plastic strip which must be removed before you insert the NIC. It's probably held in with a screw. Remove the screw and the thin strip. You can throw this away, but hang on to that screw! You need it to secure your NIC. Carefully place the NIC into the slot, and press it firmly into the computer board. It should feel solid and secure, almost popping into place. Use the screw to anchor it down so it won't shake loose.

Before putting lid back on, make sure wires or ribbon cables aren't sticking out the sides; they could get pinched. Carefully replace the cover and all screws; fasten tightly. Now you can plug the thing back in, and reconnect any cables you had to remove.

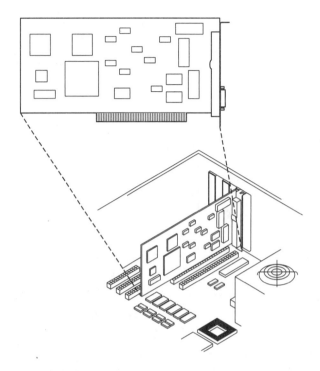

Inserting the NIC into your computer.

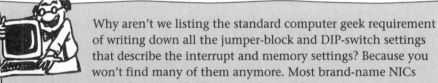

Why aren't we listing the standard computer geek requirement of writing down all the jumper-block and DIP-switch settings that describe the interrupt and memory settings? Because you won't find many of them anymore. Most brand-name NICs manufactured today have standard settings that work in most computers, and let you change settings as needed *through the use of software*. No more twiddling bits with NICs.

Configuring Your NIC with Software

Almost all NICs come with a diskette containing the software required to configure or test your adapter once it is installed inside your computer. This is a good time to use the diskette, for a very basic reason—to make sure our computer actually recognizes the NIC you just installed.

Place the NIC diskette in drive A: and power up your computer. In our example, let's say we use the 3Com EtherDisk Diagnostics and

Configuration diskette. This is a good diskette to keep track of, so we keep all of them in a locked drawer.

We're asked if we want to autoconfigure our NIC—and we reply, "Go ahead, make our day." To our surprise, everything goes quickly and smoothly. If you're ever in doubt about what a configuration or setup program is asking you, take the defaults. Suppose we see something like this:

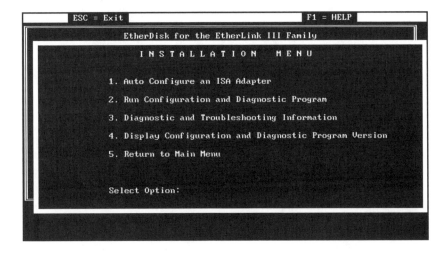

Checking the software settings of the NIC.

Now that wasn't so bad! Less than one hour to open up the computer, install the NIC, close the computer back up, and check the software settings with the NIC diskette. Now to install the NICs in the other computer. Then on to cables!

Connecting the Cables

People get paid a lot of money to install cables. We won't get a nickel. But then again, our cabling isn't hidden cleanly inside our walls, or guaranteed for a certain number of years. We don't even know if it works at all yet.

Bend and Stretch

It helps to unwind the cabling to begin shaping it into the straight or curved shape you are going to need. After making sure the cable will reach between the first two computers, you are ready to connect it to the first NIC. Using the T-connector, connect your cable to one end. Then connect the base of the T-connector to the NIC, carefully pushing in and turning the BNC connector for a solid and snug fit.

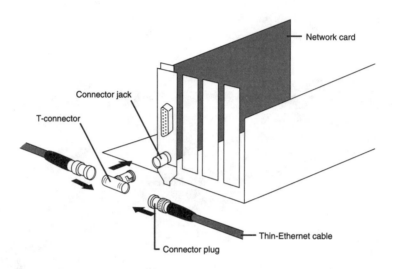

Connector jack

T-connector

Network card

Thin-Ethernet cable

Connector plug

Connecting the cable to NIC.

After connecting one cable end to the first computer, we notice we have another end! We connect it to our second computer. These were our top priority machines to start our network, but could we possibly be finished after only five minutes and a single cable?

Our book that came with the NIC says yes, as long as we've terminated both ends. We find the two terminators (there are only two) and try connecting them to the other end of the T-connector on each NIC. That's it! A small network of two computers has just entered the universe! We could stop here (while we're ahead) if we want, but decide to go further since we're ahead of schedule.

The third computer gets connected with the second cable. We remove both terminators until we are finished cabling. The fourth and fifth computer get connected with the third and fourth cable. We're left with an extra cable—which could come in handy if anyone chews through one. Our five-computer network is now connected in a line (daisy-chained) using four cables. On each end we connect the terminators.

Hiding Them Before the Tripping Starts

Before celebrating, we think it best to clean up after our creation. The empty boxes and wrappers are easy enough to throw out, but what in the world do we do with our cables?

Hiding the cabling is a smart move. It's dangerous to leave them lying on top of the carpeting because people can easily trip over them. But there aren't many other options! Our cable is too thick to hide under the carpeting (nobody could figure out how to get under the carpeting anyway), and it's not long enough to reach the ceiling and hide under the tiles. Incidentally, if you can afford it, the cabling that runs through the ceiling is best. It stays out of harm's way.

Some people wonder where they can get the diskettes for Windows for Workgroups if the software comes pre-installed on their computer. The answer should be: in the user's manual for your computer. All pre-installed computers should have an option to create all the diskettes from compressed images stored on your hard drive. It's very smart to create your diskettes very early in the life of your computer—especially before you accidentally erase them from your hard drive (or even intentionally erase them to make room for more important things).

We make a major decision: We know we saved money by not hiring a professional cable installer to run the cables cleanly throughout our office, and we'll have to live with our mess for awhile. We also know we'll get in trouble from management if we leave cables lying around, since someone will end up tripping and suing us for every penny we have. We decide to turn our desks around so the backs line up against the wall. Then we lay the cabling against the wall, behind the desks. We can live with it. And it looks neat.

Total time installing cables—one-half hour. Total time moving furniture and re-organizing the office—three hours. Total time cleaning the gross carpeting after moving the desks—two hours.

Installing WFW

Although four of the five machines in the example have Windows for Workgroups already installed on them, we still have to initialize the networking part of it. But first, we decide to install the complete Windows for Workgroups from scratch on our single computer that had none.

Running Setup

Start by turning on the computer and waiting until it completes the booting process. Stick the WFW diskette 1 into drive A:, type **A:SETUP** at the DOS prompt and press **Enter**.

If you already have a network installed (like a Novell NetWare file server or Banyan VINES), Windows for Workgroups will automatically be set up to work with it. You don't even have to be logged into those other servers right now. Also, you will be able to gain access to shared resources on a Windows NT computer, NT Advanced Server computer, IBM LAN Server, DEC Pathworks, and 3Com 3+Open networks.

Choosing the Setup Method You Need (Express or Custom)

If you are using the Microsoft Workgroup Add-On to upgrade a previous version of Windows, the Express Setup is the only option, and you must set up Windows for Workgroups in the same directory as the previous version. If it's a brand-new installation of windows, the Custom setup allows you specify a different installation drive or directory. The default of C:\WINDOWS should be good enough for anyone.

When you use Express Setup, all you do is type your name, answer a single question (what type of printer you have), and insert diskettes when the program requests them. Actually, the printer question is more important than you think. It wants to know all printers you intend to use, including those on the network. Tell it to load the printer drivers for every possible printer you may use. If you leave one out, or add a new printer in the future, you will be asked for WFW diskettes 6 and 7 at the time you try to print, which may be inconvenient. Doing it now saves you time.

After asking you for the printer type, WFW will ask you for the port it's connected to. If you have a printer on your desk connected directly to your computer, select **LPT1**. If you are installing for a printer on the network, you can choose **LPT2** or higher (**LPT3**, **LPT4**, etc.); it doesn't matter, and it doesn't have to be the same LPT number at each computer.

Starting and Logging On to Windows for Workgroups

After running Setup, you are prompted to either restart your computer or return to the command prompt. You should restart your computer now. If your computer does not have **WIN** as the last statement in the AUTOEXEC.BAT file, you should put it there, using any text editor. If you can't do that, simply type **WIN** at the DOS prompt and press **Enter** each time you start your computer, and you'll be running Windows for Workgroups (WFW).

When you start WFW, the logon dialog box appears, displaying a *logon name* that matches your *computer name* (you entered this computer name when installing WFW). You can use this name or type a new one. If several people use a single computer, each person can have their own logon name.

Congratulations! Behold the logon screen to Windows for Workgroups.

The first time you log on to Windows for Workgroups (and any time you log on using a new logon name, you are prompted to create a password-list file. You use the passwords in this list to connect to any shared resources (like printers) that require passwords.

If you choose to create a password-list file, the password for each shared resource you connect to is added to the list. When you log off of Windows for Workgroups, the password list is "locked" so nobody else can use it. Each person using a single computer must have an individual password-list file.

To protect this resource password list, you can use a *logon password*. When you log on, you supply this password, which unlocks your password list and restores your connections to networked resources. Your password can contain up to 14 characters.

The Networking Part of WFW

The remaining four workstations in our example have already come with Windows for Workgroups installed, but since they weren't purchased with the NICs, the networking part was left uninstalled until now.

To install the networking portion, be sure to have your WFW diskettes available (just in case), and select the **Windows Setup** icon from your **Main** group. You will notice that it says **No Network Installed** on the last line of the dialog box. Select the Options menu and then Change Network Settings... and you will find the familiar Network Setup dialog box. Now you can follow the same instructions as provided earlier in this chapter, since you are now at exactly the same place as a brand new installation of Windows for Workgroups.

Double-click on this icon.

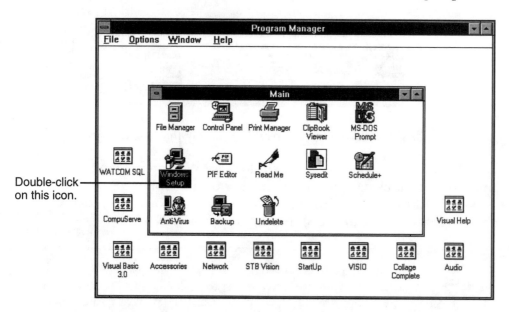

The Windows Setup icon for adding the networking software to WFW...

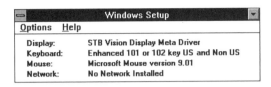

...Which takes you back to a familiar starting place.

Once you have successfully installed Windows for Workgroups, you will notice a new program group: the Network group. It contains the icons for some decent network applications.

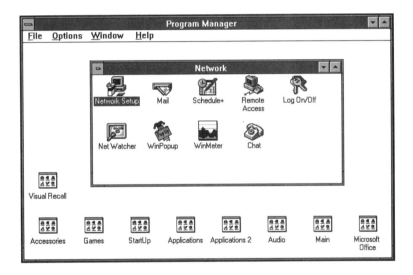

The WFW Network Programs group.

Total time for this whole activity: 2.5 hours for all of the computers, including 20 minutes spent looking for a screwdriver (car keys and paper clips just wouldn't cut it).

The Least You Need to Know

Some of us can live by the defaults. Others have to read the manual. Installing stuff in this chapter made us feel like pros. We can:

➤ Install a NIC blindfolded and underwater.

➤ Configure a NIC with both hands tied behind our back.

➤ Explain that WFW stands for Windows for Workgroups, and is a complete network operating system for a small group or business.

➤ Install WFW using either express or custom installation.

Chapter 22

Sharing Things on Your New Network

In This Chapter

➤ Sharing your files, directories, printers, and CD-ROM

➤ Connecting to others who are sharing their resources

➤ Setting up network applications

➤ How to find out who's using your shared directories and printers

---

With the hardware installation out of the way, we are itching to get started with the logging in and sharing stuff. A quick review of our plan helps us decide where to start:

➤ Kim (our boss) has the color printer we all want to use. Her computer is a laptop she takes home every night. She wants to have everyone's final business proposals stored on her laptop. She also stores payroll information on the laptop she doesn't want anyone to see.

➤ Dan has a big computer with lots of disk space, so all work in progress could be stored there. He has the HP4 laser printer that everyone wants to use. His machine also has a CD-ROM drive that would be great to use on a network. Everyone could use it to research the legal database that comes out quarterly on CD-ROM.

➤ The other three simply want a better way to get to the printers or files on Kim's or Dan's computer.

➤ Everybody wants to use e-mail and a scheduling software.

We start on Dan's machine (since he thought up this bright idea), and we need the practice before touching Kim's laptop. Kim's machine is next so we can reach the color printer. With any luck, the rest can connect in before the end of the day!

Setting Up Sharing for Files in WFW

First it's important to understand the words used by WFW to network so you won't be confused later. If Kim has a color printer, she can *share* it on the network. Dan can *share* his CD-ROM and disk space on the network. The others don't have anything of value to *share* on the network.

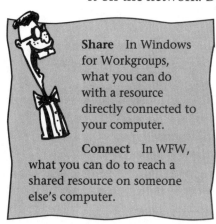

Share In Windows for Workgroups, what you can do with a resource directly connected to your computer.

Connect In WFW, what you can do to reach a shared resource on someone else's computer.

To reach a resource on the network, you *connect* to it. Dan can *connect* to Kim's color printer. Everyone can *connect* to Dan's CD-ROM.

Draw any basic conclusions? We did: You have to *share* something before anyone else can *connect* to it. Also, don't confuse the basics. Dan doesn't have to connect to the printer he's sharing. It's his. He continues to use it the way he always did; it's his local resource on LPT1.

Directory Sharing

Since everyone wants to connect to the files stored on Dan's machine, we start by sitting at his machine and setting up to share his directory. To share a directory, we first select it in File Manager. In this case we click on C:\WINWORD\DOCS. Then click the **Share As** button on the toolbar (you can also choose **Share As** from the **Disk** menu). Type any name you would like to use to identify this directory in the **Share Name** box (or use the name shown).

Share As ─┐ ┌─ Stop Sharing

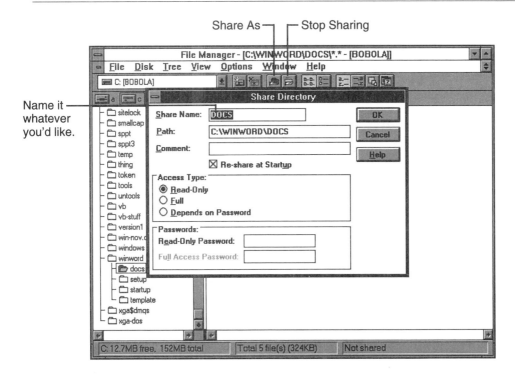

Name it
whatever
you'd like.

Setting up to share a directory.

Click on the
drive list.

Drive bar.

These are the
files that can
be shared.

The hand
signifies you
are sharing
this directory
with others.

Shared directory.

Entries referring to the arbitrary Workgroup and Computer-Name that you choose should be limited to 15 characters (for example: BRANCH-OFFICE-3 or DAN'S-COMPUTER). All other share names should conform to the DOS file-naming convention, which consists of an eight-character-maximum file name and an optional extension (limited to three characters).

To reduce confusion since others might have a \WINWORD\DOCS directory on their own computer, we decide to use the Share Name **ALL-WORK**. We skip the control access options for ALL-WORK, since everyone needs full access to these files, which is the default. We also skip the password protection for the same reason. You can also enter a comment to appear next to the directory, and specify whether the directory will be automatically shared every time you start WFW. Finally, choose **OK**; the directory is now made available for sharing with others on the network. They will now look for something called "All-Work."

Your shared directory can be seen only by other Windows for Workgroups users. Other computers on your network using only the NetWare requestor (without WFW) will *not* be able to access your shared directory.

Sharing a directory is easy, but doing it automatically each time you start your machine is even easier! Just keep the check box labeled **Re-share at Startup** checked, and your directory will be shared every time you start WFW.

To stop sharing a directory, click the **Stop Sharing** button on the toolbar (you can also choose **Stop Sharing** from the **Disk** menu). If this button appears dimmed, it simply means that no directories are currently shared. When the list appears, double-click on the name of the directory you want to stop sharing (or select it and choose **OK**). You can extend this selection to include more than one directory.

If other people are connected to your directory when you stop sharing it, a dialog box will appear, asking you to confirm your request. *If you choose the Yes button, these people may lose their data.* You might want to ask them to disconnect from your network drive first.

Here's a quick review of the security. You can use passwords to protect your files. If you assign a password to your shared directory, only those people who know the password can use files in that directory. If you don't assign a password, anyone on the network can use the files.

You can also use the following settings to control whether others who have access to your shared directory can make changes to the files in it.

➤ **Read-Only** lets others read files and run applications. This is also the default selection.

➤ **Full** allows others to create, change, delete, rename, move, or read files, and run applications. Could be dangerous in the wrong hands.

➤ **Depends On Password** is the best of both worlds. It allows others to have either read-only or full access, depending on the password they provide.

Connecting to Shared Directories

Now we are ready to see if the boss can see and use this shared directory. We go to Kim's computer and start Windows for Workgroups. This automatically asks Kim for her user ID, and then logs her on to the network. Now bring up File Manager. Click on the **Connect Network Drive** button in File Manager (you can also choose **Connect Network Drive** from the **Disk** menu). When you connect to someone else's shared directory, File Manager assigns the directory to the next available drive letter (or you can assign a letter of your choice). This creates a *network drive*. After you are connected to a shared directory, you can use the resulting network drive (as you would any other drive) to move quickly to the shared directory.

If you select **Depends On Password** and leave one password blank, people requesting access to your directory will always be prompted to enter a password. Simply pressing **Enter** at the password prompt will give them access to the file.

227

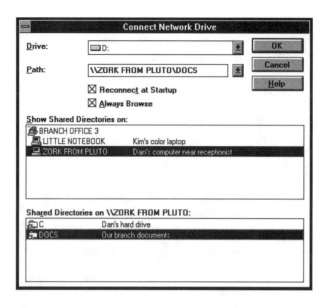

Connecting to a shared directory.

You can also specify whether to connect to the network drive automatically every time you start Windows for Workgroups. Just keep the default check box labeled **Re-connect at Start-up checked**, and the drive will be avail-able every time you start WFW.

It's easiest to fill in the **Path** box by opening the **Path** list and clicking on the most recently entered paths. (There's nothing listed now, of course; we haven't connected to a network directory yet. When we do, it will appear in this list the next time we try it.) In the **Show Shared Directories On** box, you can click on the name of a workgroup and select a computer listed below it. In this case, select **Dan's computer near receptionist**. Then you can select a shared directory by clicking on your selection from the **Shared Directories** box. To connect to this directory, choose **OK**.

To disconnect from a network drive, click on the **Disconnect Network Drive** button (you can also choose **Disconnect Network Drive** from the **Disk** menu). When the list is displayed, double-click on the drive you want to disconnect from, or select it and choose **OK**. You can also extend your selection to include more than one drive.

228

When you assign a network drive to a shared directory, you might need to know the shared directory's path. This path contains the *computer name* and the *share name*, using the format *computername**sharename*.

To display the directories on a file server or computer that isn't in your local workgroup (like a NetWare file server), type *fileservername* or *computername* in the **Show Shared Directories** box and choose **OK**.

Changing Drives and Directories

The File Manager toolbar lets you easily view and work with the files you want. To change your current drive, select the drive you want from the list of drives on the toolbar. You can also click on a drive icon in the drive bar. You can even double-click on the icon to create a new directory window that displays information about the new drive.

Discovering Who Is Using Your Shared Directory

This is helpful when trying to open files on your own computer, and you are told you cannot because *someone else has them open* already. Who's the wise guy?

Select the directory in File Manager (or you can select only the file) and from the File menu, choose Properties. Then choose Open By and you will see a dialog box naming the person that has your file open.

You can also press down and hold **Ctrl** while typing the letter of the drive you want. This shortcut works even if the drive bar is not displayed.

If you get tired of this person keeping your file open, you can close it. This only works for files stored on your computer (meaning you can't force a file closed on someone else's computer). With the selected directory or file in File Manager, choose Properties from the File menu. Finally, choose Open By and select the file or files you want to close, and choose Close Files. A dialog box will appear asking to confirm your decision. If you choose Yes, then anyone currently using the file may lose data or changes entered since the last time they saved it. Maybe it's better to send them a quick note first. See the section titled "The

Freebies: Chat, Net Watcher, Schedule+, and WinPopup," later in the chapter, to learn how to send messages to others on the network.

The easiest way to see who is using your shared directory is with the Net Watcher application. Simply choose this icon from the **Network** program group in Program Manager, and the names of all users currently sharing any of your directories will be displayed in the window.

Sharing a CD-ROM on Your WFW Network

To share a CD-ROM drive using Windows for Workgroups, use these steps:

➤ Work at the computer that has the CD-ROM attached. Make sure everything is connected and turned on.

➤ Load the CD-ROM driver in the CONFIG.SYS file. If your CD-ROM is already working, this is already in place.

➤ Load **MSCDEX.EXE /S** in the AUTOEXEC.BAT file. MSCDEX.EXE must be version 2.21 or later and loaded with the /S switch to allow sharing capability.

➤ After you make these modifications, save the files, restart the computer, and start Windows for Workgroups.

➤ The CD-ROM drive can be shared in the same way any other local hard disk drive can be shared. Choose the CD drive in File Manager, and then select the directories to be shared. In File Manager, choose **Share As** from the Disk menu. In the **Share Directory** dialog box, type the **Share Name** information, and the rest is optional. You can share the entire CD-ROM, or just certain directories on it. The choice is yours.

Setting Up Sharing for Printers in WFW

Happy with our success from sharing directories and CD-ROMs, we decide to try our luck with printers. Our main goal is to share Kim's color printer, and share Dan's laser printer with everybody. Remember that a printer must be *shared* before others can *connect* to it. Here's how.

Sharing Your Printer

Start by sitting at the computer that has the printer attached directly to it. The printer must be set up normally in Windows, assigned to a port. Double-click on the **Print Manager** icon from the **Main** program group to display the Print Manager window. Select the printer you want to share. On the toolbar, click on the **Share Printer As** button (you can also choose **Share Printer As** from the **Printer** menu). In the **Share Printer** dialog box, type any share name or password you want in the appropriate box, and then choose **OK**. You can also specify a comment to appear next to the printer, and specify whether to share the printer automatically each time you start WFW (just keep the check mark in the default box labeled **Re-share at Startup**, and the printer will be shared every time you start WFW).

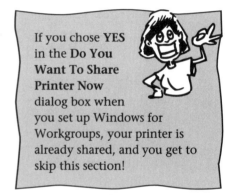

If you chose **YES** in the **Do You Want To Share Printer Now** dialog box when you set up Windows for Workgroups, your printer is already shared, and you get to skip this section!

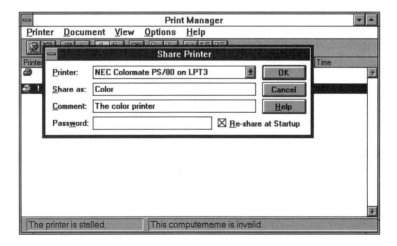

Setting up to share a printer.

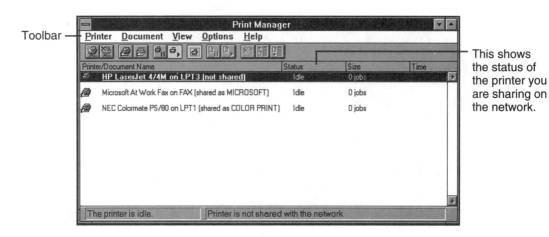

Toolbar

This shows the status of the printer you are sharing on the network.

Sharing a printer.

To stop sharing a printer, click on the **Stop Sharing Printer** button on the toolbar (you can also choose **Stop Sharing Printer** from the **Printer** menu). If this button or command appears dimmed, it simply means that no printer is currently shared. In the **Shared Printers** box, double-click on the name of the printer you want to stop sharing. (Another approach is to select it, and then choose **OK**.) You can extend the selection to stop sharing more than one printer.

That's it! Our color printer and laser printer are shared. Others should be able to connect to it from the network.

What are the differences between Windows for Workgroups Print Manager and Print Manager in Windows 3.1?

➤ You must disconnect printers from Print Manager only; you can no longer disconnect printers from the Control Panel.

➤ The toolbar in Print Manager is a new feature. Unlike the toolbar in File Manager, the Print Manager toolbar cannot be customized.

➤ Print Manager cannot pause print jobs locally.

232

Before You Try to Print

Two things have to be done before anyone can print, and it's related to how Windows uses Print Manager in applications. You must have printer drivers loaded on your local computer to print to a printer, no matter where it is. This means we *all* need to have the color printer drivers loaded if we want to print to the color printer on the network. First load and set up—on each computer—the printer drivers for all printers to be used by any computer on the network.

The print drivers come on diskette with your printer, or you can usually find them on your WFW diskettes. To install a new print driver, select the **Printers icon** in the Windows Control Panel. Click on Add and select your printer from the list. If it's not on this list, click on Install and place your driver diskette in drive A:. You will be prompted if you don't have the correct diskette for the printer you've chosen. Once finished, you'll be able to assign this new printer to one of your printer ports.

Next connect to the printer, wherever it may be. If it's your local printer, use **LPT1**. If it's a shared printer on the network, use any LPT number; you can have as many as you want (up to nine), and others won't have to worry about which number you've chosen; they will simply see it as another printer. Now you are ready to print!

Connecting to a Network Printer

Here we go. Make sure you have set up a printer driver on your computer for the network printer you desire. Start the Window's Print Manager. On the toolbar, click on the **Connect Network Printer** button (you can also choose **Connect Network Printer** from the **Printer** menu).

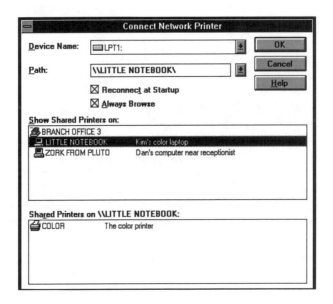

Connecting to a network printer.

If the port shown in the **Device Name** box is not the one associated with the appropriate printer driver, open the list and select the port name you desire. Notice that this list shows connections that already exist. If you select a port that is already connected to a network printer, you will be prompted to replace that connection. You can also type the port number (**1** for LPT1, **2** for LPT2, and so on) in the **Device Name** box.

You can use the Net Watcher application to display the names of people using your shared printer.

Fill out the **Path** box next. Once again, WFW uses the term "path" to describe the shared directory on someone else's computer. If you want to use a path that you've used recently, open the Path list and select a path. In the **Show Shared Printers On** box, you can choose your workgroup, select a computer listed below the workgroup name, and select a network printer from the **Shared Printers** box. Finally choose **OK**.

You probably want to use this network printer every day. You can specify to connect to the printer automatically every time you start Windows for Workgroups by keeping the check in the **Re-connect at Startup** box; the printer will be available every time you start WFW.

To disconnect from a network printer, click on the **Disconnect Network Printer** button on the toolbar (you can also do this by choosing **Disconnect Network Printer** from the **Printer** menu). In the list, double-click on the name of the printer you want to disconnect. You can also select it and then choose **OK**. You can also extend the selection to disconnect more than one printer.

Your own (local) printer is physically connected by a cable to a parallel or serial port on the back of your computer. The port is represented by a name in Windows (such as LPT1, 2, etc., or COM1, 2, etc.).

A network printer is connected to a port in the back of another computer in a workgroup, and is connected to a port name in your computer by network hardware and software.

When a port name in your computer is connected to a network printer, your computer does not need port hardware corresponding to that name. This allows you to use multiple network printers, even though your computer does not have a physical port for each one.

Choosing Your Default Printer

Many Windows-based applications use the *default printer* when you choose the Print command. This is probably the printer on your desk, not the laser or color printer. If you want to set the shared printer as your default printer, in the Print Manager window, select the printer you want documents sent to. On the toolbar, click on the **Set Default Printer** button (you can also choose **Set Default Printer** from the **Printer** menu). From now on, you can simply print in an application and it will be sent to the shared network printer.

Pausing and Resuming Printing

Let's say you've been kind enough to share your printer, and some bozo decides to print a 200-page document just before your boss asks you to print a brief message. You can pause the printing of another person's document (or pause your entire printer) by selecting the print job in the print queue and clicking on the **Pause** button. If there are other print jobs behind it in the queue, the next one in the queue will start to print. To pause the entire printer (and all its print jobs), select it and click on **Pause**.

In the print queue for a network printer, you can pause only the printing of your own document. In other words, you cannot pause the printer or anyone else's document.

Canceling a Print Job

You can cancel the printing of a document by deleting it from the list of documents waiting to print. When using a network printer, you can delete only your own documents and only before it starts to print. When using your own printer (local) you can delete anyone's documents displayed in your Print Manager at any time.

In the Print Manager window, select the document you want to delete. Click on the **Delete Document** button on the toolbar (you can also choose **Delete Document** from the **Document** menu). You can also use the **Delete** key on your keyboard. Regardless of how you do it, a dialog box will appear, asking you to confirm your decision.

If you want to cancel the printing of all documents queued to your printer, simply close the Print Manager. All documents in the queue will be deleted.

Installing Applications in WFW

DOS and Windows applications are typically loaded using the Program Manager in Windows for Workgroups. Several free networked applications were loaded when you installed WFW. These are *Chat*, *Net Watcher*, *WinMeter*, and *WinPopup*. They are loaded at each workstation running WFW. Other applications (like word processing, spreadsheets and database) can also be loaded and shared on the network, but are intended to be used only by the person sitting at the computer where they are installed.

The Freebies: Chat, Net Watcher, Schedule and WinPopup

Use Chat, Net Watcher, WinMeter, and WinPopup to perform workgroup tasks such as exchanging messages or monitoring workgroup activities and resource usage. Use Schedule+ to schedule events and communicate with others who are using the network. Schedule+ is always installed, regardless of the network you are running. There is also a **Log On/Off** icon in the Network group, used to enter or leave the network, and especially useful if two or more people share a computer at different times of the day.

Using Chat, you can have an conversation with up to seven other people by exchanging typed messages. Chat messages are interactive, meaning they are visible to the recipient as you type it.

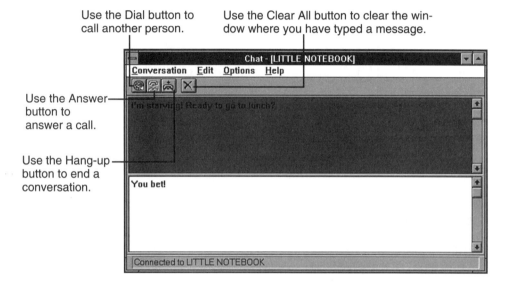

Use the Dial button to call another person.

Use the Clear All button to clear the window where you have typed a message.

Use the Answer button to answer a call.

Use the Hang-up button to end a conversation.

The Chat utility, used for conversing over the network.

You can use Net Watcher to find out which of your computer resources are being used by other people on the network. You can also see which computers are connected to your computer and, if necessary, disconnect them. You can also view the event log file (but it's boring, so don't bother).

Schedule+ is a personal scheduling tool you can use to keep track of appointments and tasks, and to record notes. You can also use Schedule+ to check the schedule of other people on the network, and share your schedule with them.

If you double-click on an appointment created by someone else, the name of the person who created it is displayed at the bottom of the appointment details. However, the appointment is not identified by an icon or special color in the appointment book.

You do not need to sign in as another user to open that person's calendar. Schedule+ allows you to grant access privileges to other users with the **Options/Set Access Privileges** command. Once you have assigned privileges to another user, that person can view your calendar while signed in under his or her own account by choosing **Open Other's Appointment Book** from the **File** menu.

WinPopup can be used to communicate with others on the network, but it's much more limiting than Chat. WinPopup can come in handy if you like to be notified on your screen the instant your print job has printed on a network printer. WinMeter is a simple tool for measuring how much the other network users are using your computer. It provides a graphical chart that compares your usage to everyone else's.

Major Apps (Word Processing, Spreadsheets, and Databases)

Spare yourself the headaches if you can. All your networked computer users should have their own copies of any major application software they may require; in Windows for Workgroups, these applications should be installed locally.

If you must share major applications like these over the network, make sure you own enough application licenses to cover everyone who can possibly get the directory you share.

A Word About Licensing

When you are using a file server network like NetWare, it is common to place one copy of an application like WordPerfect on the file server and share it with everyone. It is important to note that the network administrator is responsible for having as many licenses to WordPerfect as you have users accessing it.

Our simple Windows for Workgroups network is not intended to share major applications this way. It could, of course, but it would be too slow and difficult to manage. Most important, *it is illegal to share most applications on a network unless you have purchased the license to do so.* You need to purchase a licensed copy of software for each user, and it should be loaded onto each user's computer (which also provides the best performance).

Use the network effectively and appropriately—sharing the working and data directories of applications, not the applications themselves.

The Least You Need to Know

Sharing things on a network doesn't have to be hard; you just have to know the basics. In this chapter we learned:

➤ Directories can be easily shared by using the **Share** button in File Manager. There is also a **Stop Sharing** button.

➤ You can reach directories on other computers with the **Connect** button in File Manager.

➤ Others can share your printer (or you can connect to someone else's) by using the new buttons in Print Manager.

➤ You can find out who's using your shared stuff by using the Net Watcher utility that can be found in the Network group.

Creating Your Post Office for E-mail in WFW

With the network running smoothly and directories and printers being shared, it's time to tackle a major-league networking application: electronic mail, or *e-mail* for short. Just like in real life, we first need a post office before we can expect to send or receive mail. But instead of using postal carriers, we will use our network.

If your post office is already set up and you just want to know how to use e-mail, skip to the "Using E-mail in WFW" section.

Setting Up a Post Office for E-mail in WFW

E-mail in Windows for Workgroups consists of the Mail application and the post office. The mail application runs on each person's computer. The post office is stored in a directory on only one of the computers, and it is shared by all members of the workgroup.

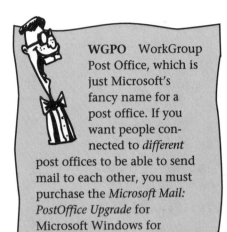

WGPO WorkGroup Post Office, which is just Microsoft's fancy name for a post office. If you want people connected to *different* post offices to be able to send mail to each other, you must purchase the *Microsoft Mail: PostOffice Upgrade* for Microsoft Windows for Workgroups.

Before people in your network can use Mail, they need to connect to something called a *workgroup post office* (WGPO). The post office contains information about mail accounts. To communicate by mail, people must be connected to the *same* post office, and each person must have a mail account. Two people connected to different post offices cannot exchange messages.

The PostOffice Manager command, used to manage the post office, is available only on the computer where the post office is located.

Planning the New Post Office

Creating a post office is easy. The hardest part is finding a computer to load it on. It has to have enough disk space to last for awhile, and post office directories can become big. Really big. In fact, they're huge. So first verify that there is enough disk space on the computer where the post office will be stored. Remember also that the PostOffice Manager utilities will be available only on the computer containing the post office.

Since mail takes so much disk space, we decide (in our example) to use Dan's machine, which has a 720MB drive—larger than anyone else's, with plenty of empty space left. Dan will still be able to use his workstation normally, even while it is performing post office functions in the background. For your planning, there should be about 400K of available disk space for an empty post office, and you'll need plenty more for the user accounts. For a small post office with three or four accounts, only a few megabytes of disk space are required. Plan on almost a megabyte each if there are many users in your post office.

Watch out if you do have many users, because the computer running the post office can get really busy. This becomes annoying for the user trying to get work done on this computer. Quite often a machine has to become dedicated to the task of running a post office, so get this guinea pig a new computer and let the post office computer sit in the corner unattended.

The post office can be created on any computer in the workgroup, but this computer must also contain the PostOffice Manager utilities, so place the post office on a permanent computer in a safe and secure location. A laptop or notebook computer is *not* a good choice.

The computer where your post office is located must be turned on at all times so that people can exchange mail. Take this into consideration when deciding what computer will house the post office.

Creating the New Post Office

There can be only one post office, but it can service many workgroups. The administrator account is the first *account* you create in the post office. You can modify this account but not remove it, so try to get it right the first time.

1. From the **Network** program group, double-click on the **Mail** icon.

2. In the **Welcome to Mail** dialog box, select Create a new Workgroup Postoffice, and then choose **OK**.

In mail terminology, an **Account** is simply a mailbox.

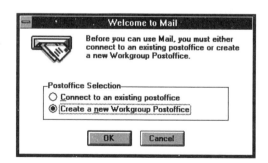

Starting Mail for the first time. Pick defaults to stay safe.

3. Select **YES** in the dialog box that asks whether you want to create a post office.

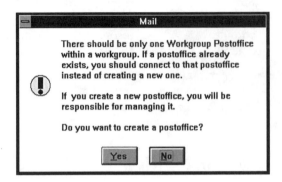

A warning and reminder.

4. In the **Create Workgroup PostOffice** dialog box, select a location for your post office. Although you can select a network computer, it is more difficult. Do this activity sitting at the machine that will be the post office, and select the local hard drive (C:) from the **Drives** box and a directory from the **Create WGPO In** list. Unless you specify otherwise, this creates a new subdirectory named WGPO in the postoffice administrator's Windows directory by default.

5. Choose **OK** and you will get the **Enter Your Administrator Account Details** dialog box.

6. Enter your administrator account details in the dialog box. You must include entries for **Name** and **Mailbox**. A password is optional. The Name value is simply the name that Mail will use to recognize you. Keep it simple—use your network user ID. The Password value defaults to the word "password"; however, you can change this value or remove it if you choose not to have a password. Click on **OK** when you're done.

Enter an easy, short name here, or use the default Windows logon name.

Type the mail administrator's full name here.

You will need this password to sign in to Mail.

The remaining entries are optional.

Entering the Mail Administrator information.

The following name-length limitations exist in Microsoft Windows for Workgroups Mail:

Server Name: 15 characters (including spaces)

Share Name: 12 characters (including spaces)

Workgroup PostOffice Share: 8 characters

Windows for Workgroups Mail clients cannot connect to a Workgroup PostOffice if the share name contains more than eight characters, or if the Workgroup PostOffice server name or share name contains any spaces. For example, the following are examples of invalid Workgroups PostOffice server or share names:

\\Zork From Pluto\Galactic Post Office

\\Our Server\WG PO

\\server\post office

The following is a valid Workgroups PostOffice server or share name:

\\server\wgpo

Microsoft recommends that the share name "WGPO" be used for consistency across all Workgroup PostOffices.

Sharing Your New Post Office

After the post office is created, it must be shared with all people connected to it. Following the same instructions for sharing a directory provided in Chapter 22, start with File Manager and select the WGPO directory that you just created. On the toolbar, click on the **Share As** button. In the **Share Name** box, type a name for your post office. The default is WGPO, and this dumb name is recommended by Microsoft, so we use it. Select the **Re-share At Startup** check box; you always want to have the post office running and available. Under the **Access Type**, select **Full Access**. Under the **Password**, you can type a full-access password for your WGPO. This is recommended only if you do not want some workgroup members to have access to your mail. You may want to type **PostOffice** in the **Comment** field so people at other workstations can identify this directory when they connect to the post office. Choose **OK** to complete this process.

After you create your post office, the PostOffice Manager command appears on the Mail menu when you start mail. This command will only appear on the computer that stores the post office.

Adding Users to Your Post Office So They Can Send E-mail

You can add people to the post office, or people can add themselves. People adding themselves can be a problem for new users, so it's best to create all mail accounts before people click on the mail icon for the first time.

To start the PostOffice Manager, mail must be running. Select the **PostOffice Manager** from the **Mail** menu. Using this dialog box, you can add names to the post office, modify accounts, and remove names. In the **PostOffice Manager** dialog box, choose **Add User**. Supply the appropriate information and choose **OK**. If you choose to include a password, be sure to write it down and give it to that user. That's it!

Maintaining Your New Post Office

There is an important file someone needs to be responsible for, especially once you've become dependent upon your new e-mail system. It's the MSMAIL.MMF file. Everyone's mail is stored in this file and it can become very large.

Since the MSMAIL.MMF file contains all your messages, you should back it up regularly. If you don't have a tape drive, at least make a copy of it to another workstation. The file will soon become too large to use DOS or Windows backup utilities conveniently for backing up to diskettes, but it can be a great start for a new post office. When you back up and restore this file, all your folders are backed up and restored.

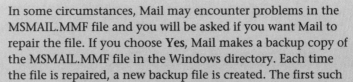

In some circumstances, Mail may encounter problems in the MSMAIL.MMF file and you will be asked if you want Mail to repair the file. If you choose **Yes**, Mail makes a backup copy of the MSMAIL.MMF file in the Windows directory. Each time the file is repaired, a new backup file is created. The first such backup file will be named MSMAIL.BAK, and subsequent backup files will be named MSMAIL.001, MSMAIL.002, and so on. After your MSMAIL.MMP file has been fixed, you can delete these backup files to save space on your computer.

Managing the disk space where the post office is located is one of the most important administrative tasks in maintaining Mail. You must check the status of shared mail folders and determine if you need to take action on these folders to recover unused disk space. To check the status of shared mail folders, choose the **Shared Folders** button in the PostOffice Manager dialog box. You can see the number of mail folders, the total number of messages, the space being used, and most importantly, the amount of space that can be recovered.

What To Do if Your Post Office Runs Out of Disk Space

If you run out of disk space, you need to *compress* shared folders. If you require even more disk space, you can delete old messages and unused

Compress To shrink the size of disk space used by shared folders in mail.

folders. If shared folders contain a large number of messages, it may take a long time to compress them.

Before trying to compress anything, ask all users to close shared mail folders. From the **Mail** menu, choose **PostOffice Manager**. In the PostOffice Manager dialog box, choose **Shared Folders**. Choose **Compress**, and when it's finished, choose **Close**.

Using E-mail in WFW

Before your users can connect to a post office, the person managing Mail should give them the appropriate computer name and the name of the shared directory where the post office is located. If there is a password for the shared directory, it should also be provided.

Connecting to Your Post Office

When we installed WFW on each computer, all the necessary Mail programs were also installed. The only task required to start using Mail is to connect to your post office. It's time to see whether our new post office stored on Dan's computer really works. We move to Kim's computer to try it. In the Network group, choose the **Mail** icon. In the **Welcome to Mail** dialog box, select **Connect to an Existing PostOffice** and choose **OK**.

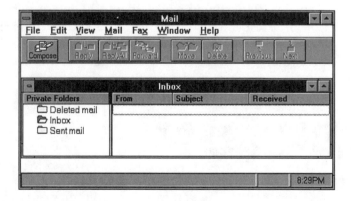

Using Mail.

Select the post office you want by selecting the computer name for your post office in the **Show Shared Directories On** box. Then in the **Shared Directories** box select the shared directory of your post office. Choose **OK** and enter the password if it is required for the shared directory. A dialog box will appear. Choose **YES**, since you have already been set up with a mailbox (the Mail account). You will be prompted for a password. If you weren't given a password, then it is the default, which is PASSWORD.

Signing In to Mail

To sign in to mail, choose the **Mail** icon in the **Network** group. Include your password. To protect your privacy, do not share your password with other people, and do not select the Remember Password box.

If you want your mail password to be supplied automatically each time you start Mail, select the **Remember Password** check box.

Changing Your Password

If security is a concern, change your password regularly. If you forget your password, see your Mail administrator. To change your password, choose **Change Password** from the **Mail** menu. In the **Old Password** box, type your previous password, and then press the **Tab** key. For security reasons, you won't see the characters you type. Type the new password in the **New Password** box, and again in the **Verify New Password** box, and press **Enter**. If your second attempt to type the new password does not match the first, your computer will give a warning beep, and you will have to start over with entering the new password and verifying it again.

Sending an E-mail

On the toolbar, click the **Compose** button (you can also choose **Compose Note** from the **Mail** menu). You will see the following:

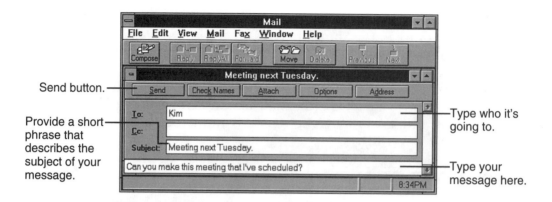

Send button.

Provide a short phrase that describes the subject of your message.

Type who it's going to.

Type your message here.

Sending mail.

In the **To** box, you can type the names of the people you want to send this message to—but it's easier to use the **Personal Address Book** to store the names of people you send messages to. Simply select the name of the person from the list and press **Enter** (or just double-click on the desired entry).

Next, click on the **Subject** box and type the subject of your message. Then you are ready to type your message. Click anywhere in the message area (or press **Tab** to move to it), and then type your message. When you are finished and ready to send the message, click on the **Send** button. Congratulations! You've sent e-mail!

Reading an Incoming E-mail

Your Inbox displays information about each e-mail that has been sent to you, including the name of the sender, and the date and time the e-mail was received. To read your e-mail, double-click on it, or use the **arrow** keys to select the e-mail and then press **Enter**. The message will be displayed.

Replying to Your E-mail

To reply to your e-mail, click the **Reply** button on the toolbar (you can also choose **Reply** from the **Mail** menu). When you send a reply, your e-mail is already addressed for you. Your response includes the original message, and you can add comments to the original message if you would like. If you choose the **Reply All** button or command, the e-mail is addressed and will be sent to everyone in the **To** and **Cc** (Carbon Copy) boxes.

The setting in the Options dialog box that determines how often your Mail application checks for new e-mail also determines how often Mail checks the Outbox for outgoing e-mail to submit to the post office. A message first waits in the Outbox for the amount of time specified, and then waits again for the same amount of time until Mail checks for new messages. For example, if you specified that Mail should check for new messages every three minutes, it can take up to six minutes before you receive new mail.

If it's taking longer than you expect to receive your new e-mail, try specifying a lower value.

Deleting an E-mail

To keep your mailbox from becoming cluttered, you can delete e-mail you no longer need. To delete a message, first select it. On the toolbar, click the **Delete** button (you can also choose **D**elete from the File menu). The message will be moved to your **Deleted Mail** folder. By default, the Deleted Mail folder is emptied each time you quit mail. You can change this option by using the Options command on the Mail menu.

Getting Out of E-mail

There are two ways you can exit the Mail application. You can select either one from inside the Mail application.

Use the Exit command to quit Mail *without signing out*. This is useful if you are running an application like Schedule+ that uses Mail to communicate with other people's calendar and appointment programs. Schedule+ can continue to run, even though you have quit Mail. Just as a warning, if you use this command and leave your computer unattended, another person can start Mail and read your messages without being prompted for a password.

Delete an important e-mail accidentally? You can retrieve any e-mail from the Deleted Mail folder at any time until you quit Mail. You can also use the Options command and request that Mail never empties your Deleted Mail folder, but this is foolish and wastes disk space. Just pay attention to what you delete.

The other way to exit is to use the **Exit and Sign Out** command to quit Mail and sign out. Other applications that use Mail to communicate with other people will also stop running automatically. If you restart Mail, you need to sign in again.

Other functions of Mail include organizing your e-mail by using folders, finding a specific message, using the address book, creating and using a message template, embedding an object, and sorting messages. These are all good things to learn, and the details can be found using the Help (the **F1** key) feature during your Mail session.

The Least You Need to Know

Neither sleet nor rain nor the calling of our boss could keep us from setting up our own e-mail system in record time. We learned that:

➤ Setting up a post office is easy! Just start Mail the first time on the computer you want to be the post office.

➤ Connecting to a post office is automatic when you start e-mail.

➤ Creating and sending e-mail is almost too easy. Our disk space is filling up much faster than we predicted.

➤ We can even bring back a deleted e-mail by looking in the Deleted Mail folder.

Chapter 24

(Trouble)Shooting Your New WFW Network

In This Chapter

➤ How to fix simple bugs found often in new networks

➤ How to tackle the tougher bugs in Windows for Workgroups

➤ Solving the most common e-mail problems

If you've made it this far, congratulations! Well, *almost*, since this is the chapter on solving problems you may be experiencing with your new Windows for Workgroups network. Cheer up! At least you're on the leading edge of technology, and you're not alone. Try to find your problem among the more commonly observed bugs, and try out the solutions provided.

Some Problems Frequently Observed

If something appears not to be working, start with some simple checkpoints:

➤ Make sure the outlet has power, and that the cables are still plugged into the power strip or the wall outlet.

➤ Double-check to see that all power cables are securely plugged into the connectors on the back of the computer and the back of the monitor.

➤ Are all power switches set in the ON position?

➤ Make sure the NIC is firmly installed. If you feel any movement with the card while attempting to connect the cable, stop everything, unplug the power, go back inside and re-seat the NIC; secure it firmly with the mounting screw.

Don't forget to check out Chapters 16–19! Even though they don't describe a Novell NetWare network, the common problem-solving techniques still apply! Most problems related to hardware—especially the NICs and the cabling—will haunt you no matter what network operating system you choose.

Other Inside Problems

If the computer was working fine before you took the cover off, but won't boot—after you put the cover back on, run and hide. No, just kidding; this happens a lot. You probably bumped a data cable just enough to loosen it from the system board or adapter. Power down the system, unplug all power cables, remove the cover screws and remove the cover. Check all the cables and replace the cover. Before you slide it all the way on, carefully tuck in the data cables so you won't bump them. Power up and try again.

If you've turned everything on, but see nothing on the computer display, get your eyes fixed. But first, check your hearing. You should be able to hear the computer booting up; the noise comes from the cooling fan and the hard disk spinning up to speed. That's good. It means that either the monitor is not correctly plugged in, or the brightness control is too dark. Try adjusting the brightness control knob. If this does not bring anything up on the display, power down and recheck all connections. It's cheaper than seeing an eye doctor.

If the display screen is visible, but the mouse pointer is not on-screen, the mouse cable is probably not connected properly.

I Think My Network Card Is Defective

You are allowed to come to this conclusion if other workstations that have a similar card are working fine, you've re-seated your cabling connections for good contact, you've tried a known good replacement patch cable, and you're really tired and angry. Seriously, cheaper NICs do go bad once in awhile, and even the brand names will have a defect, but it's usually not the case. More than likely it is a hardware conflict relating to interrupts or memory. It's best to get a network administrator to help you at this point.

Windows Won't Start After Network Setup

Make sure the proper hardware is specified for your system. Sometimes when Express Setup runs, it doesn't correctly detect the actual hardware. In DOS, change to the Windows directory, and then type **SETUP** and press **Enter**. Look at the System Information screen; make sure your hardware is correctly identified. If it is not, press **Enter** on the item that is wrong, and try to find the correct entry from the list. The item most likely to be incorrect is the video display adapter. Worry about advanced graphics later; select generic **VGA** and make sure Windows installs. You can tweak the graphics from the Control Panel by choosing the Windows Setup—later.

Also make sure you have properly connected your NIC to the network cable. A common mistake when using Thinnet cable with BNC connectors is connecting cable directly to the NIC. You should only connect the T-connector to the NIC, then attach the cabling to your T-connector.

Windows needs all the memory it can get. Check your amount of memory with a DOS utility like **MEM /C**. If your AUTOEXEC.BAT or CONFIG.SYS include small programs that chew up memory, you will see them listed. Try to remove as much as possible first, get Windows running, and then put them back. A good DOS book like *The Complete Idiot's Guide to DOS* can show you how to do this.

No Network Features Are Available

Make sure the cables that connect your computer to the network are connected properly and securely. Make sure your computer meets the minimum requirements for running Windows for Workgroups. You may want to run diagnostics on your network adapter. These diagnostics came on a diskette along with your NIC. They are DOS-based, so exit Windows and run them from the diskette.

On rare occasions, you may be experiencing some file corruption. It's worth the few minutes to re-install WFW and watch closely for any error messages.

You Forget Your Logon Password

This demonstrates one of the weaknesses in security of Windows for Workgroups. All you have to do when you forget your password is find your password file and delete it. It's easy. There is usually more than one, so make sure you delete the correct one. Go to your Windows directory and type **DIR *.PWL** and press **Enter**. You will see all of the password listing files. Find the one that has your name and delete it. Don't bother trying to view or edit this file; it's scrambled worse than an omelette. When you restart Windows you will be asked if you want to create a new password list.

Other Computers Are Not Listed

Don't laugh, but this happens a lot. Check to make sure the other computers are turned on and running Windows. Once your network grows a bit, some computers may be placed behind closed doors, and you may forget which computer controls the resources you require. You don't notice it until the day it's not turned on and you need it, and then you must go looking for it.

If the other computer is turned on and running Windows, but still can't be seen, the problem is in the cabling or NIC settings. These may include nasty INI files (the Windows INItialization files for each Windows application) that may have been changed or become corrupted.

Problems with E-mail

E-mail really bites the dust when it isn't working. Here are some of the more challenging bugs, after you've checked the obvious (like making sure the post office computer is up and running).

"Cannot Connect to the Workgroup Postoffice"

If you receive the error message "Cannot establish a DOS or Windows Mail Server" or "Cannot connect to the Workgroup Postoffice," a post office may not have been created yet, or your post office's server may be down. Check with the workgroup or system administrator to find out if a post office has been created. If a post office has not been created, determine who will be the post office administrator, and refer to Chapter 23 for the procedure for creating a post office.

If a post office has been created and you are still getting these error messages, you may need to modify the MSMAIL.INI file to reflect the location of the post office. Use the following steps. Quit Mail. Open the MSMAIL.INI file from the **Windows** directory in an ASCII text editor, such as Microsoft Windows Notepad. Note the entry beside the **ServerPath=** setting. This should match the server name and the shared directory name of the post office. The proper syntax is as follows:

serverpath=\\\servername\directoryname

Once this is corrected, simply restart Mail; you'll be back in business.

Can't Even Bring Up the Mail Application

This problem occurs when more than one post office exists within a workgroup. Extra post offices must be deleted. If you delete the extra post offices, those computers that were formerly post offices must connect to the existing post office. To delete extra post offices, follow this procedure. First, exit the mail application. Next, from File Manager, select the **MSMAIL.INI** file, which can be found in the **Windows** directory. From the **File** menu, choose **Rename**. In the **To** box, type **msmail.bak** (creating a backup just-in-case), then choose the **OK** button.

Now restart Mail. In the **Welcome To Mail** dialog box, select the **Connect To An Existing Postoffice** option. Select the server name and shared directory for the post office. If you do not have an account, add your information to the post office.

Don't forget! You must have entries for the Name, Mailbox, and Password boxes. Be sure to use the same entries you were using before you renamed the MSMAIL.INI file—that way you can access your old mail messages.

Can't Move or Delete E-mail From a Folder

If you cannot move or delete mail messages from a folder, you may have a corrupt MSMAIL.MMF file. This file contains all your mail folders and messages. To repair the MSMAIL.MMF file, use the following procedure. From the File menu in Mail, choose Exit and Sign Out. Restart Mail. If the built-in Mail utility detects any corrupt mail files, a dialog box should appear with the message **Your database file is corrupt, repair now?** Choose the **Yes** button. The Mail Message File utility should repair any damage to the MSMAIL.MMF file, and return you to Mail when it's finished.

Bad Network Connection Icon In Status Bar

Mail sometimes shows a **bad network connection** icon in its status bar when the network is functioning correctly. For example, you may see this icon and still be able to use File Manager to connect to your mail server. You may also receive mail while Mail is displaying the bad network connection.

The icon is displayed because you are very low on disk space. The icon is trying to tell you that it failed to download a message because there was insufficient space in your mail file. Mail waits and retries five minutes later.

Your best bet is to quickly free up some disk space in your post office.

Problems with Schedule+

It was free—what do you expect? Okay, here are some of the more common bugs that throw a wrench into people's Schedule+s.

Password Problems Between Mail and Schedule+

Some people try to do good, and get bitten by the network anyway. Changing your password is always good. Changing your password in Microsoft Mail does a weird thing in Schedule+. Don't worry about it, it's not your fault, and here's the scoop:

If you change your password in Mail, the Schedule+ password is affected. After you successfully create a new password in Mail, you are prompted for your old password in Schedule+ before you can enter the application. If you change your password in Schedule+, Mail accepts your new password without prompting you for your old password. That's all there is to it.

"Schedule+ File Could Not Be Opened"

When you choose Open Other's Appointment Book from the **File** menu in Schedule+, you may receive the error message *"Schedule file could not be opened. You may not have the necessary access privileges or the file may not be available."*

This error occurs when the person whose file you are trying to access has not granted you access privileges. You must have at least the Read Appointments and Tasks privilege to open another's Appointment Book. The default setting for privileges is View Free/Busy Times, which allows you to view other schedules from Planner.

Schedule+ defaults to the Appointment Book. To access Planner, you must select the tab labeled **Planner** from the left side of the Schedule+ screen. To set access privileges for other users, choose Set Access Privileges from the Options menu.

My Schedule+ Has Stopped Reminding Me of Things

The Reminders application is something we forgot to tell you about. It is a separate application from Schedule+. The default installation (that is, Express Setup) installs Reminders into the Windows Startup group. (This explains why you are asked to sign in when you start Windows, but after you sign in, no application seems to be started.)

In actuality, Reminders has started, but because it is a hidden application, this is not apparent. Reminders continues to run until you exit Windows or choose Turn Off Reminders from the File menu in Schedule+. You will be reminded of upcoming appointments while you are running Windows.

So if you experience the problem of missing reminders, you may have accidentally turned it off. To turn Reminders back on, choose Turn On Reminders from the File menu in Schedule+.

Other Problems Out in DOS-Land

The DOS networking part of Windows for Workgroups works great, too. You don't have to be in Windows to benefit from the networking capabilities of WFW. Before starting Windows, at the DOS prompt, type **NET START FULL** and you will be given full network access, even though it's a bit harder to navigate than it is in Windows. This approach takes 100K of memory, so some programs might not have enough left over to run. You can try **NET START BASIC** to save more memory at the expense of less network function; your application may work.

To learn all the networking commands in this DOS state, simply type **NET HELP** and you'll get several screens of help.

Novell NetWare Connectivity on Your WFW Network

In case you are also running on a network cabling system that has a Novell NetWare file server hanging around somewhere, you may be experiencing some problems trying to access both networks at the same time. Here's how to do it.

You can add the Novell NetWare network-specific features either during or after Windows for Workgroups Setup. If you have already installed Windows for Workgroups, use all four of the following steps. If you are adding Novell NetWare connectivity during setup, skip the first two steps.

In the **Control Panel** window, choose the **Network** icon. Then choose the **Networks** button at the bottom of the **Network Settings** dialog box. In the **Available Network Types** dialog box, select **Novell NetWare**, and choose the **Add** button. After you provide the appropriate files from the setup disks, **Novell NetWare** appears in the box titled **Other Networks In Use**. Choose the **OK** button. You must restart Windows before this change can take affect.

Your Novell NetWare server may be running protocols in addition to what you have already installed. Windows for Workgroups supports only the MSIPX protocol with Novell NetWare. Ask your NetWare networking administrator if you need further assistance. I'm sure they'd be thrilled to see what you've been doing.

The Least You Need to Know

Nobody's perfect! Neither are our networks! But this chapter showed us how we can solve common problems found with new Windows for Workgroups networks, including:

➤ Simple bugs can usually be fixed by making sure everything is plugged in correctly and turned on.

➤ If you can't connect to your post office to use Mail, make sure the person who set it up included you as a user, along with any password that might have been assigned.

➤ If not much of anything seems to be working correctly, you can always re-install Windows for Workgroups on your computer.

Part 5
Networking Command Reference Guide

Did you ever have one of those days where you couldn't remember your own name, let alone some stupid networking command? More often than you care to admit? Or just curious about stupid networking commands? This section is for you!

Have you ever mixed up the NDIR and NLIST commands? If we all had great memories there would be no reason for dictionaries. We will always have dumb computer manuals, however, because the companies come and go, and their commands go with them. This set of chapters represents the more common commands from the more common networks. Enjoy!

OH **THAT**, HE'S BEEN ACTING THAT WAY EVER—
SINCE HE GOT HIS PASSWORD TO FINALLY WORK...

Chapter 25

NetWare (Versions 3.x and 4.x) Command Reference

Introduction to the Commands

Although there are almost a zillion commands available at the DOS command prompt in NetWare, you only need a few to get around. Although we've included a bunch, you'll probably find you can get by with only MAP, CAPTURE, NDIR, FLAG, RIGHTS, SETPASS, and SEND.

Notation Explanation

To describe and understand the commands, you should first review the convention and format used to describe them. Here it is:

COMMAND [/*option /option*] *variable* [*optional variable*]

Everything between square brackets is optional. The /**OPTIONS** are specific command options or switches that affect command execution. The **Variables** are items that must be inserted into the command line, such as server names, user IDs, and file names.

ATTACH

What's it for? The attach command is used to connect to another file server. You can't use it until you are logged into a file server. Then you can attach to a second file server. If you just want to map a drive to another server, it's easier to simply use the MAP command and include the name of the server.

Commonly heard: "Are you *attached* to that server?" "I didn't want to run the login script on that other server, so I just *attached* to it instead of logging in." "Who uses ATTACH anymore?"

Syntax: ATTACH *[server/userid]*

Example: ATTACH SERVER2/MYNAME

CAPTURE

What's it for? You have to use the CAPTURE command before you can print on the network. It prepares your computer to send print jobs to your NIC instead of your parallel port. The network takes it from there. Most capture statements are created by your network administrator; they are usually stored in the login script so you don't have to worry about them.

Commonly heard: "What do you mean you can't print? Is your LPT1 *captured* to the network printer?" "I can *capture* 9 ports to 9 different network printers at once, and my computer has only one LPT connector on it!"

Syntax: CAPTURE *[/][options][=][names or values]*

Available options you can use:

(Spaces or slashes can be used to separate options.)

B	Banner (optional; the default includes a banner with your user ID).
C	Number of copies (the default is 1).
CR	Create a print file instead of printing.
E	End the capture.
FF	Place a form-feed sheet after the print job (this is the default).
L	Local port.
NB	No banner included.
NFF	No extra sheet of paper desired after the print job.
NT	Don't interpret tabs, especially printing graphics.
P	Identify which printer.

Q	Identify which queue.
S	Identify which server.
SH	Displays your current capture status.

Examples:

CAPTURE /SHOW	Display your current captured status (very useful!).
CAPTURE LASER3 NOTI	Capture LPT1 to the laser printer and notify when complete.
CAPTURE L=3 B=Me NFF	Use a banner that says "Me," no form feed, and LPT3.

FLAG

What's it for? The flag command is used to see or change the attributes of a file or directory stored on the network.

Commonly heard: "I can't seem to update that file. Did someone flag it read-only?" "Gosh, someone flagged that game hidden, but management thought they erased it!"

Syntax: FLAG *[filename] [attributes] [options]*

All wild card rules apply to file and directory names.

Attributes:

A	Archive
DI	Delete Inhibit
X	Execute Only
H	Hidden
RO	Read-Only
RW	Read-Write
RI	Rename Inhibit
SH	Shareable
SY	System
T	Transactional

267

ALL	All (turns on all attributes)
N	Normal (turns off all attributes)

Switches you can use:

/DO	Directories only
/FO	Files only
/S	Include the subdirectories

Examples:

flag H:*.*	To see all attributes of all files on home directory.
flag H:*.bat H	To make all BAT files hidden on your home directory.
flag H:*.bat -H :	
or	
flag H:*.bat N	To bring the BAT files back into view.

GRANT

What's it for? You can use the GRANT command to give others the ability to see and use your network storage areas. The opposite of this command is REVOKE.

Commonly heard: "Can you *grant* me full access to your home directory? I promise not to harm anything!" "Too bad we don't have the Modify right *granted* to us in the PUBLIC directory. Then we could flag all the files hidden, just for fun."

Syntax: GRANT *[RIGHTS]* FOR *[LOCATION]* TO *[USER]*

Examples:

GRANT ALL FOR H: TO KIM	Giving user Kim the right to use your home directory.
GRANT F FOR H: TO MELISSA	Giving user Melissa only the right to see files in your home directory.

LOGIN

What's it for? The login command is used to log in to a file server. It also logs you out of anything you might be in at the time.

Commonly heard: "You can't see my files? Are you sure you are *logged into* this file server?" "Wow! I can see the *login* command on drive F: and I'm not even logged in yet!"

Syntax: LOGIN *[SERVERNAME\USERNAME]*

Examples:

LOGIN TEST5/FRED	To log in to file server TEST5 as user FRED.
LOGIN	To log in to the default server and be prompted for a name.

LOGOUT

What's it for? Real tough command. It's used for logging out of a file server. Don't run it while inside of Windows, or else you confuse the heck out of your computer.

Commonly heard: "I'm totally lost. I think I'll just *log out* and start over." "Rats! The *logout* command logged me out of all of my servers, not just one of them!"

Syntax: LOGOUT

MAP

What's it for? The map command is common; you should feel comfortable using it. Use MAP at your workstation to view your current drive mappings, or to create or change network or search-drive mappings. You can have up to 26 mappings, including local drives. Search-drive mappings begin with the letter Z and continue backward through the alphabet. You can have up to 16 search drives.

Commonly heard: "I like to run plain old *MAP* when I've forgotten what network drive letters I'm using." "Okay, I've granted you rights to see my home directory, so go ahead and *map a drive* to it."

Syntax: MAP *[type] driveletter:=volume:\path*

269

where *type* could be **root** or **search** or nothing; *driveletter* is any letter A through Z; *drive* is a letter you may currently have, and *path* is the complete location you desire. Don't forget the colon after the mandatory volume! This is the most common error!

Available types you can use:

C	Change a drive mapping to a new one.
DEL	Delete a drive mapping.
INS	Insert a search-drive mapping without replacing an existing mapping.
N	Map the next available drive to the specified path.
ROOT	Map a drive to a fake root directory for applications that require rights in a root directory.

Examples:

MAP	Viewing your current mappings.
MAP G:=SYS:\HOME\DAN	Map drive G: to SYS:\HOME\DAN.
MAP S4:=BIGSERV\SYS:APP\DOOM2	Map search drive 4 to BIGSERV\SYS:APP\DOOM2.
MAP DEL G:	Delete the mapping for drive G:.
MAP ROOT F:=HOME\TERRY	Map drive F: to HOME\TERRY as a fake root.

NCOPY (pronounced EN-copy)

What's it for? Use NCOPY to copy files between locations on file servers. NCOPY is better than the DOS COPY command because it maintains attributes like Shareable or Read-Only during the copying procedure.

Commonly heard: "They say it's much easier on the network to use the NCOPY command, instead of COPY, to move files from one file server to another." "Cool! The NCOPY command also brings the file attributes along with it! That's much better than the DOS COPY command!"

270

Syntax: The source (from) location is given first; the target location (to) is always last:

NCOPY *[drive:\directory] [drive:\directory] [options]*

Available options you can use:

/SUB	To include subdirectories.
/V	To verify after the copy (designed for the paranoid).

Examples:

NCOPY G:*.* H:\TEMP	Copy files from current directory on G: to TEMP directory on H:.
NCOPY G:\DATA H:\ /SUB /V	Copy files from DATA directory to home directory, including subdirectories, and verify the copy when finished.

NDIR (pronounced EN-dir)

What's it for? The NDIR command is often used to display network directories. The advantage over the DOS DIR command is that you can see network file attributes, which means normally hidden files can be seen.

Commonly heard: "Do an NDIR and see if you can find my files." "What's the craziest NDIR search you've ever seen?"

Syntax: NDIR *[filename] [/options]*

Available options you can use...

...for displaying the results:

DA	Formats the output to display *dates*.
DE	Displays more *detail* about files.
R	Formats to display *rights* and attributes.

...for listing different types of information:

FO	Displays files only.
DO	Displays directories only.

271

S   Includes all subdirectories.

/VOL   Displays volume space information.

/FI   Searches until "finding" a filename.

/?   Displays lots of help screens.

...to look for files you left somewhere you don't remember...

CR   Matches a creation date.

UP   Matches an update or modification date.

SI   Matches a particular size.

OW   Matches an owner.

...and use these comparison parameters with your searching:

=   Checks for equals.

EQ   Checks for equals.

NOT   Checks for inequality.

LE   Checks for a lower value.

GR   Checks for a greater value.

AFT   Checks for a later date.

BEF   Checks for an earlier date.

...for sorting different ways:

SORT   Displays in the sorted order.

SORT UN   Displays in an unsorted way.

REV SORT   Displays in descending order instead of ascending.

Examples:

NDIR /DE	To see all date, attribute, rights and owner information for each file in the current directory.
NDIR \DOCS /CR AFT 04-15-94	To see all files in the DOCS directory created after 4/15/94.

NDIR \DOCS /OW=FRED   To list all files owned by FRED
                          in the DOCS directory.

NLIST (pronounced EN-list)

What's it for? For those of you using NetWare 4, this command is important, so you should probably learn how to use it correctly. NLIST is used to view information about users, groups, volumes, servers, print queues, and printers.

Commonly heard: "Rats! NetWare 4 got rid of all the commands I've just learned and replaced them with NLIST!" "Is it true that entire books have been written about all the ways you can use NLIST?"

Syntax: NLIST *[class type] [=object name] [/option...]*

where *class type* = USER, SERVER, PRINTER, GROUP, or VOLUME, and *object name* = the name of the object you want information about.

Available options you can use:

/A   View users who are logged in.

/SHOW   View a specific property of an object.

/S   Search all levels.

Examples:

NLIST SERVER /S   Search for all servers.

NLIST USER /A /S   Search for all users logged in, regardless
                      of context.

NLIST PRINTER = L*   View all printers whose name begins
                      with L.

NLIST QUEUE /N   View print queue names.

NPRINT (pronounced EN-print)

What's it for? The NPRINT command is used for fast printing of text files. It's like the DOS PRINT command except it understands all of the network options. Commonly used for README files.

Commonly heard: "Who uses NPRINT?"

Syntax: NPRINT *filename [/][options][=][names* or *values]*

Available options you can use (similar to CAPTURE):

Spaces or slashes can be used to separate options.

B	Banner (optional; the default includes a banner with your user ID).
C	Number of copies (the default is 1).
FF	Place a form-feed sheet after print job (this is the default).
NB	No banner included.
NFF	No extra sheet of paper desired after print job.
NT	Don't interpret tabs, especially printing graphics.
P	Identify which printer.
Q	Identify which queue.
S	Identify which server.
SH	Displays your current capture status.

Example:

NPRINT C:\DOWNLOAD\README.TXT /Q=HP4 NB NFF

PCONSOLE (pronounced pee-console)

What's it for? Use the PCONSOLE menu command to manage print jobs in queues, kill an existing print job, and check status of printers and print servers.

Commonly heard: "Quick, kill that print job! Bring up PCONSOLE and delete the print queue entry!" "We use PCONSOLE to see any new printers that the network administrator might be installing on our network."

Syntax: PCONSOLE (It will bring up the PCONSOLE menu.)

REVOKE

What's it for? Use REVOKE to remove security rights previously given with the GRANT command.

Commonly heard: "Who erased my stuff? I'm going to *revoke* every right I ever gave to anyone."

Syntax: REVOKE *[RIGHTS]* FOR *[LOCATION]* FROM *[USER]*

Examples:

REVOKE ALL FOR H: FROM KIM	Taking away the rights given to Kim for your home directory.
REVOKE F FOR H: FROM MELISSA	Revoking only the ability to see files in your home directory from user Melissa.

RIGHTS

What's it for? The RIGHTS command is used to display or grant security rights for the user in the desired directory.

Commonly heard: "Why can't I copy my file to this directory? Don't I have the *rights* to do it?" "Hey LAN administrator, could you please give me all *rights* to the SYSTEM directory?"

Syntax: RIGHTS *[directory* or *filename] [rights list] [options]*

Available options you can use:

(no parameter)	Displays effective rights.
/S	Applies command to all subdirectories.
/T	Displays trustees of a directory or file.

Rights List:

S	**Supervisor**	All rights, king of the hill.
R	**Read**	You can open and read a file.
W	**Write**	You can change the contents of a file.
C	**Create**	You can create or copy in a new file.
E	**Erase**	You can get rid of a file.
M	**Modify**	You can change the attributes of a file.
F	**File Scan**	You can see a file.
A	**Access Control**	You can give your rights to others.

275

Examples:

RIGHTS H:	Displays current rights for the current directory on H:.
RIGHTS SYS:\PUBLIC /T	Displays who has what rights for the PUBLIC directory.

SALVAGE

What's it for? This is a very useful command for bringing back files that are accidentally erased. Salvage can be used until the PURGE command is run for that directory; then nothing can be salvaged.

Commonly heard: "Oops! I erased everything. Lucky for me someone invented the SALVAGE command." "I had better PURGE that incriminating file or else someone might find it with the SALVAGE command."

Syntax: SALVAGE (It's a menu utility.)

SEND

What's it for? The SEND command is used to send short, simple messages to one or more people. The message will appear in one or two lines at the very top or bottom of a DOS screen, or in a message box on a Windows screen. The received message on a DOS screen must be cleared away with the keystrokes **Ctrl+Enter** before you can do anything else.

Commonly heard: "I don't know where she is, SEND her a message on the network and tell her to get back here."

Syntax: SEND *[options]* "*Message*" *[TO] userid*

Available options you can use (but can't include message):

/A=N	To block incoming messages.
/A=C	Block all messages except from the file server.
/A=P	Hold messages until you run SEND /A.
/A	Allows messages to be received again.
Example:	SEND "Time for our meeting!" to BOB HEIDI CLOWNS

SETPASS

What's it for? Use SETPASS to changing your password at the DOS command prompt.

Commonly heard: "Change your password with SETPASS, okay?"

Syntax: SETPASS *[old password] [new password] [new password]*

or just type **SETPASS** and it will prompt you.

SLIST (pronounced ES-list)

What's it for? The SLIST command is used in NetWare 2 and 3 for providing a list of currently available file servers. NetWare 4 now uses NLIST SERVER to provide the same function.

Commonly heard: "Are you sure our file server is down? Did you check and see if it shows up in SLIST?"

Syntax: SLIST

USERLIST (pronounced user-list)

What's it for? This command is used to obtain a listing of all people currently logged on to the network. It is useful just before sending a message to know that the person will get it. This command can also be used to obtain the NIC address.

Commonly heard: "Run a USERLIST and tell me who's still logged in this evening."

Syntax: USERLIST *[options]*

Available options you can use:

/A   Displays the NIC address where the user ID is logged in.

WHOAMI (pronounced who-am-I)

What's it for? This command is used to identify the current userid logged into a computer.

Commonly heard: "What happened? Where am I? WHOAMI?"

Syntax: WHOAMI *[options]*

Switches you can use:

/A   List all the information available.

Chapter 26

Jimmy's personal
Netware...

Personal NetWare Command Reference

A total of 35 commands are available at the DOS command prompt in Personal NetWare. All of these commands start with the command **NET**. An easier alternative to these compound commands is to use the menu utility in either DOS or Windows. To obtain the DOS menu, simply type **NET** and press **Enter**. For the Windows alternative, select the **NetWare Tools** icon in the **Personal NetWare** group.

To describe and understand the commands, you should first review the convention and format used to describe them. Here it is:

COMMAND *[/OPTION /OPTION] variable [optional variable]*

Everything between square brackets is optional. The **/OPTIONS** are specific command options or switches that affect command execution. The **variables** are items that must be inserted into the command line, such as server names, user IDs, and file names.

NET ADMIN

This command starts the main DOS administrative program for Personal NetWare. Use it to add users, grant access, and start audit trails.

Syntax: NET ADMIN *["message"]*

Available Option:

"**Message**"   Allows you to place a message in the audit log.

Example: If you wanted to add another user to your workgroup, and you have only a DOS station available, this is the place to start.

NET CAPTURE

The capture command lists the currently captured printer port assignments, and connects a printer port to a workgroup printer.

Syntax: NET CAPTURE *[options] [device]*

Example: net capture del lpt1

NET CONNECT

This command lists all servers, including regular NetWare servers, that you have connected.

Syntax: NET CONNECT *[ServerName\UserName]*

Example: Try using this command when you are logged into many NetWare servers. You'll see the difference between a Personal NetWare server and a regular NetWare server (version 2, 3, or 4).

NET CONSOLE

Use this command to display all users connected to your computer (if it is set up as a server). It will also display their open files, and it acts as a useful screen saver as well.

Syntax: NET CONSOLE

Example: Use this command when you are having problems opening a file. You'll be able to see whether or not someone else is using it.

NET DIAGS

Use this command to start the DOS-based network diagnostic program.

Syntax: NET DIAGS

Example: Use this command to test your network connection when you are having trouble.

NET DOWN

This command is used at a Personal NetWare server before it is shut off. It safely closes all files and disconnects all clients before stopping.

Syntax: NET DOWN *[servername]*

Example: net down idiot_server

NET HELP

This command provides help screens with a complete explanation of the command in question. Running NET HELP without a command is also helpful; it will display all net commands.

Syntax: NET HELP *[command]*

Example: net help capture

NET INFO

This command displays the names and versions of all Personal NetWare software running on your computer, including the name of your server, your workgroup, and the computer address.

Syntax: NET INFO

Example: You could use this command for inventory purposes, or to remind yourself of these network details.

NET JOIN

This command will connect your computer to a different workgroup, and modify your software to make this new workgroup your default the next time you log in.

Syntax: NET JOIN

Example: Not used very often, but useful for permanently changing to a new workgroup when it is created.

NET LOGIN

This command intitiates the login process to connect a user to the workgroup.

Syntax: NET LOGIN *[servername\username] [@filename]*

Example: This is a good line to put in your AUTOEXEC.BAT, if it's not already there.

NET LOGOUT

This command will disconnect the user from all workgroups and other network resources.

Syntax: NET LOGOUT *[/OPTIONS] [servername]*

Available options:

/B   Disconnects only the NetWare 2, 3, and some 4 servers.

/T   Disconnects only the NetWare 4 directory trees.

/W   Disconnects only the workgroup.

Example: If the big NetWare server is going down for maintenance, disconnect from it but remain connected to your workgroup with:

net logout /b

NET MAP

Use this command to see all current network drive connections.

Syntax: NET MAP *[DriveLetter:] [=ServerName:\PathName]*

Example: net map g:=workserv:\document

NET PLIST

Use this command to list all available printers in your network.

Syntax: NET PLIST *[Name*]*

Example: net plist r*

This lists all printers whose name starts with the letter R.

NET PRINT

This command is used to print files on the network. To use this command you must already have a captured printer.

Syntax: NET PRINT *FileName [PrinterName] [PortName]*

Example: net print c:\download\readme.txt hp4

NET RECEIVE

This command controls messages at your computer.

Syntax: NET RECEIVE *[options]*

Available options:

ON   Turns on message reception.

OFF   Turns off message reception.

Seconds   Enter a number for the number of seconds the received
            message stays on your screen. If blank, the message
            remains on the screen until the user clears it off.

Example: net receive on 5

You would use this command to start receiving messages and have
them display only five seconds.

NET RIGHTS

This command displays your rights to use files in the current directory.
Remember that the security rights in Personal NetWare are less com-
plex than those for a NetWare file server. They're limited to only ALL,
NONE, READ, and finally WRITE.

Syntax: NET RIGHTS

Rights Listing:

ALL   Allows you full access.

None   Allows you no access.

Read   Allows you to read and execute files.

Write   Allows you to write, modify, create, and delete files.

Example: use NET RIGHTS to find out what rights you have in a
particular directory.

283

NET SEND

Use this command to send a short message to another workgroup user or users.

Syntax: NET SEND *"Message" [Option]*

Available options:

UserName	Send to one or more users.
All	Send to everyone in the workgroup.

Example: net send "Sorry, folks. Server shutting down." all

NET SETPASS

Use this command to set or change your workgroup password.

Syntax: NET SETPASS *[Options]*

Example: Use this command often to change your password.

NET SHARE

This command is used to share a local resource from your computer, which must first be running as a server.

Syntax: NET SHARE *[option]*

Available options:

PathName	To share a directory.
PortName	To share a printer.

Example: net share c:\document

NET SLIST

This command lists all available servers, including regular NetWare file servers.

Syntax: NET SLIST *[options]*

Available options:

/B	Shows NetWare 2, 3, and some 4 bindery file servers.

/P   Will pause after each full screen of information.

/T   Displays the NetWare 4 directory tree servers.

Example: Use this command if you are having difficulty logging in to a particular server; if the server is available, it will be displayed.

NET ULIST

This command lists the users currently logged in to the workgroup or a NetWare server. It also lists their physical address.

Syntax: NET ULIST *[servername]*

Example: Use this command before sending a message to someone to make sure they are logged in. Don't bother sending the message if they aren't logged in to see it.

NET VLIST

This command lists all shared workgroup directories and NetWare server volumes you have available.

Syntax: NET VLIST *[volumename]*

Example: If you are having trouble finding a directory located on a particular volume, you could use this command to make sure that volume is currently available to you.

285

ITS LANTASTIC!

Chapter 27

LANtastic Command Reference

A total of 46 commands are available at the DOS command prompt in LANtastic. All of these commands start with the command **NET** and are listed in this chapter.

To make things even easier in LANtastic, you can use either menus or Windows to execute any of the following commands. To run the LANtastic DOS menu, simply type **NET** and press **Enter**. You'll see menu options for selecting network drives, printers, and mail. For the Windows alternative, run LANtastic for Windows, open the LANtastic **Net** palette, and click on either the **Drives**, **Printers**, or **Mail** button.

To describe and understand the commands, you should first review the convention and format used to describe them. Here it is:

COMMAND *[/OPTION /OPTION] variable [optional variable]*

Everything between square brackets is optional. The **/OPTIONS** are specific command options or switches that affect command execution. The **variables** are items that must be inserted into the command line, such as server names, user names, and file names.

NET ATTACH

This command attaches all disk resources of the named server. NET ATTACH will only redirect disk drives, not printers or other devices. It also grabs the next available drive letter automatically. To keep your assignments the same every day, forget this command and use NET USE instead.

Syntax: NET ATTACH *[option]* *servername*

Available option:

/VERBOSE   Displays all redirection information on-screen.

Example: net attach \\Idiot_Server

NET CHANGEPW

This command is used to change your network password in LANtastic.

Syntax: **NET CHANGEPW *ServerName OldPassword NewPassword***

Example: net changepw \\Idiot_Server sotrsab tnplh

NET CHAT

This command checks all servers for mail and provides a count of incoming mail items on each server.

Syntax: NET CHAT

NET COPY

This command copies a file from one location to another on a server without passing data over the network.

Syntax: **NET COPY *frompath topath***

Example: net copy f:\research*.* g:\backup

NET DETACH

The NET DETACH command cancels all network disk drive redirections to a named server without logging out. This command works for disk resources only (not printers).

Syntax: NET DETACH *servername*

Example: net detach \\Idiot_Server

NET DIR

Similar to the DOS DIR command, this command lists a network directory.

Syntax: NET DIR*[/Option][Path]*

Available option:

/ALL   To include system and hidden files.

Example: net dir g:

NET HELP

This command is used to get help on any other LANtastic command.

Syntax: NET HELP *[COMMAND]*

Example: net help send

NET LOGIN

This command is used for logging into a server.

NET LOGIN[/WAIT] \\ServerName UserName [Password]

Available option:

/WAIT   Causes login attempts to continue until successful or
            canceled manually.

Example: net login \\Idiot_Server Kimba

NET LOGOUT

This command cancels all redirections and logs out of a server.

Syntax: NET LOGOUT *servername*

Example: net logout \\Idiot_Server

NET MAIL

In LANtastic, mail is nothing more than a file sent from one person to
another. To send a file as mail:

NET MAIL*[/VOICE] filename \\servername [username] ["comment"]*

Example: NET MAIL C:\MAIL\NOTE33.TXT \\MAIL_SRV KIM
            "Read ASAP!"

289

NET MESSAGE

This command is used to turn messages on or off.

Syntax: NET MESSAGE*[/ENABLE /DISABLE] [BEEP POP]*

Available options:

BEEP   Provides sound when message is received.

POP   Provides pop-up message box.

NET POSTBOX

Checks all servers for mail; provides a count of incoming mail items on each server.

Syntax: NET POSTBOX

NET PRINT

This command is used to print from the DOS command prompt.

Syntax: NET PRINT*[options] filename device ["comment"]*

Available options include:

/BINARY   Used for graphics.

/DELETE   Deletes file after printing; use it when using the DIRECT switch.

/DIRECT   Sends job directly to network printer without using the queue.

/NOTIFY   Tells you when your print job has printed.

/NONOTIFY   Doesn't bother you with the NOTIFY message.

/VERBOSE   Displays the names of the files sent to the queue.

Examples:

NET PRINT README.TXT LPT1 "The readme file"

NET PRINT/VERBOSE C:\DOWNLOAD*.*
\\IDIOT_SERVER\@@PRINTER

NET QUEUE

This command is used with options to manage the printing environment.

Syntax: NET QUEUE *option* *servername [device* or *ALL]*

Available options include:

HALT   Same as stopping the queue.

PAUSE   Temporarily suspend queue activity.

RESTART   To continue after pausing.

START   Assign a queue.

STATUS   Displays the queue status.

STOP   Stops Printing.

Examples:

Net Queue Halt \\Idiot_Server All

NET QUEUE START \\IDIOT_SERVER LPT1

NET SEND

This command is used to send a pop-up message.

Syntax: NET SEND *machine "message" [\\servername username]*

Examples: NET SEND * "Ready for lunch, Kim?" * KIM

NET UNUSE

This command is used to cancel a specified redirection.

Syntax: NET UNUSE *option*

Available options:

Drive   The redirected drive letter you want to cancel.

Port   The redirected printer port you want to cancel.

Example: net unuse lpt1

291

NET USE

This command redirects a local drive or device to a network resource.

Syntax: NET USE *[options]* *servername**resource*

Available options:

Drive   The local drive letter to redirect to a network resource.

Port   The local device port you want to redirect to a network resource.

Examples:

net use lpt1 \\idiot_server\laser

net lpt timeout=10

Receiving Mail

There is no command you can use at the DOS prompt to directly receive a piece of mail. You must access your LANtastic mail through **Mail Services** from the **Main Function Menu** in DOS (bring up this menu with the **NET** command), or users of LANtastic for Windows can click on the **Mail** icon in the **LANtastic Net** menu.

Chapter 28

Windows for Workgroups (and Windows NT) Command Reference

A total of 14 commands are available at the DOS command prompt in Windows for Workgroups. All of these commands start with the command **NET** and are listed in this chapter.

Most people don't realize these commands even exist. After all, you're using Windows, so why should you spend any time at the command prompt? One big reason is for troubleshooting your network; if you ever receive an error number, you can use the **NET HELP** *Error#* command to get further information about the problem. Whatever your reason may be, this chapter describes the most frequently used commands in Windows for Workgroups.

It gets crazier. In an attempt to make it even easier to use networking commands *outside* of Windows with Windows for Workgroups, you can use a DOS-based menu utility. To run the Windows for Workgroups DOS menu, simply type **NET** and press **Enter**. You'll see menu options for selecting network drives and printers.

To describe and understand the commands, you should first review the convention and format used to describe them. Here it is:

COMMAND *[/OPTION /OPTION] variable [optional variable]*

Everything between square brackets is optional. The **/OPTIONS** are specific command options or switches that affect command execution. The **variables** are items that must be inserted into the command line, such as server names, user names, and file names.

NET

This command loads the pop-up interface into memory and displays it on your screen.

NET CONFIG

This command is used to display your current workgroup settings.

Syntax: NET CONFIG *[/YES]*

Available option:

/YES   Carries out the NET CONFIG command without first prompting you to provide information or confirm actions.

NET DIAG

This command runs the Microsoft Network Diagnostics program to evaluate the hardware connection between two computers and to display information about a single computer.

Syntax: NET DIAG *[options]*

Available options:

/NAMES   Enables you to specify the two computers whose connection you want to test.

/STATUS   Enables you to specify a computer about which you want network diagnostics information.

NET HELP

This command provides information about NET commands and error messages.

Syntax: NET HELP *[option]*

Available options:

Command   Specifies the Microsoft NET command that you want information about.

Error#   Specifies the number of the error message that you want information about.

Example: net help 28

NET LOGOFF

This command breaks the connection between your computer and the shared resources to which it is connected.

Syntax: NET LOGOFF *[Option]*

Available option:

/YES   Carries out the NET LOGOFF command without first prompting you to provide information or confirm actions.

NET LOGON

This command identifies you as a member of a workgroup and reestablishes your persistent connections.

Syntax: NET LOGON *[options]*

Available options:

User	Specifies the name that identifies you in your workgroup. The name you specify can have as many as 20 characters.
Password	The unique string of characters that authorizes you to gain access to your password-list file.
?	Specifies that you want to be prompted for your password, even if you use the /YES option.
/DOMAIN:Name	Specifies the Windows NT or LAN Manager domain you want to log on to.
/YES	Carries out the NET LOGON command without first prompting you to provide information or confirm actions.

Example: If you would rather be prompted to type your user name and password instead of specifying them in the NET LOGON command line, type NET LOGON without options.

295

NET PASSWORD

This command is used to change your logon password to Windows for Workgroups. You can also use the options to change your password on a Windows NT network or LAN Manager domain.

Syntax: NET PASSWORD *[options] [oldpassword newpassword]*

Available options:

Oldpassword	Specifies your current password.
Newpassword	Specifies your new password. It can have as many as 14 characters.
\\Computer	Specifies the Windows NT or LAN Manager server on which you want to change your password.
/DOMAIN:Name	Specifies the Windows NT or LAN Manager domain on which you want to change your password.
User	Specifies your Windows NT or LAN Manager user name.

NET PRINT

This command displays information about the print queue on a shared printer, or controls your print jobs. When you specify the name of a computer by using the NET PRINT command, you receive information about the print queues on each of the shared printers that are connected to the computer.

Syntax: NET PRINT *[options]*

Available options:

\\Computer	Specifies the name of the computer whose print queue you want information about.
\Printer	Specifies the name of the printer you want information about.
Port	Specifies the name of the parallel LPT port on your computer that is connected to the printer you want information about.

NET START

This command starts services or loads the pop-up interface. These services cannot be started from a DOS prompt within Windows. To start the workgroup redirector you selected during Setup, type **NET START** without options. In general, you don't need to use any of the options. Use the POPUP option to load the pop-up interface, if it is not loaded by NET START.

Syntax: NET START *[options]*

Available options:

POPUP	Loads the pop-up interface into memory. Use this option if the pop-up interface is not automatically loaded each time you start your computer.
/LIST	Displays a list of the services that are running.
/YES	Carries out the NET START command without first prompting you to provide information or confirm actions.
/VERBOSE	Displays information about device drivers and services as they are loaded.

NET STOP

This command stops services or unloads the pop-up interface from memory. These services cannot be stopped from a DOS prompt within Windows. To stop the workgroup redirector, type **NET STOP** without options. This breaks all your connections to shared resources and removes the NET commands from your computer's memory.

Syntax: NET STOP *[options]*

Available options:

POPUP	Unloads the pop-up interface from memory, but does not stop the redirector.
/YES	Carries out the NET STOP command without first prompting you to provide information or confirm actions.

NET TIME

This command displays the time on your computer's clock. It can also synchronize your computer's clock with the shared clock on a Microsoft Windows for Workgroups, Windows NT, or LAN Manager time server.

Syntax: NET TIME *[options] [/SET] [/YES]*

Available options:

\\Computer	Specifies the name of the computer whose time you want to check or synchronize your computer's clock with.
/WORKGROUP: wgname	Specifies the name of the workgroup containing a computer whose clock you want to check or synchronize your computer's clock with. If there are multiple time servers in that workgroup, NET TIME uses the first one it finds.
/SET	Synchronizes your computer's clock with the clock on the computer or workgroup you specify.

NET USE

This command connects or disconnects your computer from a shared resource or displays information about your connections. To list all of your connections, type NET USE without any options.

Syntax: NET USE *[devices] [options]*

Available devices:

Drive:	Specifies the drive letter you assign to a shared directory.
Port:	Specifies the parallel LPT. port name you assign to a shared printer.

Available options:

*	Specifies the next available drive letter. If used with /DELETE, specifies to disconnect all of your connections.

Computer	Specifies the name of the computer sharing the resource.
Directory	Specifies the name of the shared directory.
Printer	Specifies the name of the shared printer.
Password	Specifies the password for the shared resource.
?	Specifies that you want to be prompted for the password of the shared resource. You don't need to use this option unless the password is optional.
/PERSISTENT	Specifies which connections should be restored the next time you log on to the network. It must be followed by either YES, NO, LIST, SAVE, or CLEAR.
/DELETE	Breaks the specified connection to a shared resource.
/HOME	Makes a connection to your HOME directory if one is specified in your LAN Manager or Windows NT user account.

NET VER

This command does nothing more than display the type and version number of the workgroup redirector you are using. Big deal.

NET VIEW

This command displays a list of computers that share resources or a list of shared resources on a specific computer. To display a list of computers that share resources, type **NET VIEW** without options.

Syntax: NET VIEW *[options]*

Available options:

Computer	Specifies the name of the computer whose shared resources you want to see listed.
/WORKGROUP:wgname	Specifies the name of the workgroup whose computer names you want to view.

299

Speak Like a Geek: The Complete Archive

The networking world is like an exclusive club, complete with its own language. If you want to be accepted, you need to learn the secret words. The following mini-glossary will help you get started.

10BASE2   The IEEE standard for a 10-megabit-per-second baseband network on thin coaxial cable.

10BASE5   The IEEE standard for a 10-megabit-per-second baseband network on thick coaxial cable.

10BASET   The IEEE standard for a 10-megabit-per-second baseband network on twisted-pair cable.

access rights   A list of rights that tell you what you can and cannot do with network files or directories.

account   What the network uses to identify who you are and what you can do on the network.

adapter card   A computer card that is plugged into an available slot in your computer and provides expanded capabilities like networking and graphics.

ADMIN, administrator   A network user who can access commands used to set up, configure, and manage the network.

AppleTalk   Apple's networking operating system for Macintoshes.

archiving   The act of backing up and moving computer files to a less expensive place of storage.

ARCnet   An alternative to Ethernet or token-ring that lots of people may still use, although nobody admits it.

attributes   Characteristics that are assigned to files and directories. DOS attributes include Hidden, Read-Only, Archive, and System. Networking creates additional attributes.

AUTOEXEC.BAT   The DOS file that executes automatically each time you start your computer.

backbone   The main transmission medium (usually coax or fiber) that interconnects the segments or workgroup areas of a network.

backing up   Creating copies of important files and storing them in a different location for security. If you lose one you have the other.

bandwidth   The amount of information that can be moved over a cable.

banner   The identifying cover sheet of a print job.

BNC connector   The childproof connector on 10BASE2 cabling that you have to push and turn to use.

bridge   A connection between two LANs.

bus   A type of network layout in which nodes are arranged in a single, straight cabling line.

CAPTURE   The NetWare command used to redirect your printer output to a printer on the network. It usually runs in the login script so users don't have to worry about it.

cc:Mail   The most popular electronic mail program for medium-sized and larger networks.

CD-ROM   Compact Disc-Read-Only Memory, similar to the music CD, but used to store lots of computer information that can't be changed.

Certified NetWare Engineer (CNE)   A title awarded to people that pass all the tests that measure your knowledge of networking.

cheapernet   Another name for 10BASE2; the cables are less expensive, but the performance of the network is the same.

client/server   Name describing two or more computers working together to complete a task.

coaxial cable   An electrical wire consisting of two primary elements: an outer braided wire that acts as a protective grounding, and an inner one used to carry signals.

COM1   Your first communications port on your computer.

concentrator   A multiport hub used in Ethernet to connect 10BASET cables together.

CONFIG.SYS   The DOS file that provides system configuration information during the boot-up of your computer.

configuration   The software settings that allow different hardware components of a computer system to communicate with each other.

console   The name for the display on the file server.

Control Panel   The Windows application that lets you configure your computer for Windows capabilities.

crash   Term used to describe the failing of a computer hard drive.

daisy chain   Describing a single cabling path going from one machine to another without crossing itself.

dedicated server   A computer left alone to do nothing but run the network.

DIP switch   A small block of switches used to configure older NICs and adapter cards. The settings represent different IRQs and memory settings.

DOS   Disk Operating System, the popular operating system used by most IBM-compatible computers; required to run Windows.

DOS prompt   The place you may need to be to run DOS commands; it looks like this: **C:\>**

double-click   Standard Windows language for selecting an item by clicking the button on a mouse twice in rapid succession.

drag   Standard Windows language for grabbing an object with the mouse and moving it somewhere else.

drive mapping   The term describing where a logical letter is pointing on the network.

drivers   A software program, usually loaded into server or workstation memory, that controls the network hardware (such as adapters or controllers), or implements the base for network communications software.

e-mail   Electronic mail, a form of communicating on a network by sending messages back and forth.

Ethernet   A local area network standard defining a physical medium and its method of placing data on a cable. It's based on CSMA/CD and 10Mbps. The Macintosh version of Ethernet is called EtherTalk.

executable file   A filename ending in .EXE, which runs automatically when its name is typed and entered.

extension   In DOS naming convention, the part of the name following the period.

file   An electronic package of information stored by computers.

file server   A networked computer used as the central storage area for other networked computers.

File Manager   The Windows utility for navigating the DOS directory structure.

FLAG   The Novell NetWare utility for viewing or changing the attributes of a networked file.

gateway   A machine used to connect two dissimilar computer components. An example is a network gateway to the mainframe.

GB (gigabyte)   Approximately one billion bytes of information.

hardware   The physical nuts, bolts, and all other pieces of computer equipment.

hub   See *concentrator*.

I/O port address   The unique address used to configure a computer component; it is set using software, jumpers, or DIP switches.

IEEE   The Institute of Electrical and Electronic Engineers, who establish standards that specify interface and protocol requirements for Ethernet and token-ring.

incremental backup   A partial backup, taken of only the files that have not been backed up since the last time.

Internet   The information superhighway of zillions of connected computer networks covering the earth.

IRQ   Interrupt ReQuest, the method used by adapters to communicate with a computer.

KB (kilobyte)   Approximately one thousand bytes of information.

LAN   Local Area Network, describing two or more computers connected together for the purpose of sharing information.

LAN driver   Software used with NIC to allow it to communicate on the network.

LANtastic   A very popular peer-to-peer network operating system.

local area network   See *LAN*.

LocalTalk   Describes the cabling system used by the Macintosh.

log in or **log on**   To go through the process of identifying yourself to the network to get access to network resources.

LOGIN directory   The directory on the file server where the LOGIN files are maintained.

login script   A series of commands that execute automatically when you log in to a network. The CAPTURE and MAP commands are commonly used in the login script.

LOGOUT   The command to end a session on the computer network.

LPT1   Line Printer One, representing your first parallel port on the back of your computer.

MAP   The NetWare command used to assign letters to directory locations.

MB (megabyte)   Approximately one million bytes of information.

memory   The temporary electronic storage where a computer stores active data and programs.

menu program   A list of programs or choices of action made available to the user. When the user makes a selection from this list, the program branches to the program of choice.

modem   Used to communicate by connecting your computer to a phone line. Stands for MOdulator-DEModulator.

NDIS   Network Driver Interface Specification. A software specification used by some operating systems (like Windows for Workgroups) to create drivers for network adapters.

NetBIOS   Network Basic Input/Output System, a networking standard used by many peer networks and also Novell NetWare.

NetWare   The most popular network operating system software.

NetWire   A location on CompuServe where a user can find the latest NetWare files.

network   A series of devices (such as computers and peripherals) interconnected by a communications channel.

Network Operating System (NOS)   An operating system that controls the behavior of two or more computers on a network.

network resource   Something valuable shared on the network; examples include storage space on hard drives, and devices such as a printer, modem, plotter, or scanner.

NIC (Network Interface Card)   A circuit board mounted inside each workstation and server on the network. It allows the device to listen and talk to other stations (or nodes) on the network.

node   A point in a network where one communication device is linked to the network, and where information can be sent or received.

NOS   Network Operating System.

Novell   The company that created NetWare.

packets   The unit of information transmitted over the network.

parallel port   Also called a printer port. The port used to connect a printer to your computer.

password   Used in combination with a user ID to provide security and privacy on the network.

PCI   Peripheral Component Interconnect, the primary standard architecture for Pentium computers.

PCONSOLE   The NetWare utility used to view print queues.

peer-to-peer network   A network in which all computers start as equivalent participants.

peripheral   Another word for a component that performs a service of value to the network; a device that qualifies as a computer resource.

port   A connector on the back of your computer used to connect a device like a printer or modem.

print job   The complete set of information sent to a printer for the printing of a document, which includes control information.

Print Manager   The Windows utility for managing local print queues.

print queue   Disk space that stores print jobs in sequential order; each one waits its turn to print.

print server   A computer that performs the network printing.

protocol   A formal set of rules that computers use to communicate.

queue   A list of things waiting to be processed.

redirection   When something appears to be local but really resides at another location on the network.

RJ-11   The little connector used on your telephone cable.

RJ-45   The slightly larger connector that looks like a telephone connector, but is used for 10BASET networks.

router   A machine used to connect dissimilar computer networks. An example is using a router to connect an Ethernet network with a token-ring network.

SCSI   Small Computer Systems Interface, a connection used for disk drives and other components.

search drive   A NetWare term used to describe a network directory that becomes an extension to your DOS path. Most NetWare utilities are stored in your search drive so you won't have to look for them.

segment   The description of a single complete section of networked computers. Bridges, routers, and gateways connect network segments.

serial port   The port on the back of your computer normally used to connect a modem or a mouse.

server   A networked computer usually dedicated to serving resources on a network.

SETPASS   The NetWare utility used to change your password.

shared resource   A resource that is made available to others on a network. Examples are printers, directories, modems, and fax machines.

shielded twisted pair   Twisted-pair cabling that has a shield covering it; used mostly by token-ring networks.

sneakernet   A term commonly used to describe sharing information between computers without a network. Still very effective.

superserver   Describes a powerful single computer that has many features making it ideal to be a server, including reliability, performance, and storage capacity.

Supervisor   The NetWare user who can do anything on the network.

SYS   The name of the first volume of disk space on a NetWare file server.

SYS:LOGIN   The network directory that holds the login files.

SYS:PUBLIC   The network directory that holds the network utilities and help information.

T-connector   A cable adapter that attaches a PC with a network interface card to the network.

tape drive   A piece of equipment used to back up files on a disk by copying them to a cassette tape.

TB (terabyte)   Approximately one trillion bytes of information.

TCP/IP   Transmission Control Protocol/Internet Protocol, a common protocol used in computer networks and the Internet.

terminator   The small connector that must be connected to each end of a 10BASE2 cabling segment. It can connect directly to the T-connector.

token-ring   A more expensive computer network alternative to Ethernet, running at 4 or 16 Mbps over shielded twisted-pair cabling.

topology   The physical geometric shape of the network. The main types of topology include bus (straight line), ring, and star-shaped.

transceiver   A hardware device that links a computer to the network and functions as both a transmitter and receiver.

twisted pair   Wiring similar to that found in the telephone system, consisting of two insulated wires loosely twisted around each other to help cancel out induced noise in balanced circuits.

UPS   Uninterruptible Power Supply, used with file servers to provide battery-powered backup in case of a power failure.

unshielded twisted pair (UTP)   Simple twisted-pair cabling without the extra electrical insulation around the outside. Less expensive than STP, but signals can't travel as far on it.

user ID   Your account name on a computer network, used when you log in to a network.

VINES   Virtual Networking System, the network operating system from Banyan.

virus   A computer program designed to spread quickly by copying itself to other computers, often creating harm by changing or deleting information stored on the computer or diskettes.

volume   The name of the major disk drive spaces on a NetWare file server. The SYS is the first volume on a NetWare file server.

WAN   Wide Area Network, describing interconnected computers spread over a wide area: city, country, or worldwide.

Windows for Workgroups   (WFW)   Microsoft's entry-level networking product.

wiring closet   A small and secure area of a building, where computer networking cables meet to be connected to one another.

workstation   Another name for your computer if it is not a file server.

zero-slot network   A slow-but-inexpensive network created without using NICs. Uses only parallel or serial ports and cabling.

Index

Q

R

S

U

V-W

X-Y-Z

Who Cares What *YOU* Think?

WE DO!

alpha books

We're not complete idiots. We take our readers' opinions very personally. After all, you're the reason we publish these books! Without you, we'd be pretty bored.

alpha books

So please! Drop us a note or fax us a fax! We'd love to hear what you think about this book or others. A real person—not a computer—reads every letter we get, and makes sure your comments get relayed to the appropriate people.

Not sure what to say? Here's some stuff we'd like to know:

- Who are you (age, occupation, hobbies, etc.)?
- Which book did you buy and where did you get it?
- Why did you pick this book instead of another one?
- What do you like best about this book?
- What could we have done better?
- What's your overall opinion of the book?
- What other topics would you like to purchase a book on?

Mail, e-mail, or fax your brilliant opinions to:

Faithe Wempen
Product Development Manager
Alpha Books
201 West 103rd Street
Indianapolis, IN 46290
FAX: (317) 581-4669

CompuServe: 75430,174
Internet: 75430.174@compuserve.com

PLUG YOURSELF INTO...

THE MACMILLAN INFORMATION SUPERLIBRARY™

Free information and vast computer resources from the world's leading computer book publisher—online!

FIND THE BOOKS THAT ARE RIGHT FOR YOU!

A complete online catalog, plus sample chapters and tables of contents give you an in-depth look at *all* of our books, including hard-to-find titles. It's the best way to find the books you need!

- ● STAY INFORMED with the latest computer industry news through our online newsletter, press releases, and customized Information SuperLibrary Reports.

- ● GET FAST ANSWERS to your questions about MCP books and software.

- ● VISIT our online bookstore for the latest information and editions!

- ● COMMUNICATE with our expert authors through e-mail and conferences.

- ● DOWNLOAD SOFTWARE from the immense MCP library:
  - Source code and files from MCP books
  - The best shareware, freeware, and demos

- ● DISCOVER HOT SPOTS on other parts of the Internet.

- ● WIN BOOKS in ongoing contests and giveaways!

TO PLUG INTO MCP: ➡ **WORLD WIDE WEB: http://www.mcp.com**

GOPHER: gopher.mcp.com

FTP: ftp.mcp.com

Home Page   What's New   Bookstore   Reference Desk   Software Library   Macmillan Overview   Talk to Us